SHADOWMAN

DEAD AND GONE

ANDY DIGGLE | RENATO GUEDES | DOUG BRAITHWAITE
SHAWN MARTINBROUGH | JOSÉ VILLARRUBIA

CONTENTS

Collection Cover Art: Tonci Zonjic

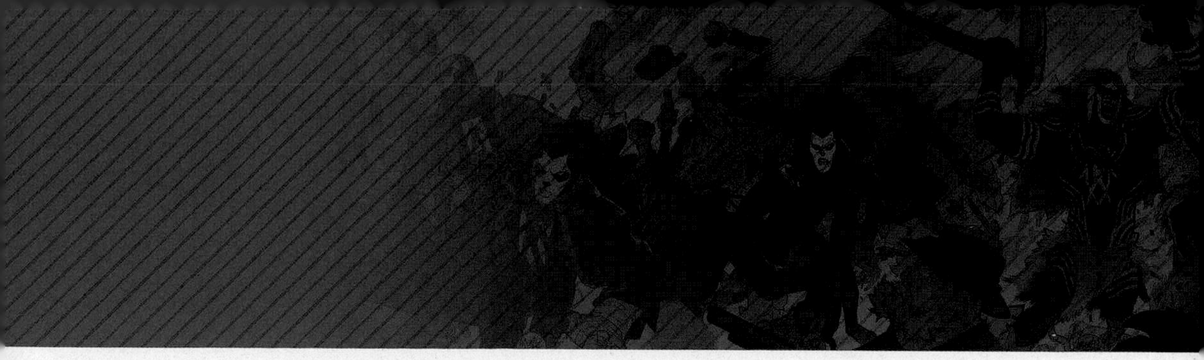

Assistant Editors: Benjamin Peterson (#4-6)
and David Menchel (#6-7)
Editors: Warren Simons (#4)
and Karl Bollers (#4-7)
Executive Editor: Joseph Illidge

VALIANT.

Dan Mintz
Chairman

Fred Pierce
Publisher

Walter Black
VP Operations

Joseph Illidge
Executive Editor

Robert Meyers
Editorial Director

Mel Caylo
Director of Marketing

Matthew Klein
Director of Sales

Travis Escarfullery
Director of Design & Production

Peter Stern
Director of International Publishing & Merchandising

Karl Bollers
Lysa Hawkins
Editors

Victoria McNally
Senior Marketing & Communications Manager

Jeff Walker
Production & Design Manager

Julia Walchuk
Sales Manager

Emily Hecht
Sales & Social Media Manager

David Menchel
Assistant Editor

Connor Hill
Sales Operations Coordinator

Ivan Cohen
Collection Editor

Steve Blackwell
Collection Designer

Russ Brown
President, Consumer Products,
Promotions & Ad Sales

Caritza Berlioz
Licensing Coordinator

Oliver Taylor
International Licensing Coordinator

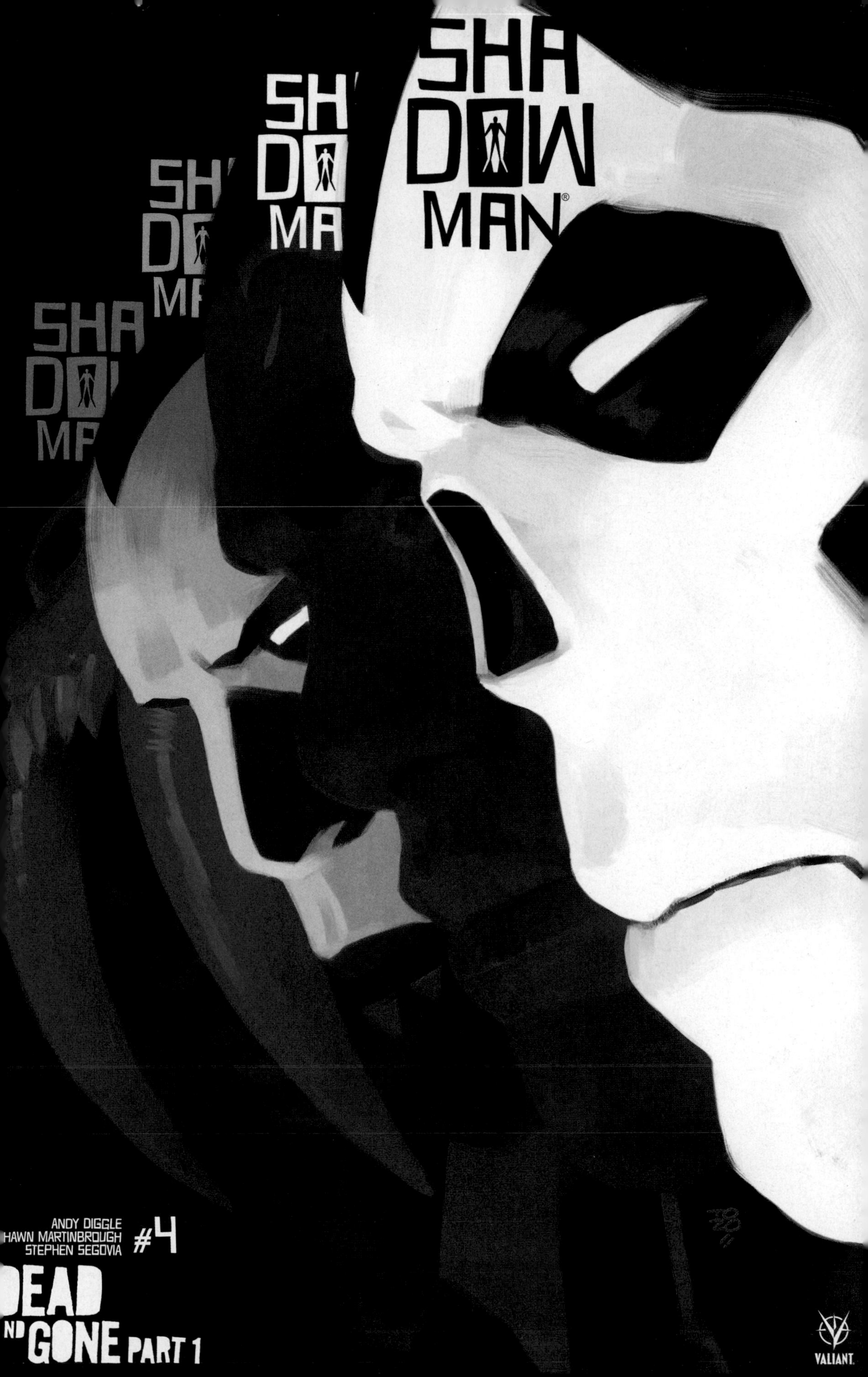
SHA
DOW
MAN®
ANDY DIGGLE
HAWN MARTINBROUGH
STEPHEN SEGOVIA
#4
DEAD
ND GONE PART 1
VALIANT

SHADOW MAN ®

Bonded to a loa, an ancient voodoo spirit, Jack Boniface is Shadowman — the guardian between the living world and what lies beyond.

Jack struggled to control the loa, fighting against the spirit's murderous urges. Ultimately, Jack succumbed to its rage, and was trapped in the demonic realm known as the Deadside for years as a result. However, with the help of his closest friend and ally, Alyssa Myles, Jack was able to return home to New Orleans, free once more.

When the deadly loa Baron Samedi took up residence in his hometown, Jack and Alyssa attempted to send the spirit back to the Deadside. However, their plan backfired, causing Jack's spirit to leave his body instead, and get lost in an unknown void...

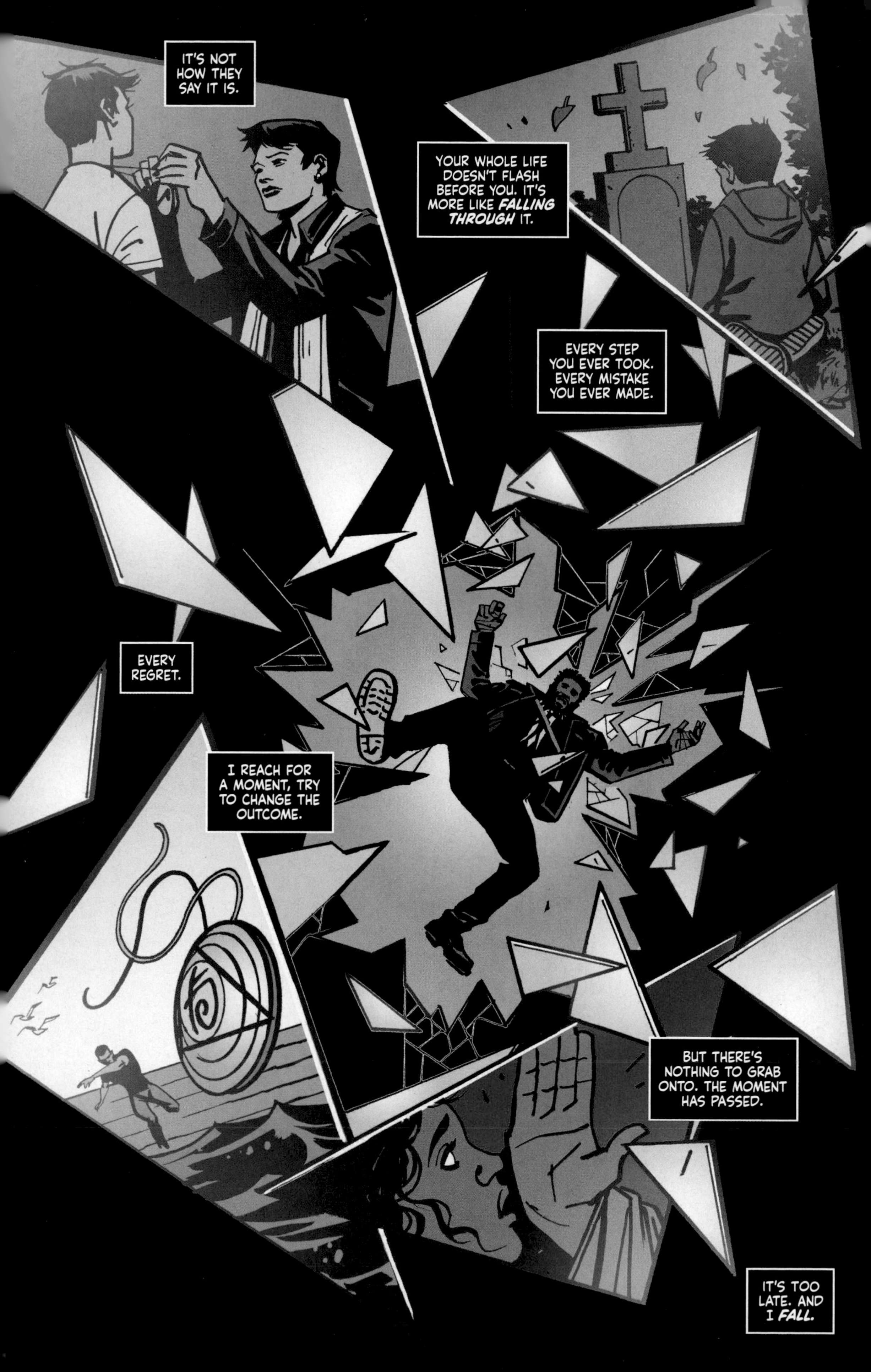
IT'S NOT HOW THEY SAY IT IS.
YOUR WHOLE LIFE DOESN'T FLASH BEFORE YOU. IT'S MORE LIKE *FALLING THROUGH* IT.
EVERY STEP YOU EVER TOOK. EVERY MISTAKE YOU EVER MADE.
EVERY REGRET.
I REACH FOR A MOMENT, TRY TO CHANGE THE OUTCOME.
BUT THERE'S NOTHING TO GRAB ONTO. THE MOMENT HAS PASSED.
IT'S TOO LATE. AND I *FALL.*

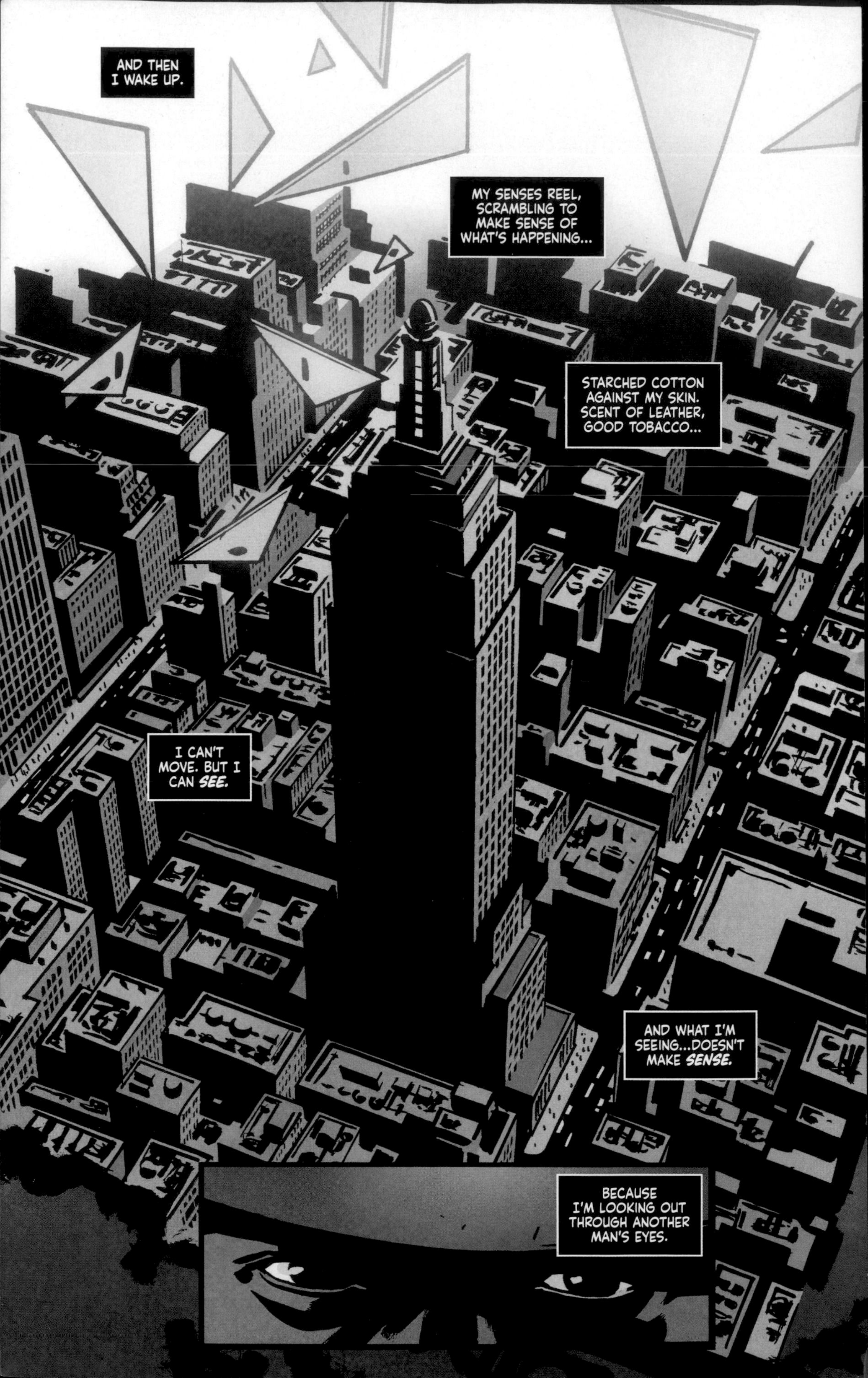
AND THEN I WAKE UP.
MY SENSES REEL, SCRAMBLING TO MAKE SENSE OF WHAT'S HAPPENING...
STARCHED COTTON AGAINST MY SKIN. SCENT OF LEATHER, GOOD TOBACCO...
I CAN'T MOVE. BUT I CAN *SEE.*
AND WHAT I'M SEEING...DOESN'T MAKE *SENSE.*
BECAUSE I'M LOOKING OUT THROUGH ANOTHER MAN'S EYES.

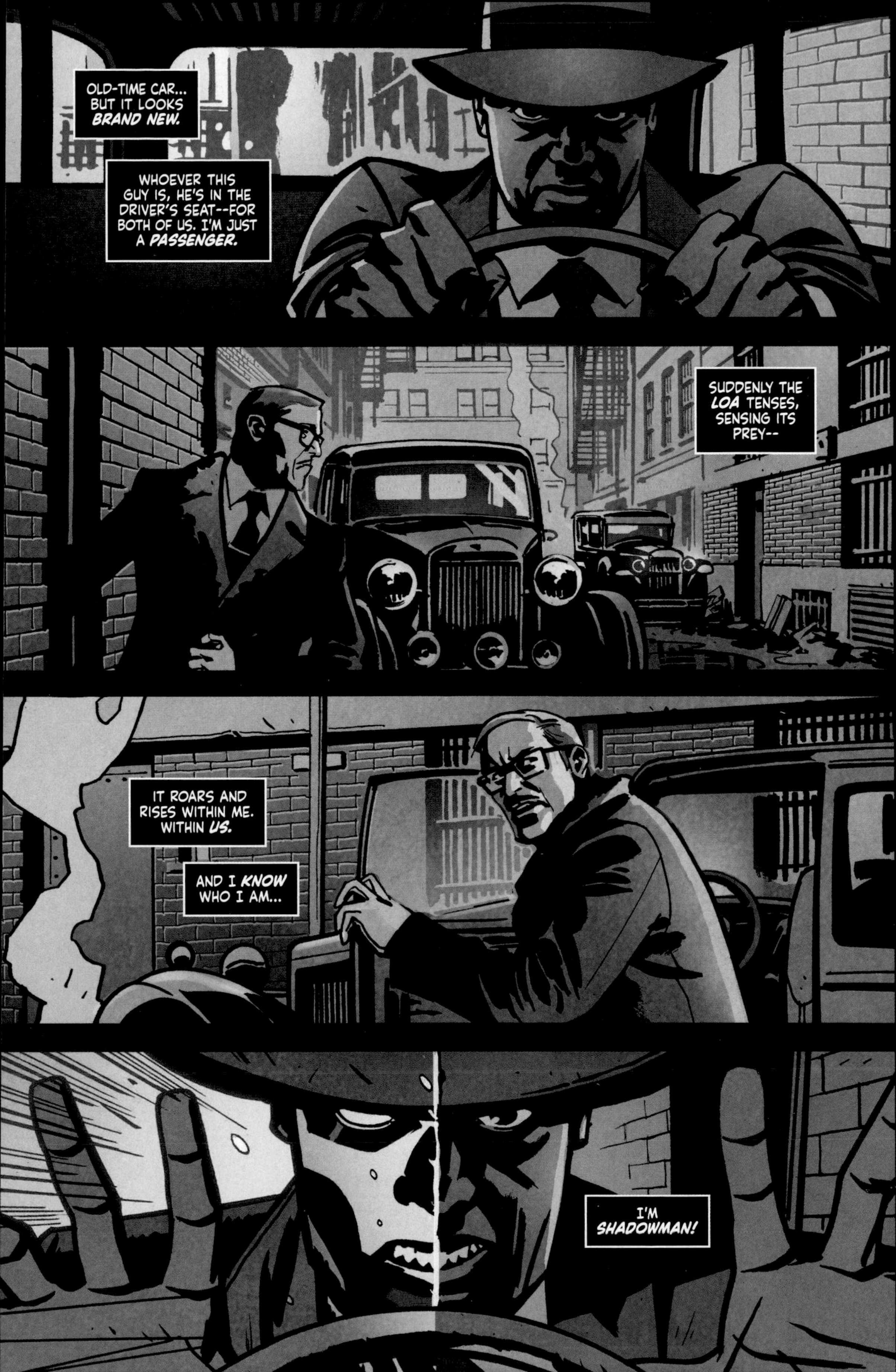
OLD-TIME CAR... BUT IT LOOKS BRAND NEW.
WHOEVER THIS GUY IS, HE'S IN THE DRIVER'S SEAT--FOR BOTH OF US. I'M JUST A PASSENGER.
SUDDENLY THE LOA TENSES, SENSING ITS PREY--
IT ROARS AND RISES WITHIN ME. WITHIN US.
AND I KNOW WHO I AM...
I'M SHADOWMAN!

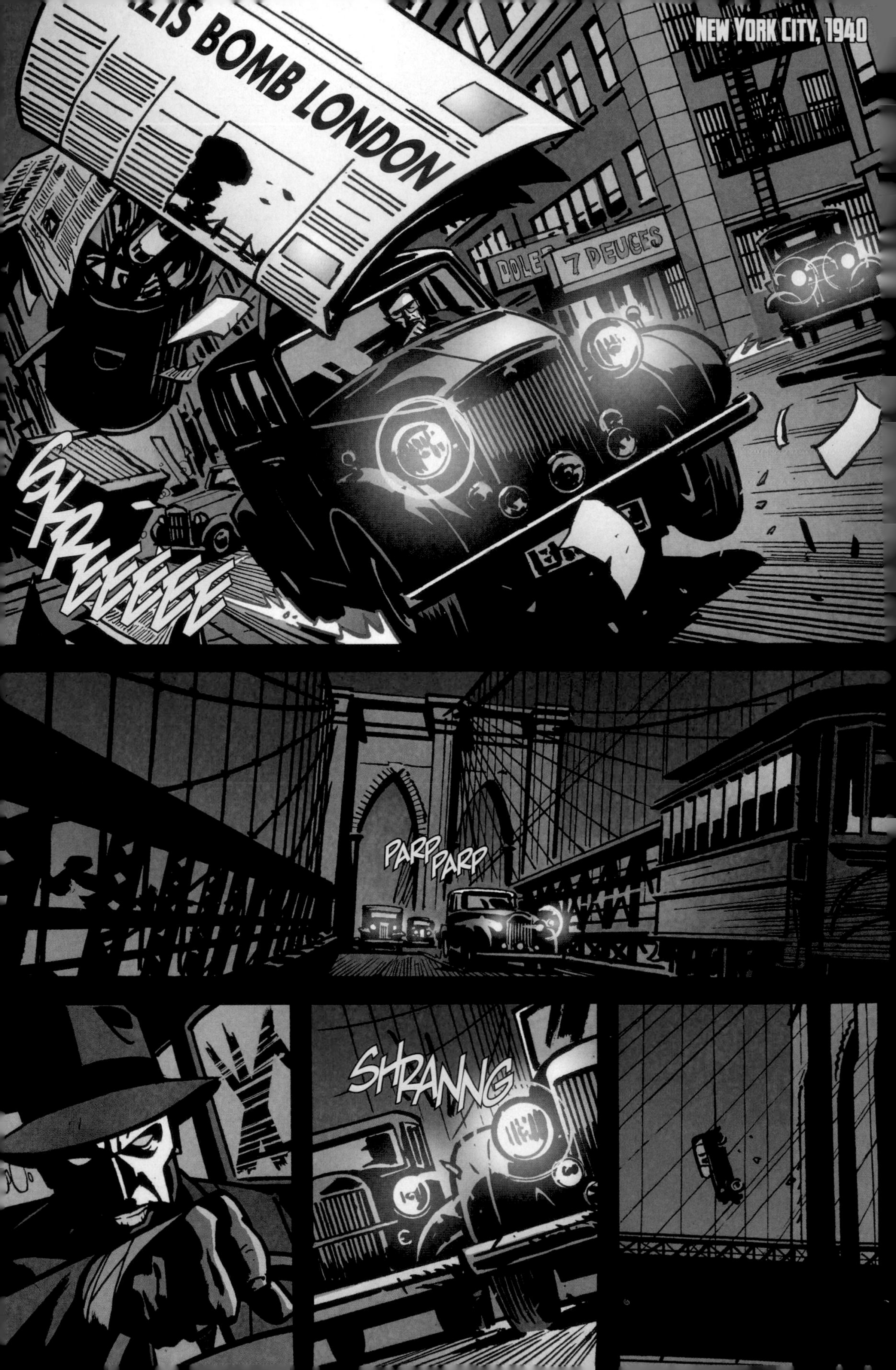
NEW YORK CITY, 1940
ZIS BOMB LONDON
DOLE
7 DEUCES
PARP PARP
SHRANNG

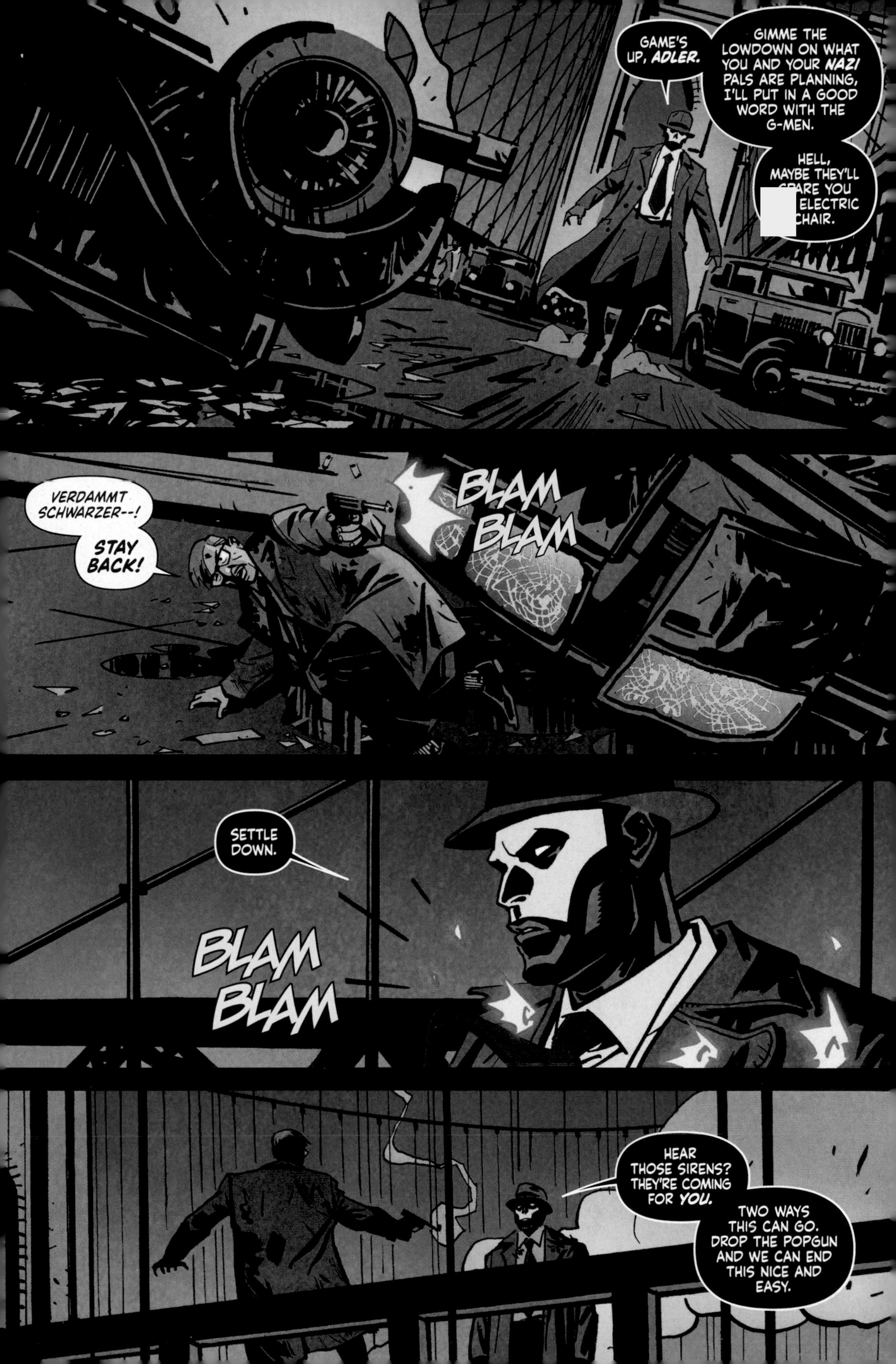
GAME'S UP, ADLER.
GIMME THE LOWDOWN ON WHAT YOU AND YOUR NAZI PALS ARE PLANNING, I'LL PUT IN A GOOD WORD WITH THE G-MEN.
HELL, MAYBE THEY'LL SPARE YOU ELECTRIC CHAIR.
VERDAMMT SCHWARZER--!
STAY BACK!
BLAM BLAM
SETTLE DOWN.
BLAM BLAM
HEAR THOSE SIRENS? THEY'RE COMING FOR YOU.
TWO WAYS THIS CAN GO. DROP THE POPGUN AND WE CAN END THIS NICE AND EASY.

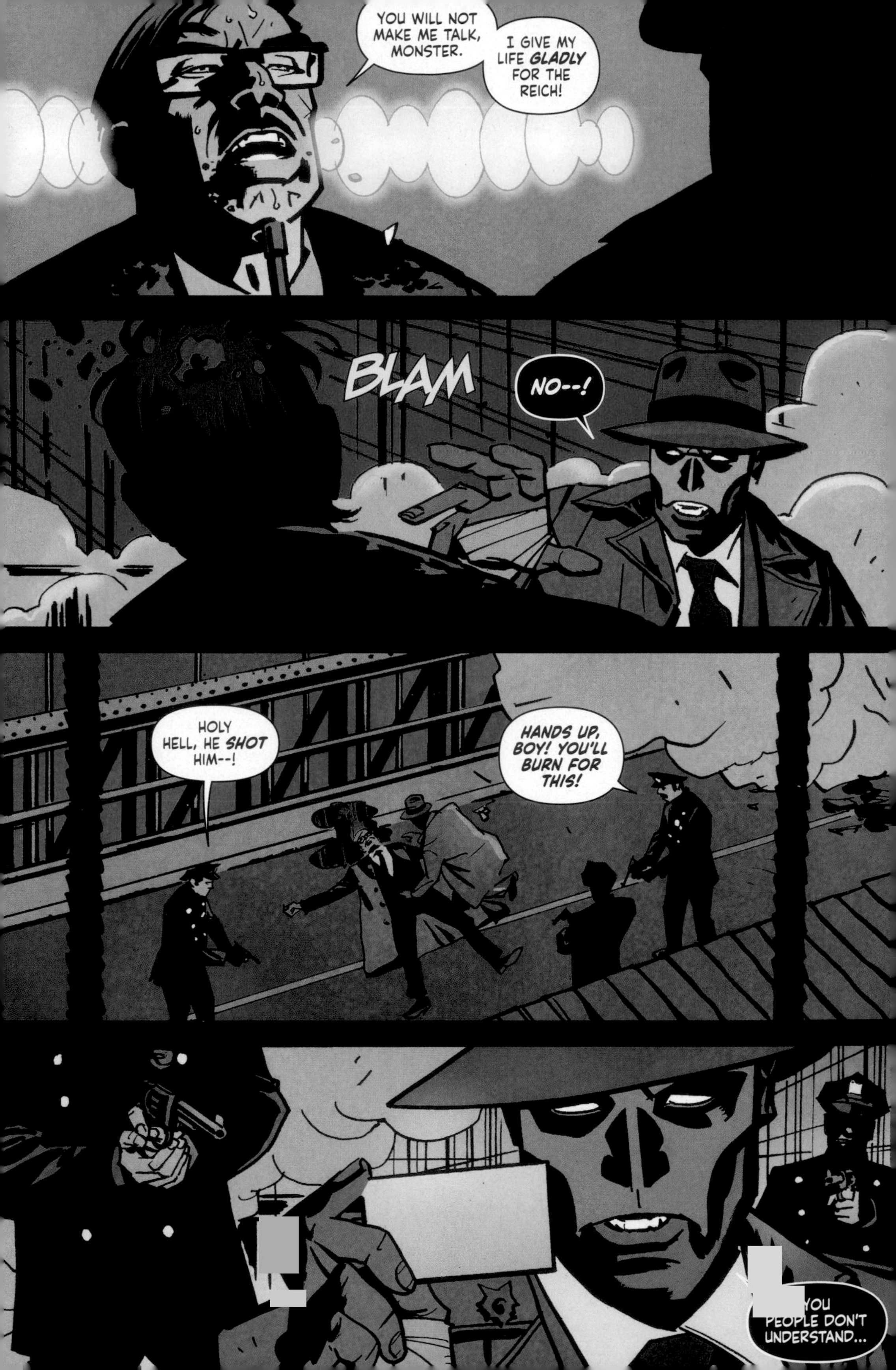
YOU WILL NOT MAKE ME TALK, MONSTER.
I GIVE MY LIFE GLADLY FOR THE REICH!
BLAM
NO--!
HOLY HELL, HE SHOT HIM--!
HANDS UP, BOY! YOU'LL BURN FOR THIS!
YOU PEOPLE DON'T UNDERSTAND...

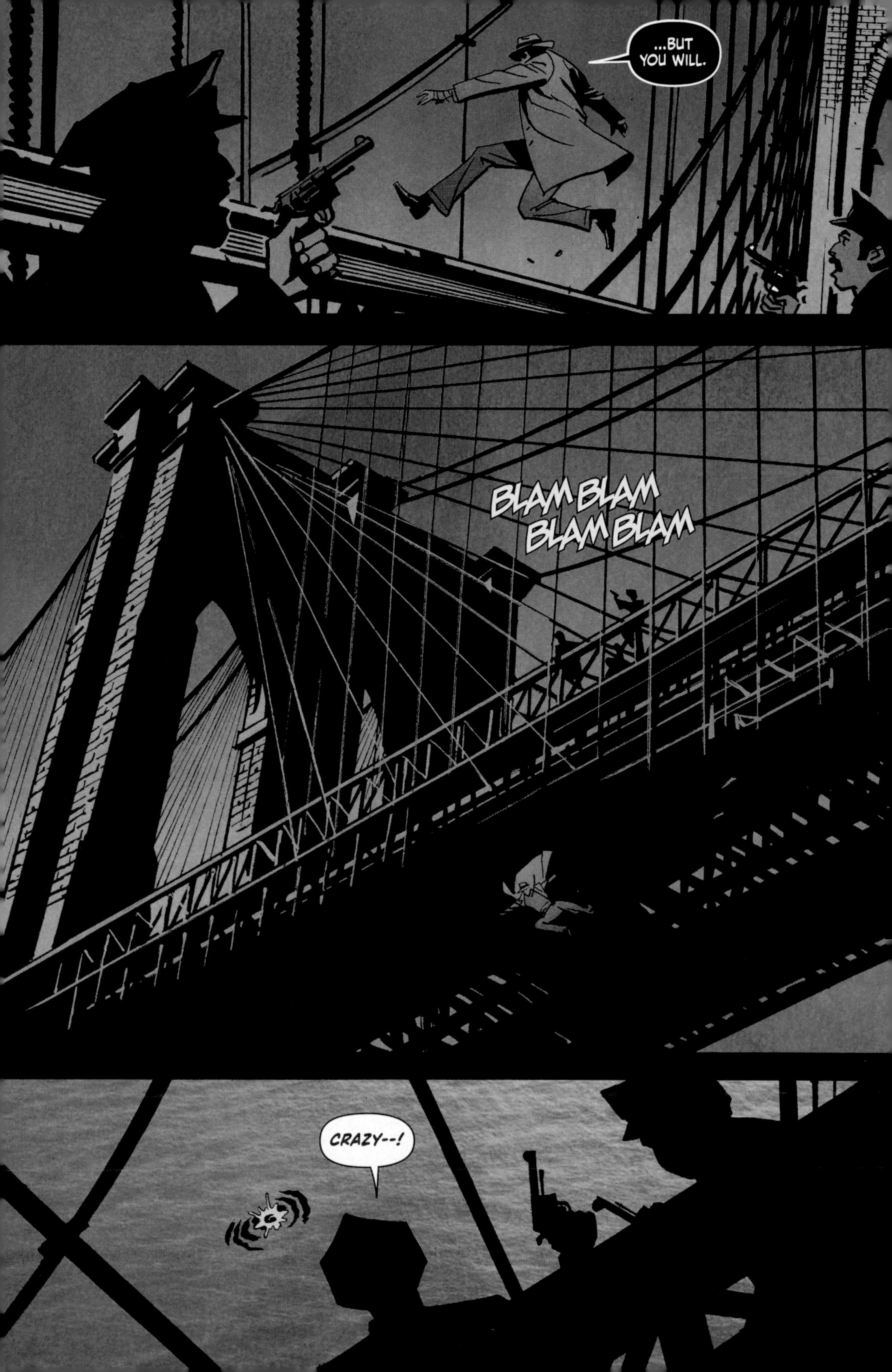
...BUT YOU WILL.
BLAM BLAM BLAM BLAM
CRAZY--!

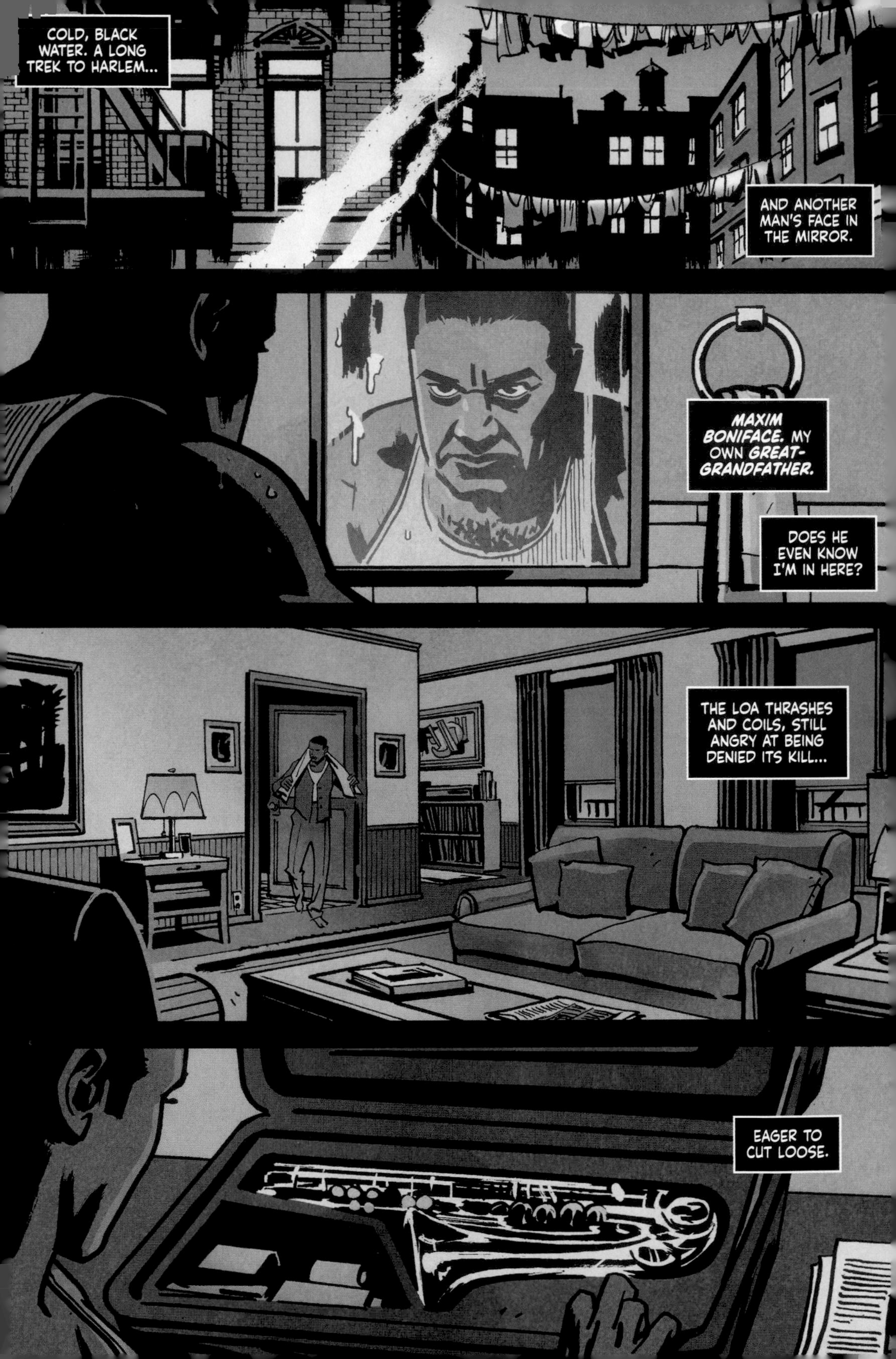
COLD, BLACK WATER. A LONG TREK TO HARLEM...
AND ANOTHER MAN'S FACE IN THE MIRROR.
MAXIM BONIFACE. MY OWN *GREAT-GRANDFATHER.*
DOES HE EVEN KNOW I'M IN HERE?
THE LOA THRASHES AND COILS, STILL ANGRY AT BEING DENIED ITS KILL...
EAGER TO CUT LOOSE.

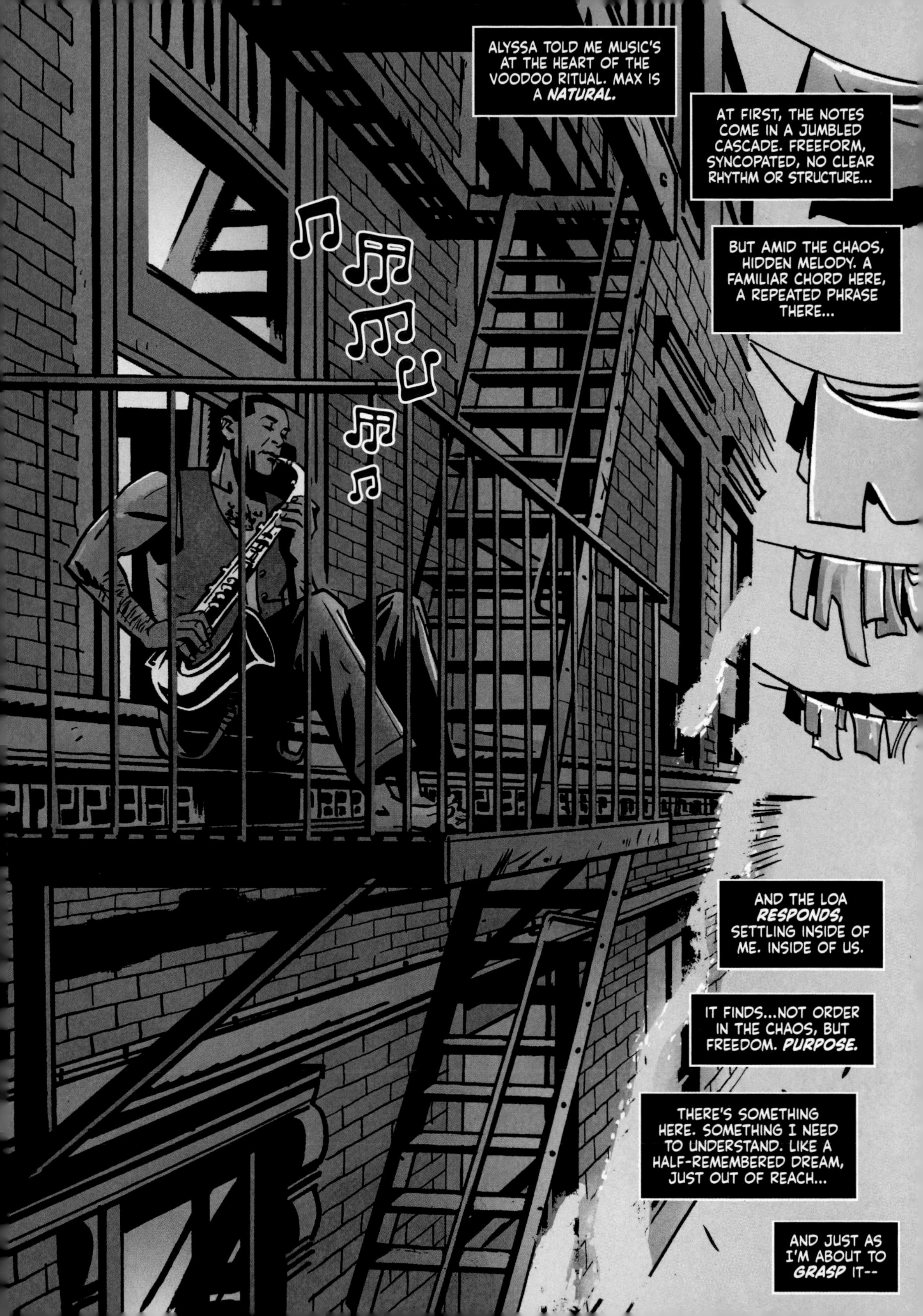
ALYSSA TOLD ME MUSIC'S AT THE HEART OF THE VOODOO RITUAL. MAX IS A NATURAL.
AT FIRST, THE NOTES COME IN A JUMBLED CASCADE. FREEFORM, SYNCOPATED, NO CLEAR RHYTHM OR STRUCTURE...
BUT AMID THE CHAOS, HIDDEN MELODY. A FAMILIAR CHORD HERE, A REPEATED PHRASE THERE...
AND THE LOA RESPONDS, SETTLING INSIDE OF ME. INSIDE OF US.
IT FINDS...NOT ORDER IN THE CHAOS, BUT FREEDOM. PURPOSE.
THERE'S SOMETHING HERE. SOMETHING I NEED TO UNDERSTAND. LIKE A HALF-REMEMBERED DREAM, JUST OUT OF REACH...
AND JUST AS I'M ABOUT TO GRASP IT--

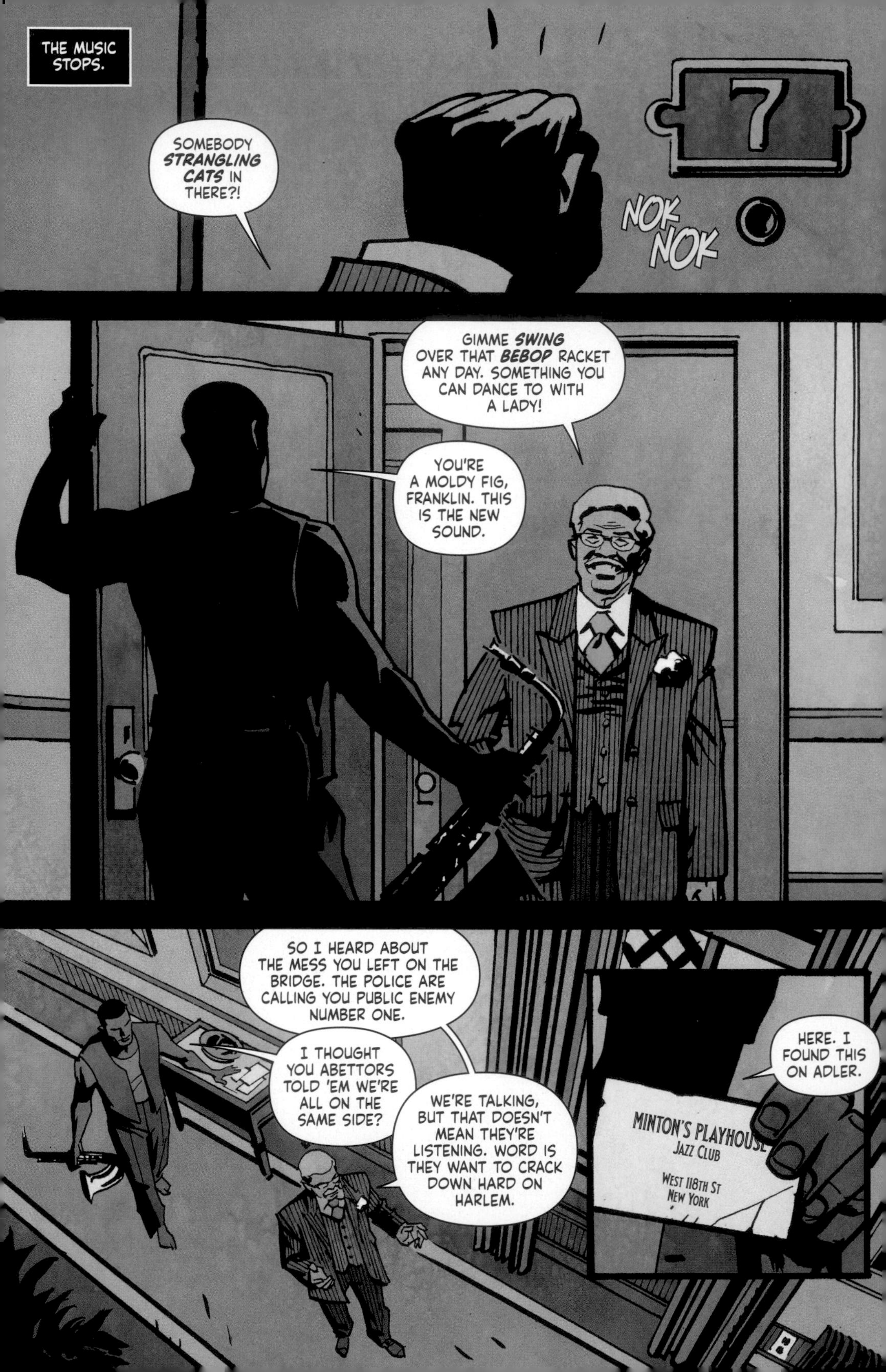
THE MUSIC STOPS.
SOMEBODY STRANGLING CATS IN THERE?!
NOK NOK
GIMME SWING OVER THAT BEBOP RACKET ANY DAY. SOMETHING YOU CAN DANCE TO WITH A LADY!
YOU'RE A MOLDY FIG, FRANKLIN. THIS IS THE NEW SOUND.
SO I HEARD ABOUT THE MESS YOU LEFT ON THE BRIDGE. THE POLICE ARE CALLING YOU PUBLIC ENEMY NUMBER ONE.
I THOUGHT YOU ABETTORS TOLD 'EM WE'RE ALL ON THE SAME SIDE?
WE'RE TALKING, BUT THAT DOESN'T MEAN THEY'RE LISTENING. WORD IS THEY WANT TO CRACK DOWN HARD ON HARLEM.
HERE. I FOUND THIS ON ADLER.
MINTON'S PLAYHOUSE
JAZZ CLUB
WEST 118TH ST
NEW YORK

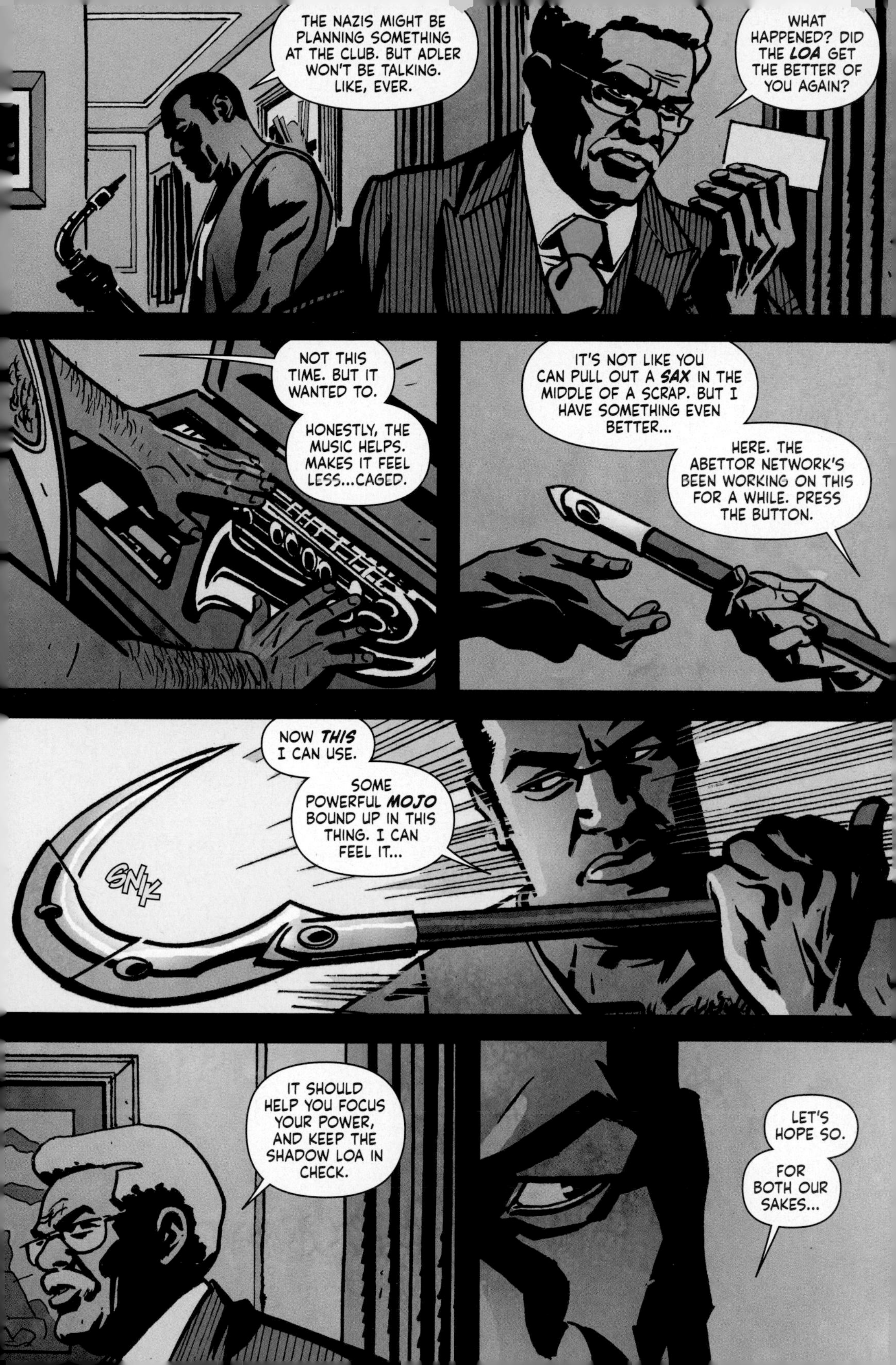
THE NAZIS MIGHT BE PLANNING SOMETHING AT THE CLUB. BUT ADLER WON'T BE TALKING. LIKE, EVER.
WHAT HAPPENED? DID THE *LOA* GET THE BETTER OF YOU AGAIN?
NOT THIS TIME. BUT IT WANTED TO.
HONESTLY, THE MUSIC HELPS. MAKES IT FEEL LESS...CAGED.
IT'S NOT LIKE YOU CAN PULL OUT A *SAX* IN THE MIDDLE OF A SCRAP. BUT I HAVE SOMETHING EVEN BETTER...
HERE. THE ABETTOR NETWORK'S BEEN WORKING ON THIS FOR A WHILE. PRESS THE BUTTON.
NOW *THIS* I CAN USE.
SOME POWERFUL *MOJO* BOUND UP IN THIS THING. I CAN FEEL IT...
SNIK
IT SHOULD HELP YOU FOCUS YOUR POWER, AND KEEP THE SHADOW LOA IN CHECK.
LET'S HOPE SO.
FOR BOTH OUR SAKES...

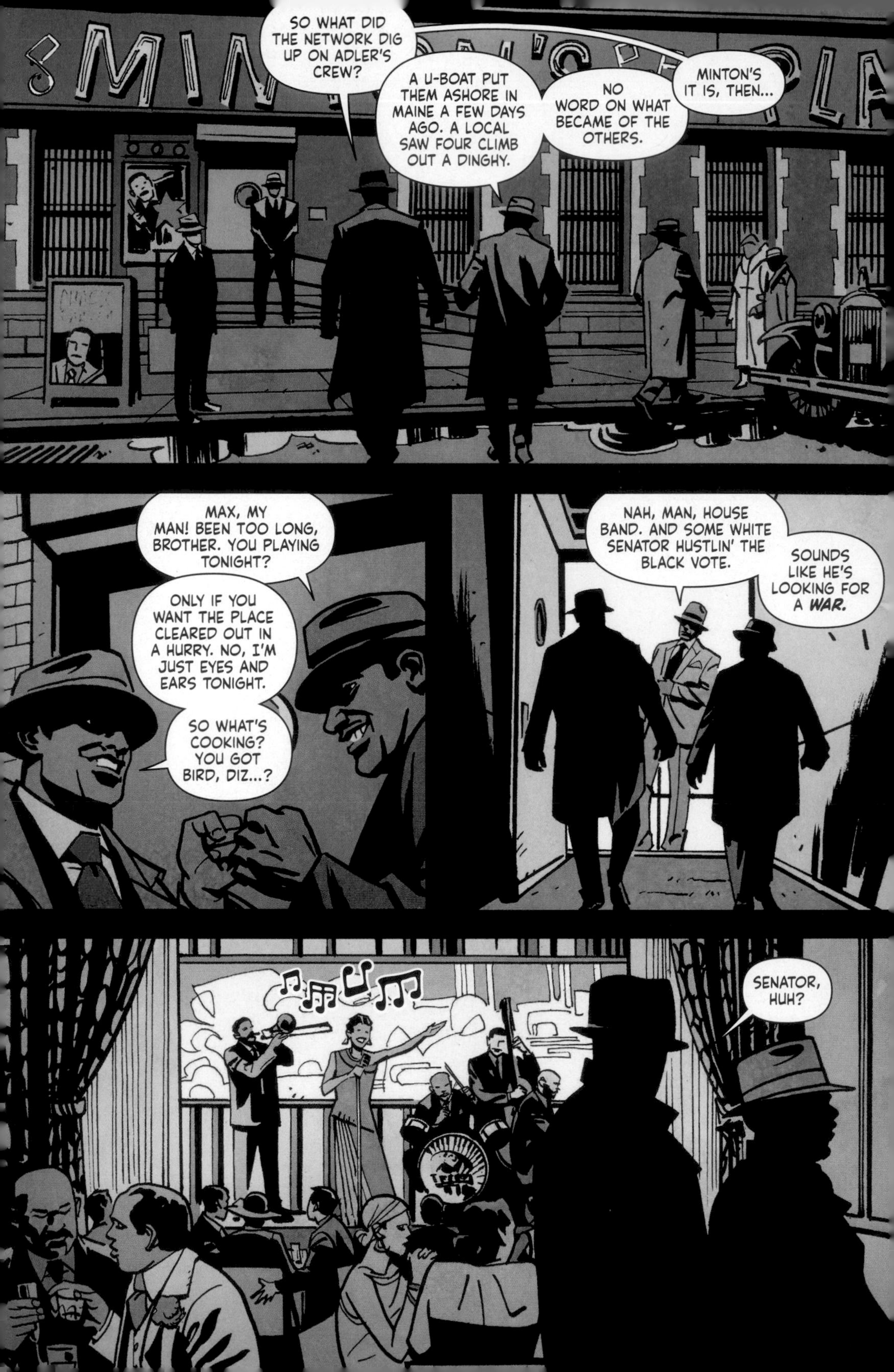
SO WHAT DID THE NETWORK DIG UP ON ADLER'S CREW?
A U-BOAT PUT THEM ASHORE IN MAINE A FEW DAYS AGO. A LOCAL SAW FOUR CLIMB OUT A DINGHY.
NO WORD ON WHAT BECAME OF THE OTHERS.
MINTON'S IT IS, THEN...
MAX, MY MAN! BEEN TOO LONG, BROTHER. YOU PLAYING TONIGHT?
ONLY IF YOU WANT THE PLACE CLEARED OUT IN A HURRY. NO, I'M JUST EYES AND EARS TONIGHT.
SO WHAT'S COOKING? YOU GOT BIRD, DIZ...?
NAH, MAN, HOUSE BAND. AND SOME WHITE SENATOR HUSTLIN' THE BLACK VOTE.
SOUNDS LIKE HE'S LOOKING FOR A **WAR.**
SENATOR, HUH?

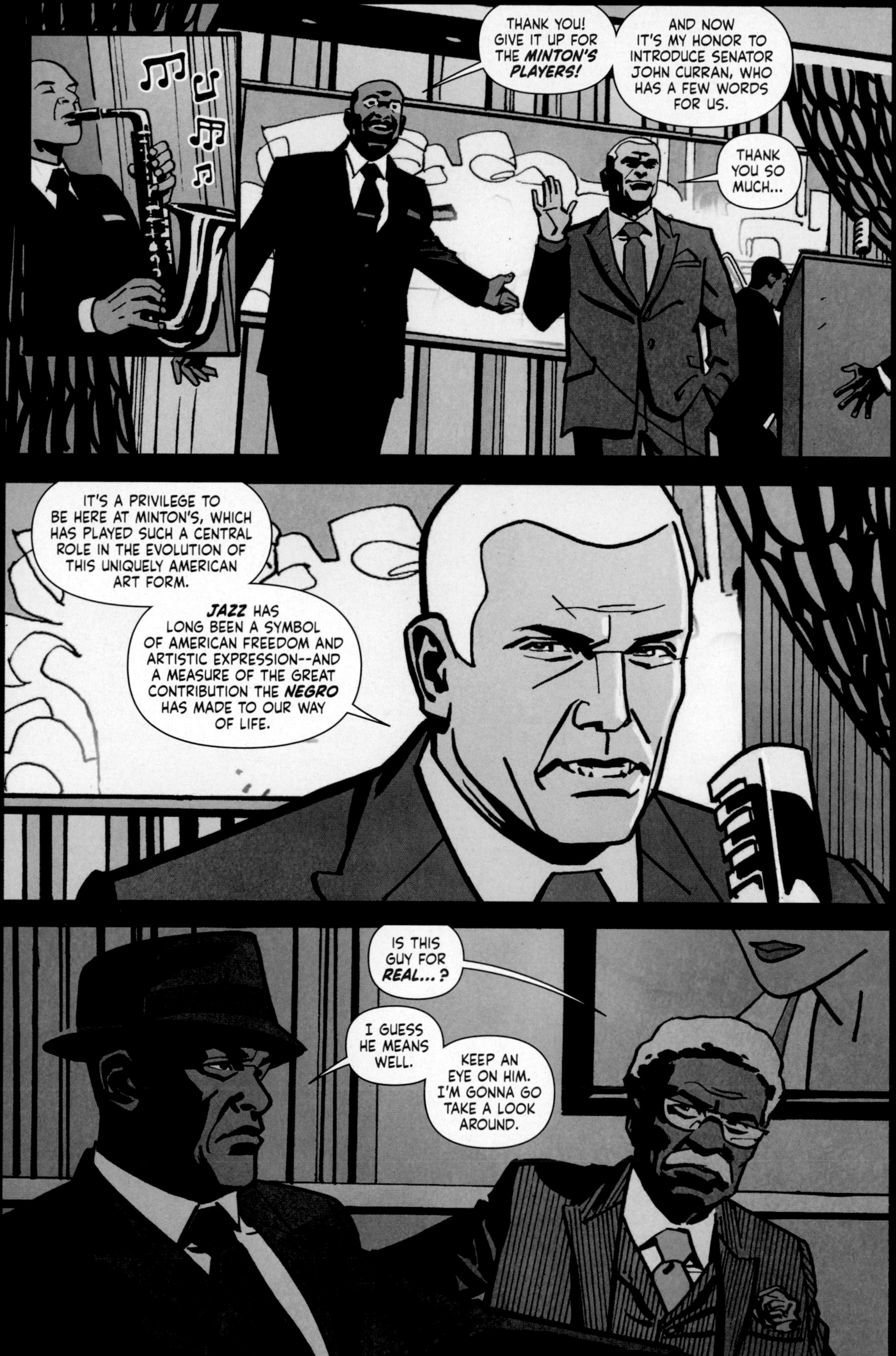
THANK YOU! GIVE IT UP FOR THE MINTON'S PLAYERS!
AND NOW IT'S MY HONOR TO INTRODUCE SENATOR JOHN CURRAN, WHO HAS A FEW WORDS FOR US.
THANK YOU SO MUCH...
IT'S A PRIVILEGE TO BE HERE AT MINTON'S, WHICH HAS PLAYED SUCH A CENTRAL ROLE IN THE EVOLUTION OF THIS UNIQUELY AMERICAN ART FORM.
JAZZ HAS LONG BEEN A SYMBOL OF AMERICAN FREEDOM AND ARTISTIC EXPRESSION--AND A MEASURE OF THE GREAT CONTRIBUTION THE NEGRO HAS MADE TO OUR WAY OF LIFE.
IS THIS GUY FOR REAL...?
I GUESS HE MEANS WELL.
KEEP AN EYE ON HIM. I'M GONNA GO TAKE A LOOK AROUND.

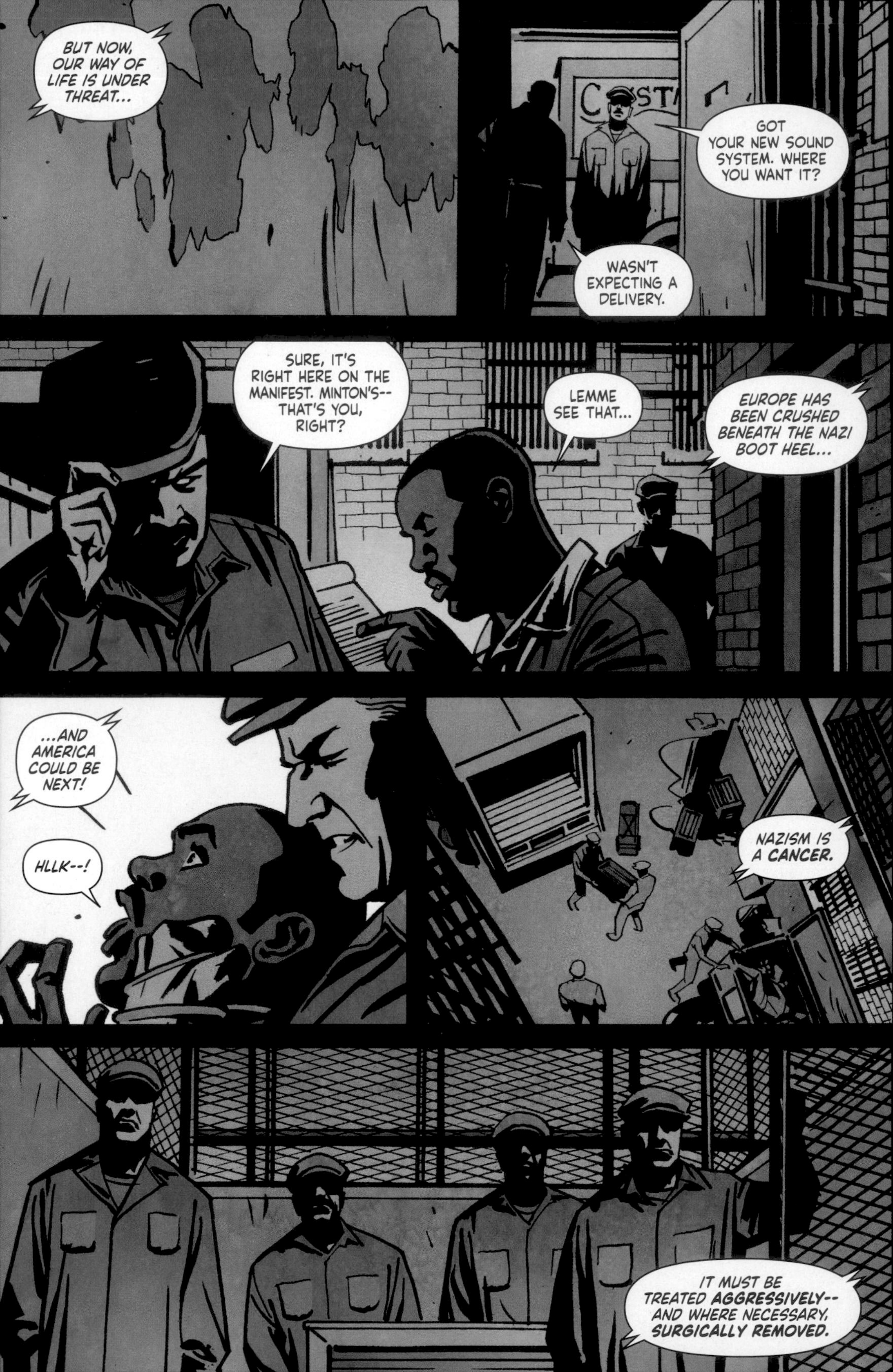
BUT NOW, OUR WAY OF LIFE IS UNDER THREAT...
GOT YOUR NEW SOUND SYSTEM. WHERE YOU WANT IT?
WASN'T EXPECTING A DELIVERY.
SURE, IT'S RIGHT HERE ON THE MANIFEST. MINTON'S-- THAT'S YOU, RIGHT?
LEMME SEE THAT...
EUROPE HAS BEEN CRUSHED BENEATH THE NAZI BOOT HEEL...
...AND AMERICA COULD BE NEXT!
HLLK--!
NAZISM IS A CANCER.
IT MUST BE TREATED AGGRESSIVELY-- AND WHERE NECESSARY, SURGICALLY REMOVED.

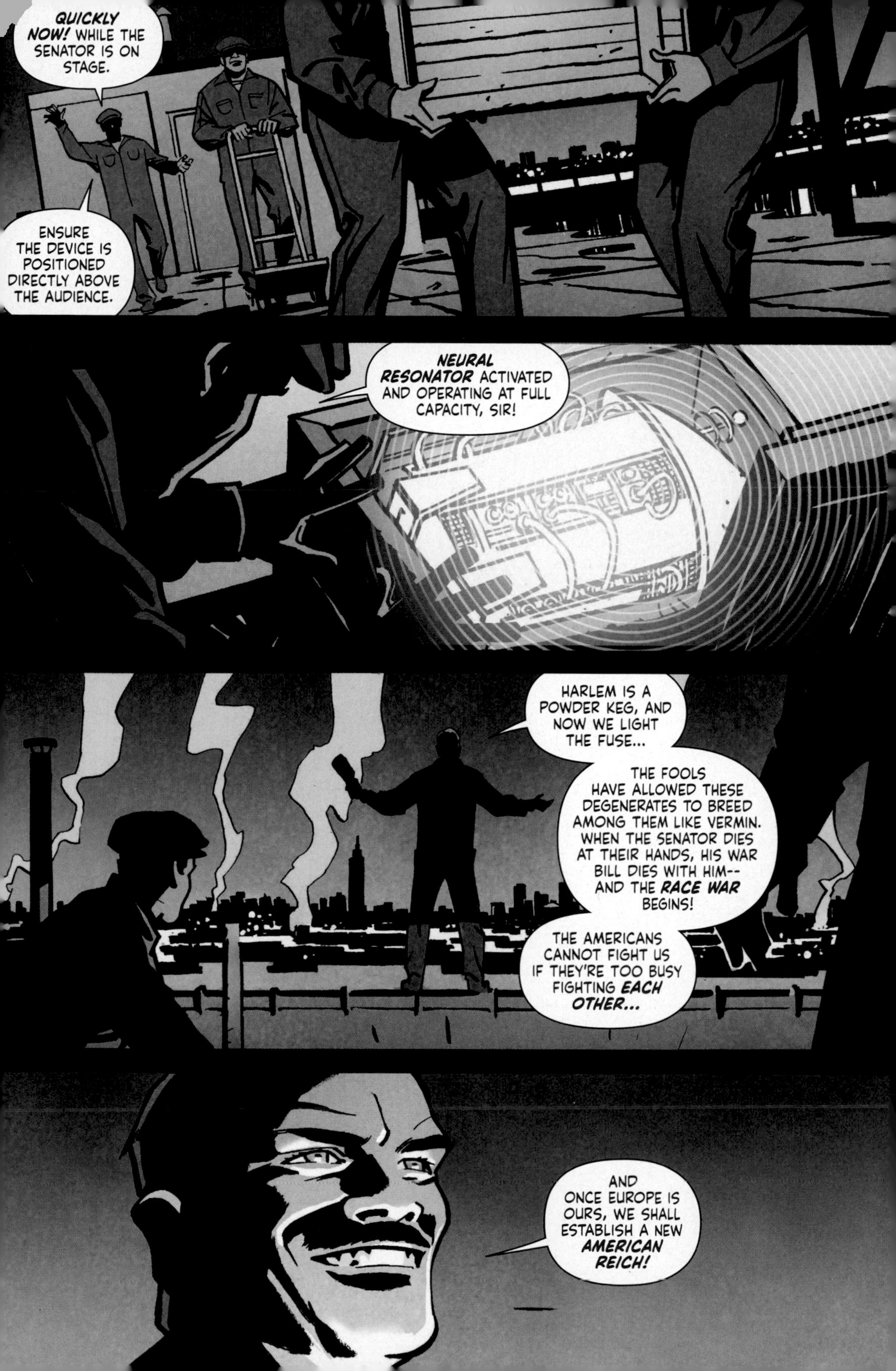
QUICKLY NOW! WHILE THE SENATOR IS ON STAGE.
ENSURE THE DEVICE IS POSITIONED DIRECTLY ABOVE THE AUDIENCE.
NEURAL RESONATOR ACTIVATED AND OPERATING AT FULL CAPACITY, SIR!
HARLEM IS A POWDER KEG, AND NOW WE LIGHT THE FUSE...
THE FOOLS HAVE ALLOWED THESE DEGENERATES TO BREED AMONG THEM LIKE VERMIN. WHEN THE SENATOR DIES AT THEIR HANDS, HIS WAR BILL DIES WITH HIM--AND THE RACE WAR BEGINS!
THE AMERICANS CANNOT FIGHT US IF THEY'RE TOO BUSY FIGHTING EACH OTHER...
AND ONCE EUROPE IS OURS, WE SHALL ESTABLISH A NEW AMERICAN REICH!

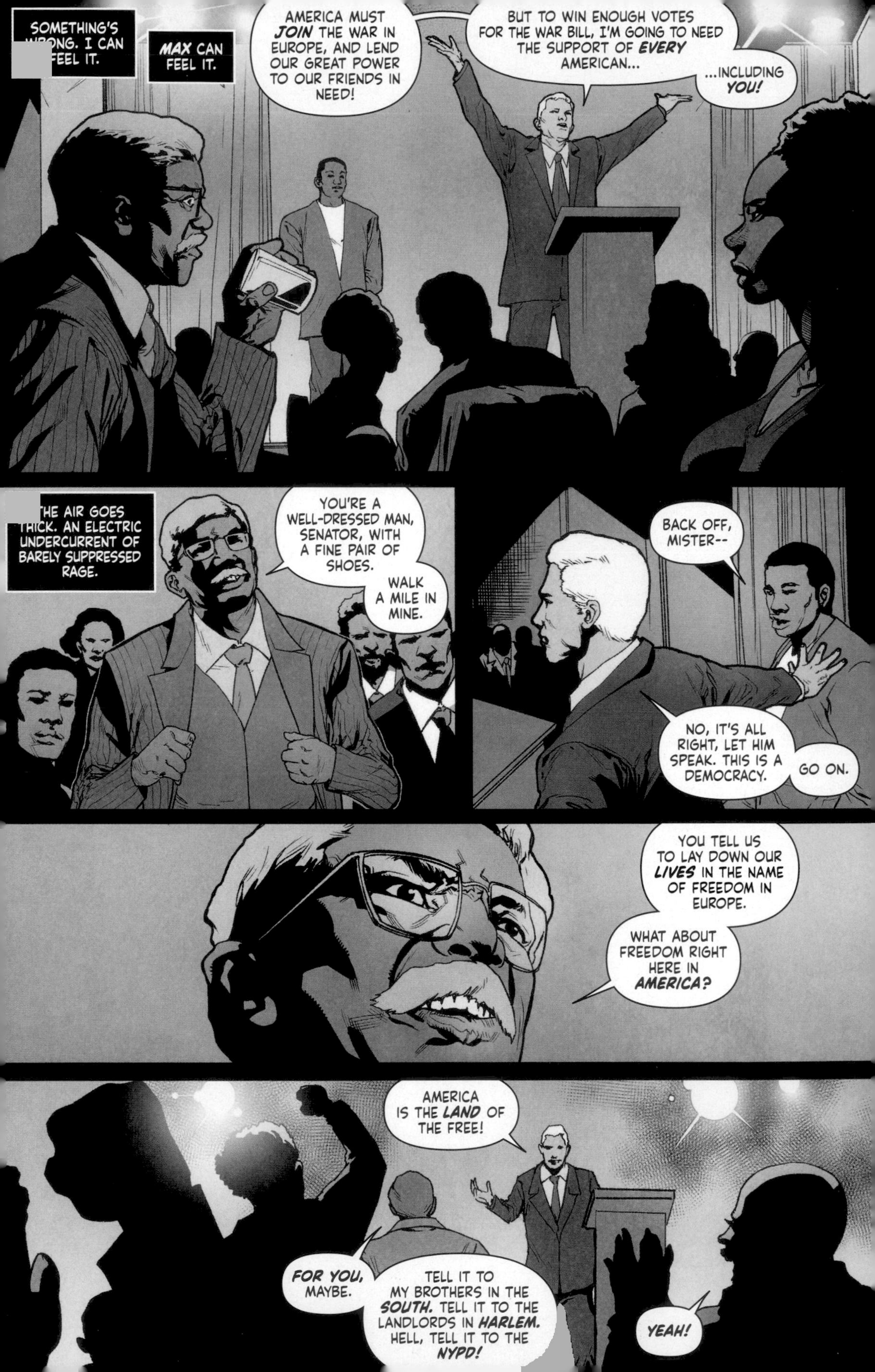

SOMETHING'S WRONG. I CAN FEEL IT.
MAX CAN FEEL IT.
AMERICA MUST JOIN THE WAR IN EUROPE, AND LEND OUR GREAT POWER TO OUR FRIENDS IN NEED!
BUT TO WIN ENOUGH VOTES FOR THE WAR BILL, I'M GOING TO NEED THE SUPPORT OF EVERY AMERICAN...
...INCLUDING YOU!
THE AIR GOES THICK. AN ELECTRIC UNDERCURRENT OF BARELY SUPPRESSED RAGE.
YOU'RE A WELL-DRESSED MAN, SENATOR, WITH A FINE PAIR OF SHOES.
WALK A MILE IN MINE.
BACK OFF, MISTER--
NO, IT'S ALL RIGHT, LET HIM SPEAK. THIS IS A DEMOCRACY.
GO ON.
YOU TELL US TO LAY DOWN OUR LIVES IN THE NAME OF FREEDOM IN EUROPE.
WHAT ABOUT FREEDOM RIGHT HERE IN AMERICA?
AMERICA IS THE LAND OF THE FREE!
FOR YOU, MAYBE.
TELL IT TO MY BROTHERS IN THE SOUTH. TELL IT TO THE LANDLORDS IN HARLEM. HELL, TELL IT TO THE NYPD!
YEAH!

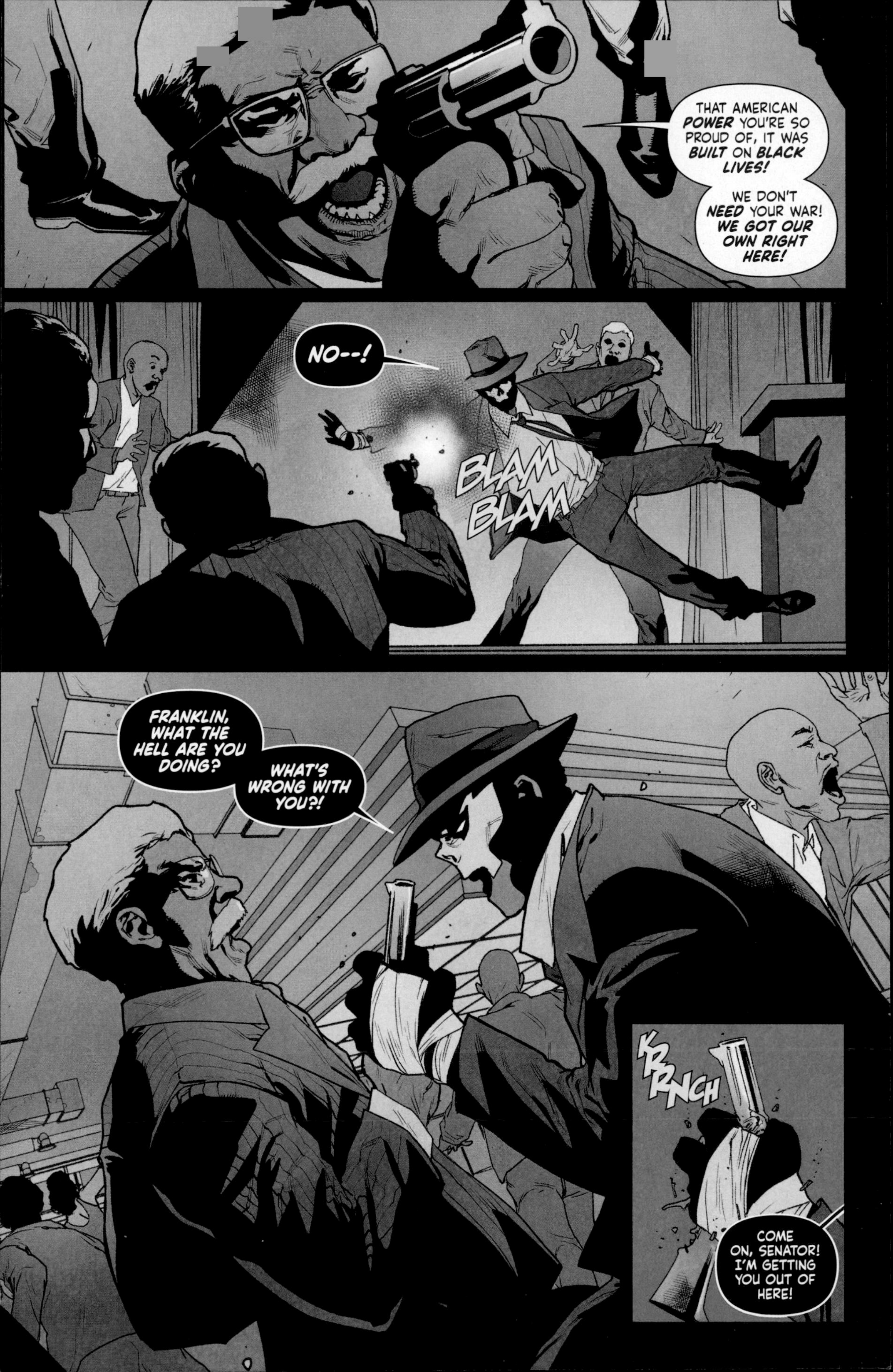
THAT AMERICAN POWER YOU'RE SO PROUD OF, IT WAS BUILT ON BLACK LIVES!
WE DON'T NEED YOUR WAR! WE GOT OUR OWN RIGHT HERE!
NO--!
BLAM BLAM
FRANKLIN, WHAT THE HELL ARE YOU DOING?
WHAT'S WRONG WITH YOU?!
KRRNCH
COME ON, SENATOR! I'M GETTING YOU OUT OF HERE!

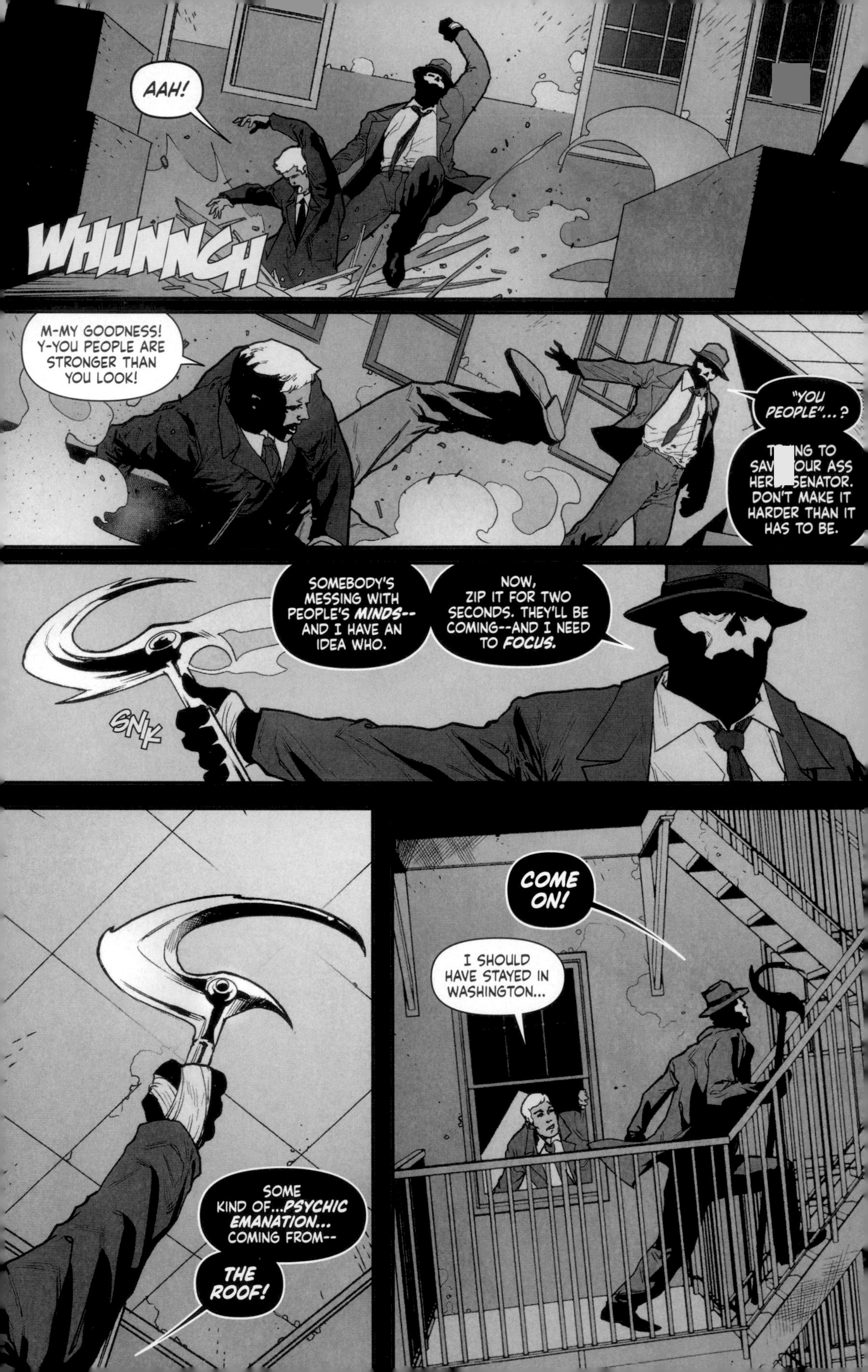
AAH!
WHUNNCH
M-MY GOODNESS! Y-YOU PEOPLE ARE STRONGER THAN YOU LOOK!
"YOU PEOPLE"...?
T ING TO SAV OUR ASS HER SENATOR. DON'T MAKE IT HARDER THAN IT HAS TO BE.
SOMEBODY'S MESSING WITH PEOPLE'S MINDS-- AND I HAVE AN IDEA WHO.
NOW, ZIP IT FOR TWO SECONDS. THEY'LL BE COMING--AND I NEED TO FOCUS.
SNIK
SOME KIND OF...PSYCHIC EMANATION... COMING FROM--
THE ROOF!
COME ON!
I SHOULD HAVE STAYED IN WASHINGTON...

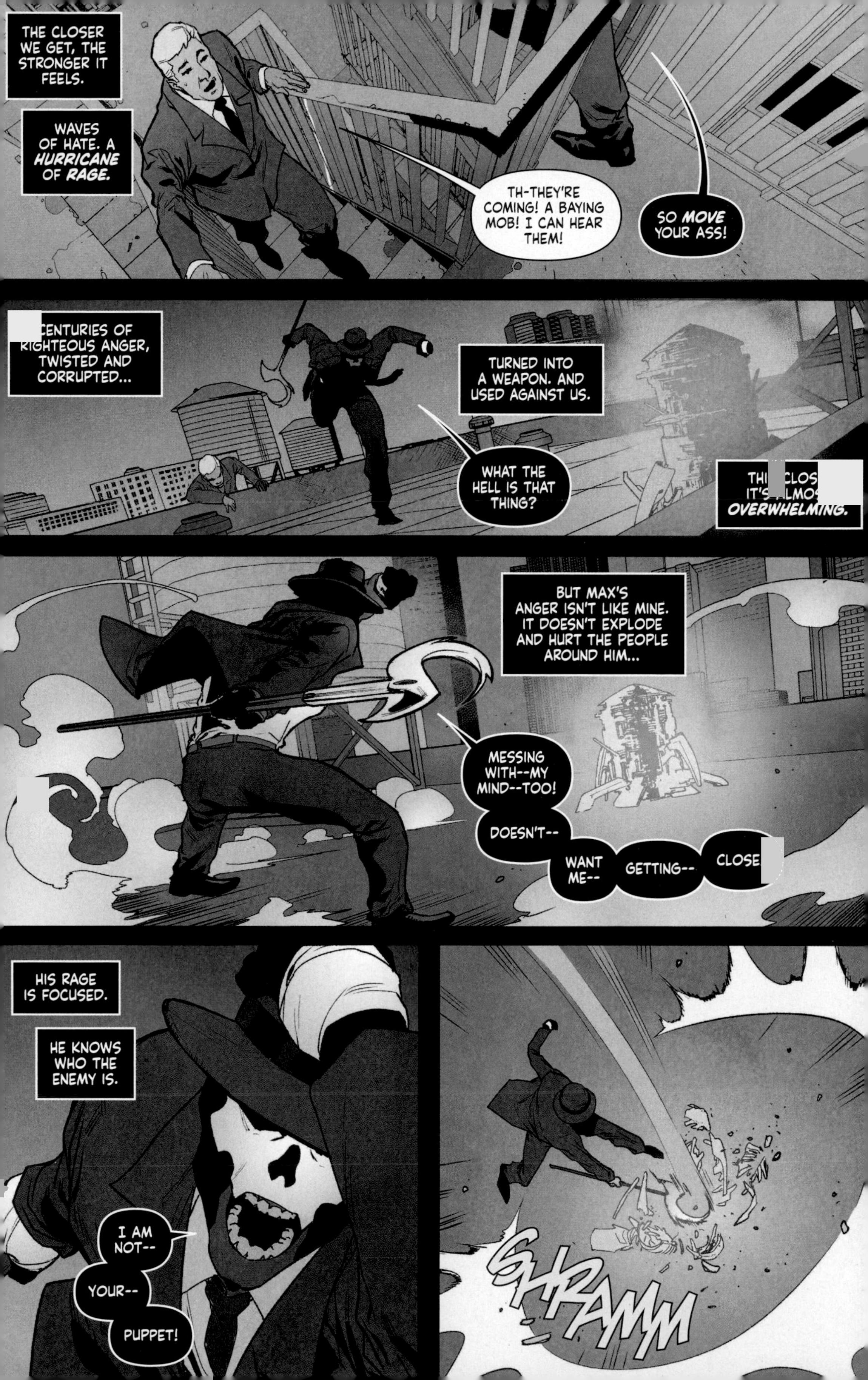
THE CLOSER WE GET, THE STRONGER IT FEELS.
WAVES OF HATE. A ***HURRICANE*** OF ***RAGE.***
TH-THEY'RE COMING! A BAYING MOB! I CAN HEAR THEM!
SO ***MOVE*** YOUR ASS!
CENTURIES OF RIGHTEOUS ANGER, TWISTED AND CORRUPTED...
TURNED INTO A WEAPON. AND USED AGAINST US.
WHAT THE HELL IS THAT THING?
OVERWHELMING.
BUT MAX'S ANGER ISN'T LIKE MINE. IT DOESN'T EXPLODE AND HURT THE PEOPLE AROUND HIM...
MESSING WITH--MY MIND--TOO!
DOESN'T--
WANT ME--
GETTING--
CLOSE
HIS RAGE IS FOCUSED.
HE KNOWS WHO THE ENEMY IS.
I AM NOT--
YOUR--
PUPPET!
SHRAMM

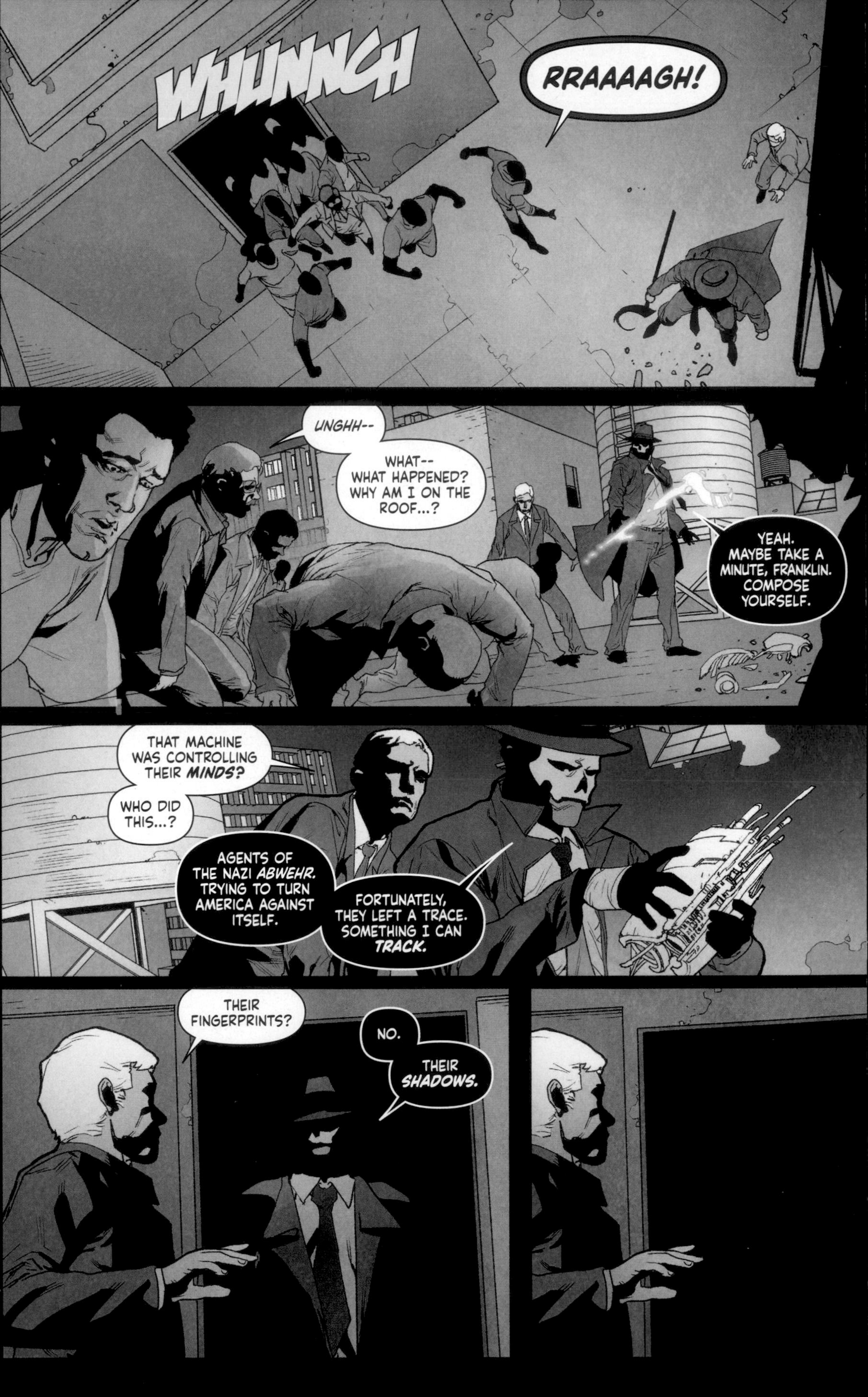
WHUNNCH
RRAAAAGH!
UNGHH--
WHAT-- WHAT HAPPENED? WHY AM I ON THE ROOF...?
YEAH. MAYBE TAKE A MINUTE, FRANKLIN. COMPOSE YOURSELF.
THAT MACHINE WAS CONTROLLING THEIR MINDS?
WHO DID THIS...?
AGENTS OF THE NAZI ABWEHR. TRYING TO TURN AMERICA AGAINST ITSELF.
FORTUNATELY, THEY LEFT A TRACE. SOMETHING I CAN TRACK.
THEIR FINGERPRINTS?
NO.
THEIR SHADOWS.

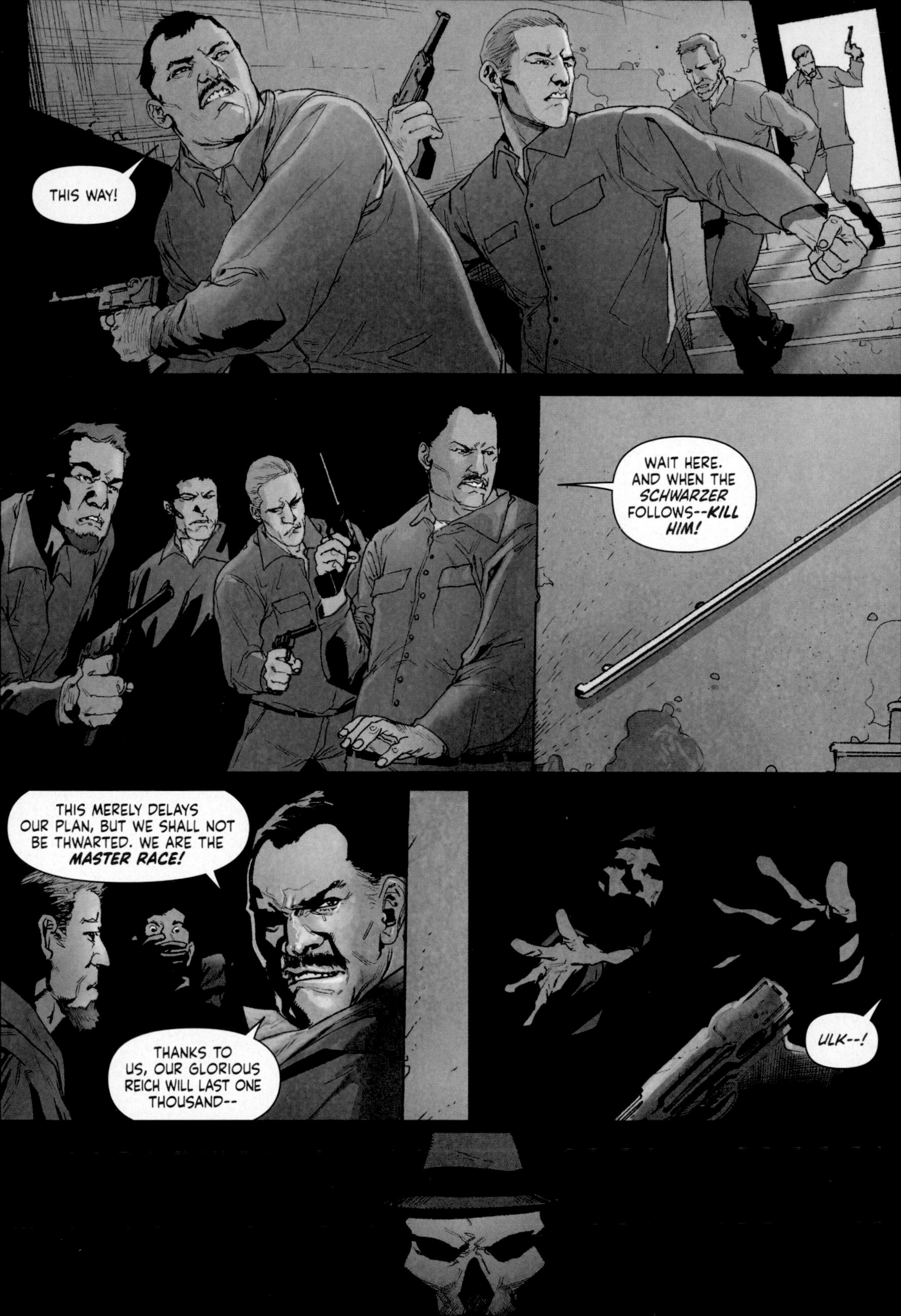

THIS WAY!
WAIT HERE. AND WHEN THE *SCHWARZER* FOLLOWS--**KILL HIM!**
THIS MERELY DELAYS OUR PLAN, BUT WE SHALL NOT BE THWARTED. WE ARE THE ***MASTER RACE!***
THANKS TO US, OUR GLORIOUS REICH WILL LAST ONE THOUSAND--
ULK--!

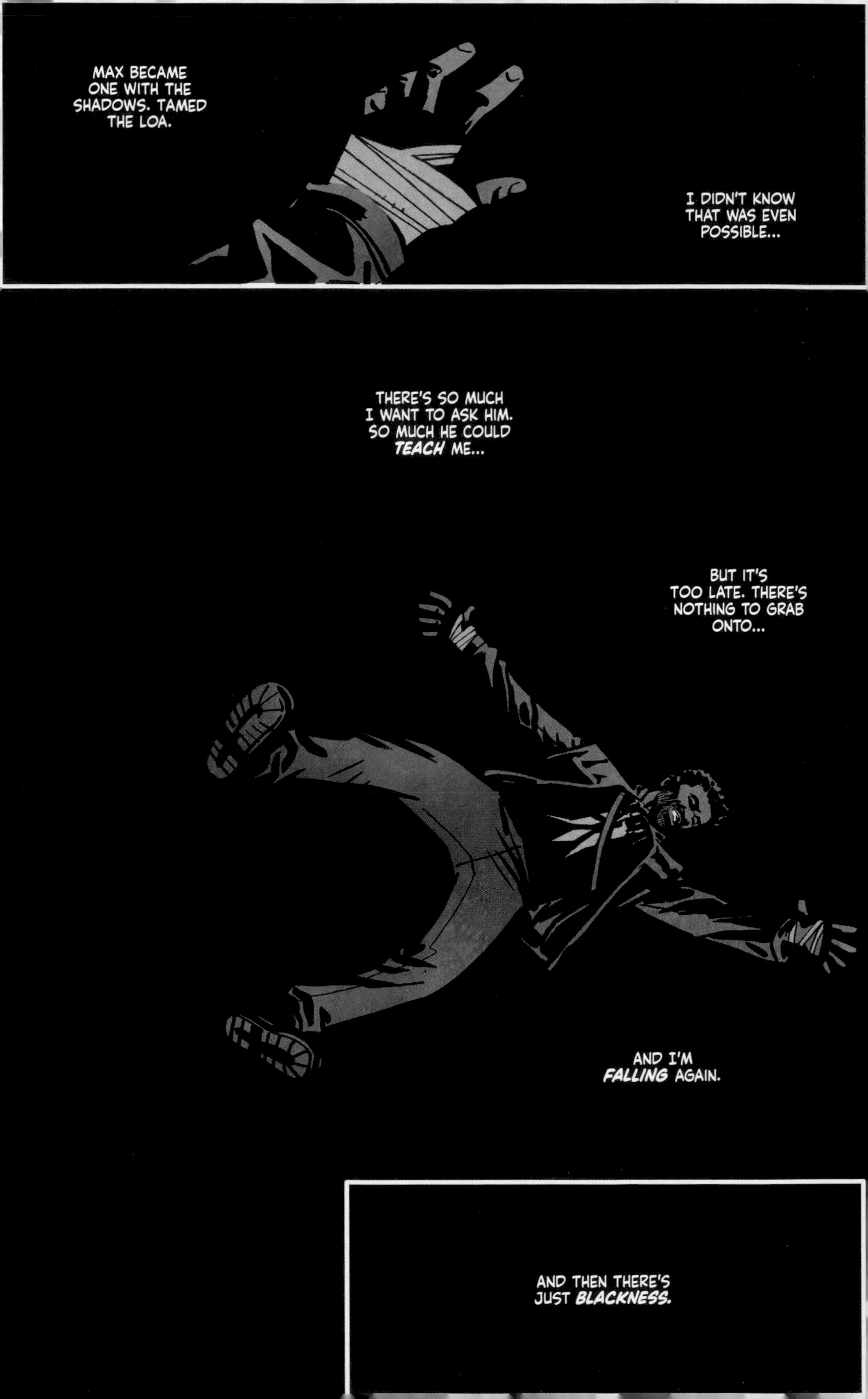
MAX BECAME ONE WITH THE SHADOWS. TAMED THE LOA.
I DIDN'T KNOW THAT WAS EVEN POSSIBLE...
THERE'S SO MUCH I WANT TO ASK HIM. SO MUCH HE COULD *TEACH* ME...
BUT IT'S TOO LATE. THERE'S NOTHING TO GRAB ONTO...
AND I'M *FALLING* AGAIN.
AND THEN THERE'S JUST *BLACKNESS.*

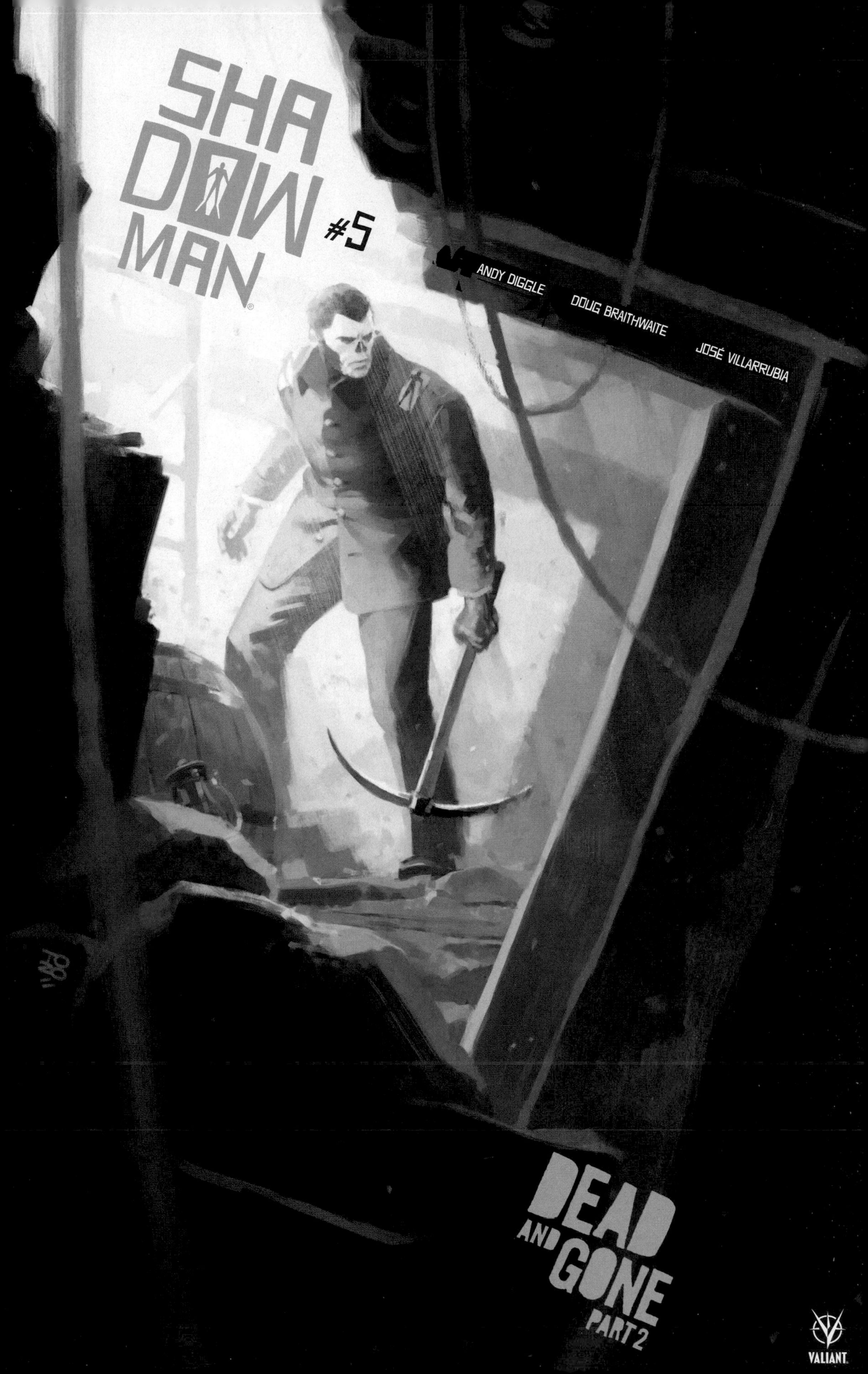
SHADOWMAN
#5
ANDY DIGGLE
DOUG BRAITHWAITE
JOSÉ VILLARRUBIA
DEAD AND GONE
PART 2
VALIANT

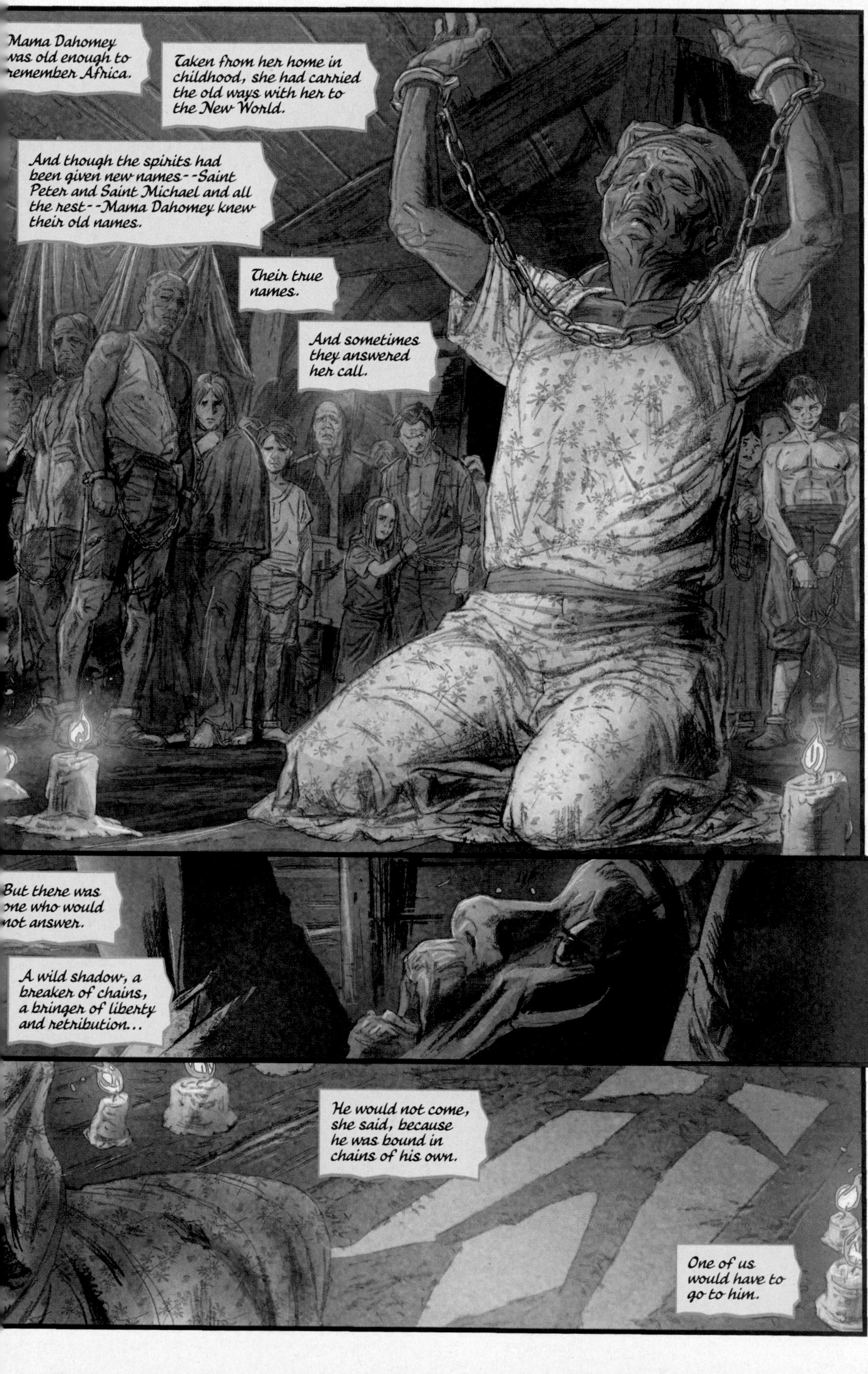
Mama Dahomey was old enough to remember Africa.
Taken from her home in childhood, she had carried the old ways with her to the New World.
And though the spirits had been given new names--Saint Peter and Saint Michael and all the rest--Mama Dahomey knew their old names.
Their true names.
And sometimes they answered her call.
But there was one who would not answer.
A wild shadow, a breaker of chains, a bringer of liberty and retribution...
He would not come, she said, because he was bound in chains of his own.
One of us would have to go to him.

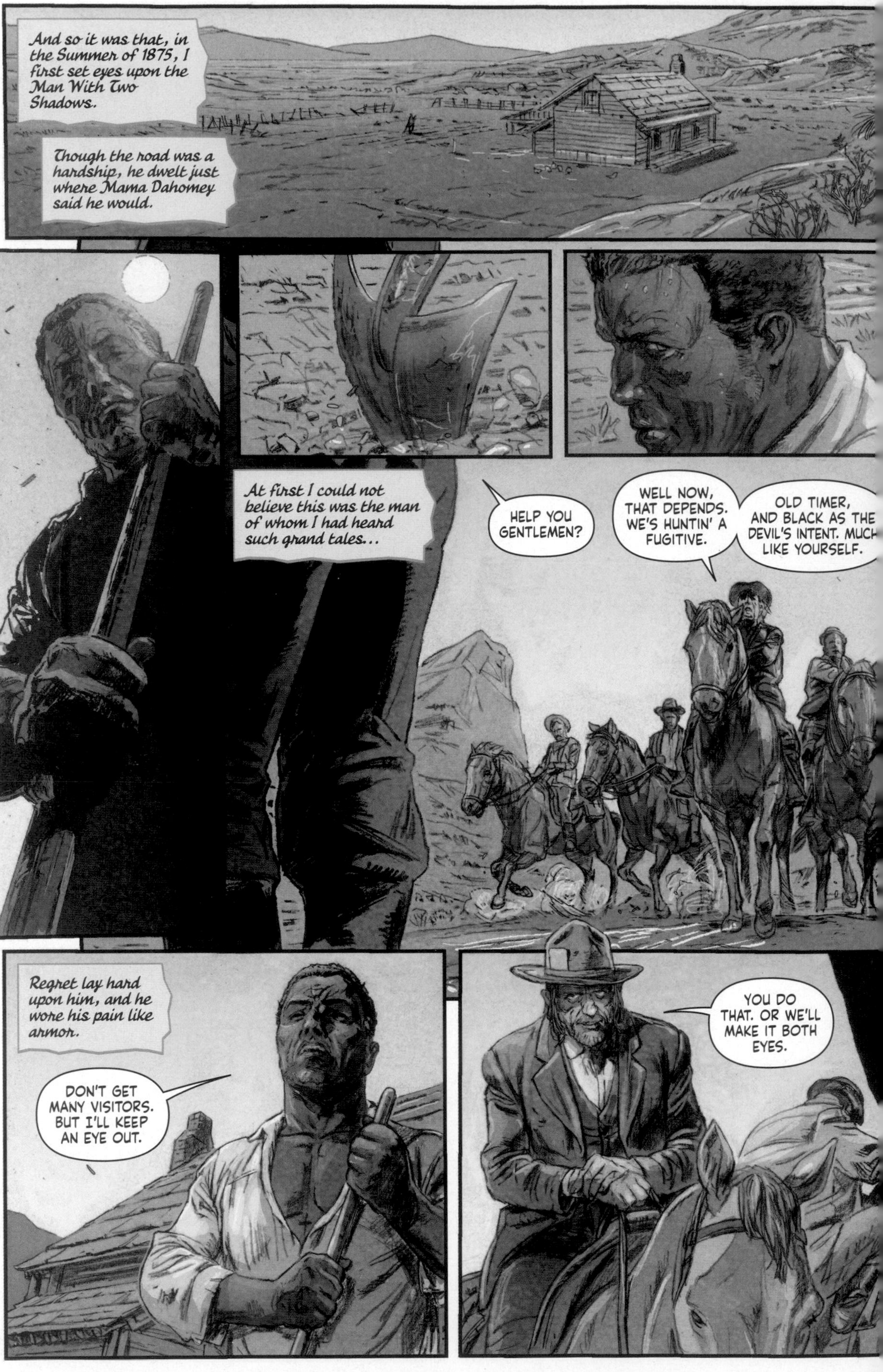
And so it was that, in the Summer of 1875, I first set eyes upon the Man With Two Shadows.
Though the road was a hardship, he dwelt just where Mama Dahomey said he would.
At first I could not believe this was the man of whom I had heard such grand tales...
HELP YOU GENTLEMEN?
WELL NOW, THAT DEPENDS. WE'S HUNTIN' A FUGITIVE.
OLD TIMER, AND BLACK AS THE DEVIL'S INTENT. MUCH LIKE YOURSELF.
Regret lay hard upon him, and he wore his pain like armor.
DON'T GET MANY VISITORS. BUT I'LL KEEP AN EYE OUT.
YOU DO THAT. OR WE'LL MAKE IT BOTH EYES.

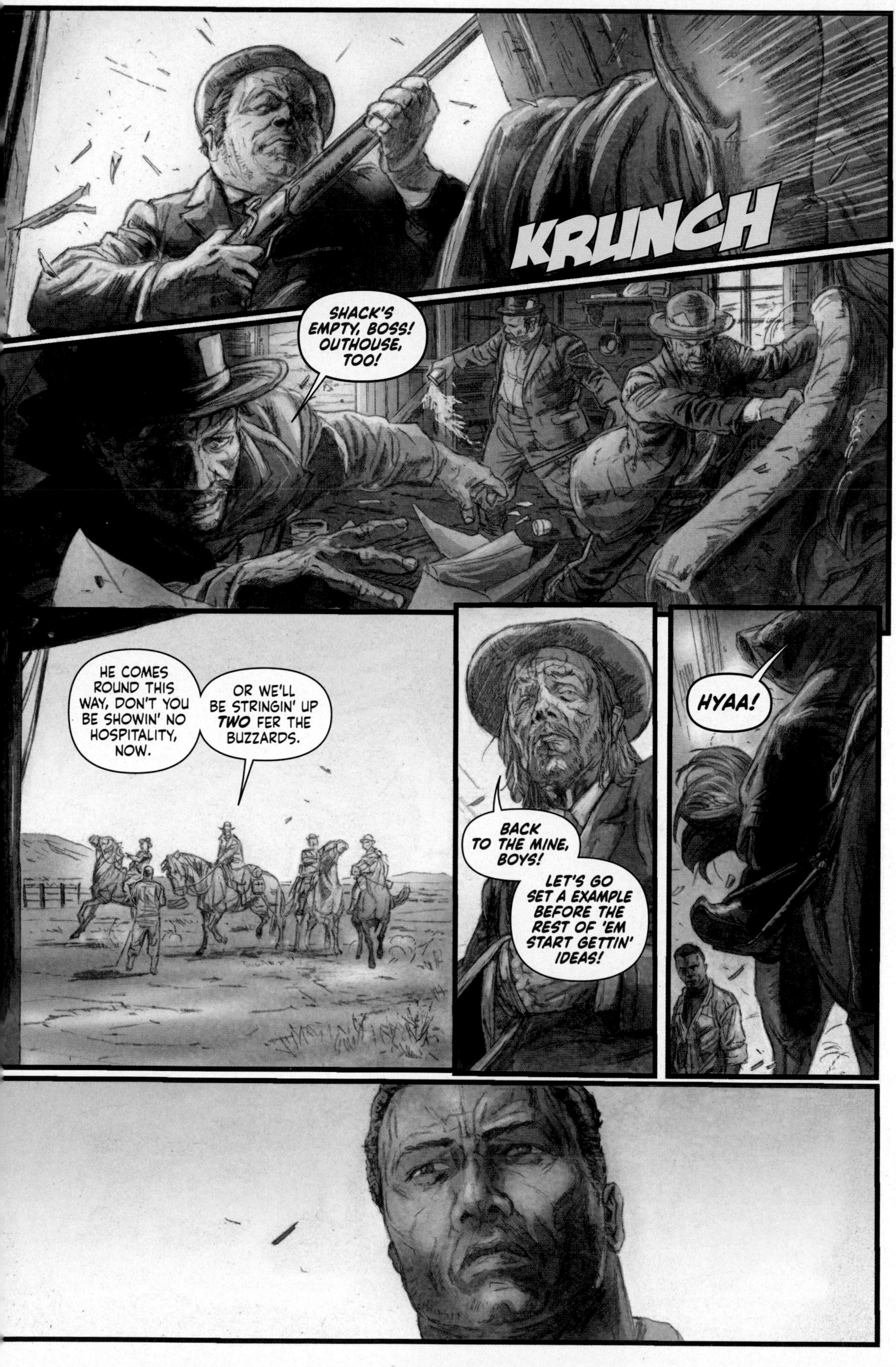
KRUNCH
SHACK'S EMPTY, BOSS! OUTHOUSE, TOO!
HE COMES ROUND THIS WAY, DON'T YOU BE SHOWIN' NO HOSPITALITY, NOW.
OR WE'LL BE STRINGIN' UP TWO FER THE BUZZARDS.
BACK TO THE MINE, BOYS!
LET'S GO SET A EXAMPLE BEFORE THE REST OF 'EM START GETTIN' IDEAS!
HYAA!

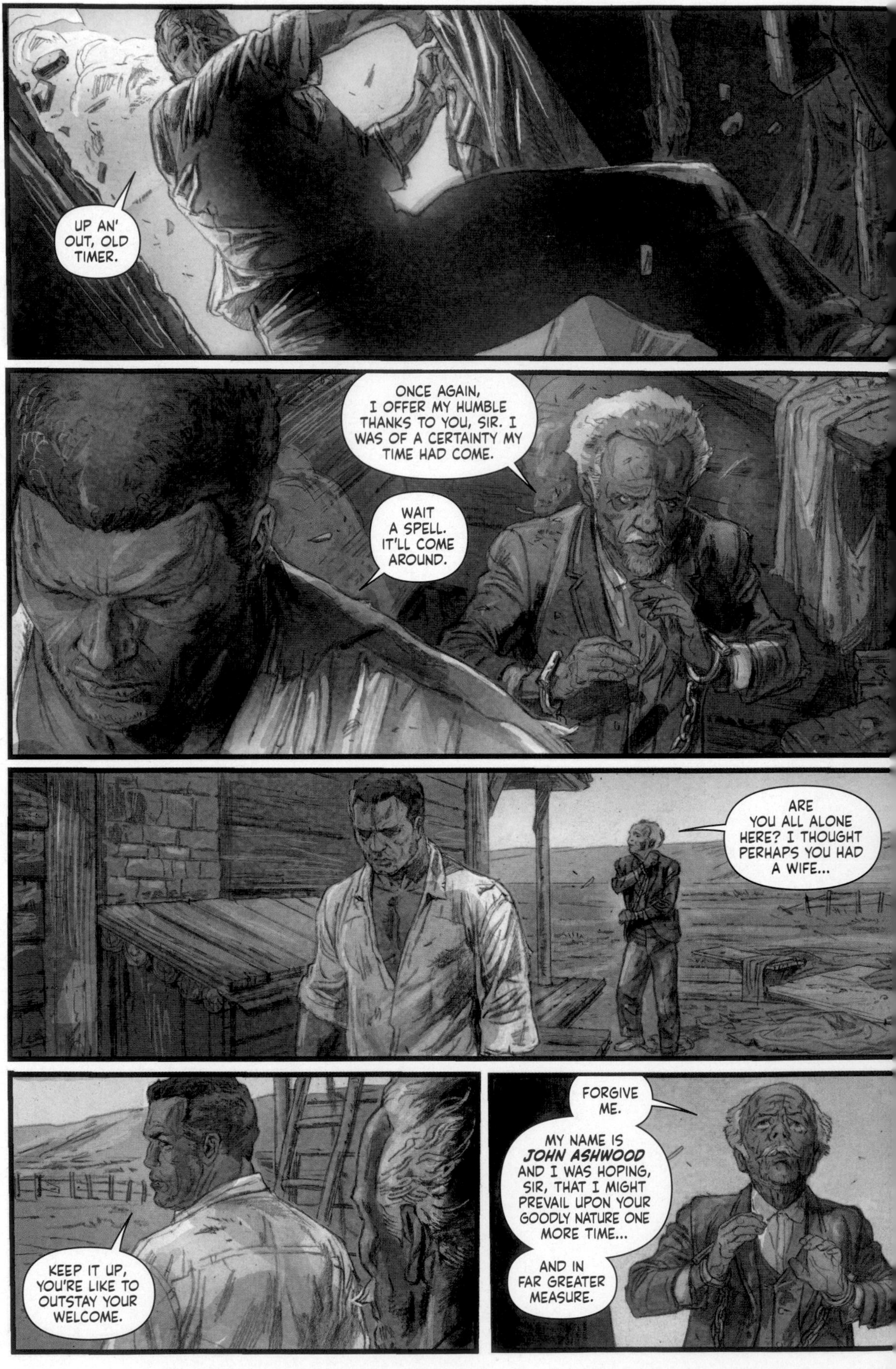
UP AN' OUT, OLD TIMER.
ONCE AGAIN, I OFFER MY HUMBLE THANKS TO YOU, SIR. I WAS OF A CERTAINTY MY TIME HAD COME.
WAIT A SPELL. IT'LL COME AROUND.
ARE YOU ALL ALONE HERE? I THOUGHT PERHAPS YOU HAD A WIFE...
KEEP IT UP, YOU'RE LIKE TO OUTSTAY YOUR WELCOME.
FORGIVE ME.
MY NAME IS ***JOHN ASHWOOD*** AND I WAS HOPING, SIR, THAT I MIGHT PREVAIL UPON YOUR GOODLY NATURE ONE MORE TIME...
AND IN FAR GREATER MEASURE.

YOU ARE *MARIUS BONIFACE*, ARE YOU NOT?

THE ONE THEY CALLED THE *SHADOW MAN.*

YOU'RE CHASIN' A FAIRY TALE.

THEY SAY YOU FELLED *TWO SCORE REBELS* AT GETTYSBURG--

WAR'S OVER. I'M *DONE* SAVIN' THE WORLD.

GOD ISN'T LISTENING, I FEAR.

THAT GENTLEMAN AHORSE FROM WHOM YOU WERE KIND ENOUGH TO CONCEAL ME? HIS NAME IS *CALVIN RAKE...*

I GOT MY FORTY ACRES. THE REST IS GOD'S COUNTRY.

LET HIM SORT IT OUT.

I'VE HEARD THE NAME. MAN EARNED HIMSELF A LOW REPUTATION BACK IN THE WAR DAYS.

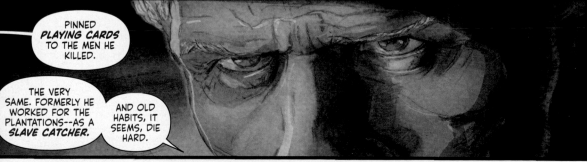

PINNED *PLAYING CARDS* TO THE MEN HE KILLED.

THE VERY SAME. FORMERLY HE WORKED FOR THE PLANTATIONS--AS A *SLAVE CATCHER.*

AND OLD HABITS, IT SEEMS, DIE HARD.

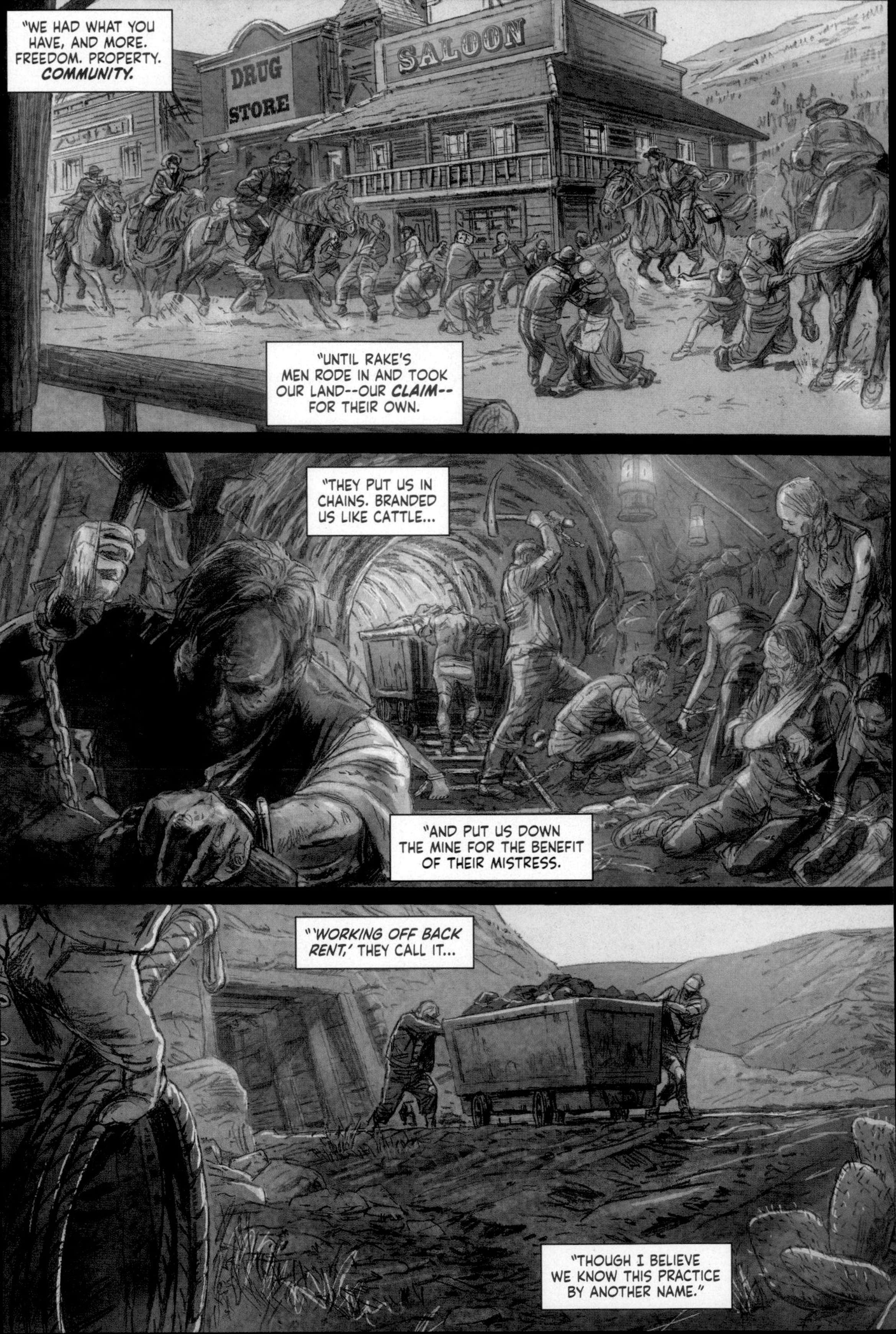
"WE HAD WHAT YOU HAVE, AND MORE. FREEDOM. PROPERTY. *COMMUNITY.*
DRUG STORE
SALOON
"UNTIL RAKE'S MEN RODE IN AND TOOK OUR LAND--OUR *CLAIM*--FOR THEIR OWN.
"THEY PUT US IN CHAINS. BRANDED US LIKE CATTLE...
"AND PUT US DOWN THE MINE FOR THE BENEFIT OF THEIR MISTRESS.
"'*WORKING OFF BACK RENT,*' THEY CALL IT...
"THOUGH I BELIEVE WE KNOW THIS PRACTICE BY ANOTHER NAME."

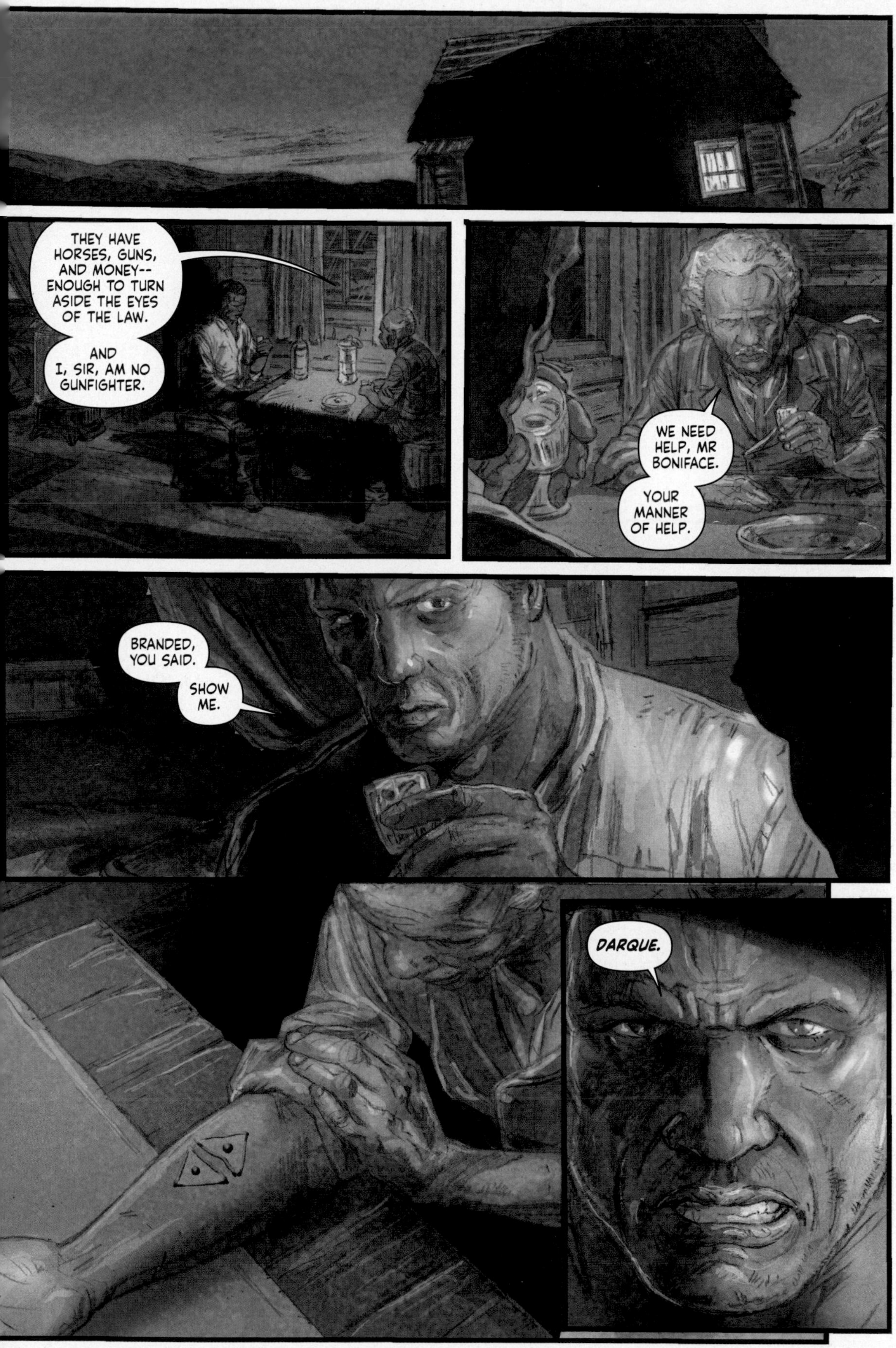
THEY HAVE HORSES, GUNS, AND MONEY-- ENOUGH TO TURN ASIDE THE EYES OF THE LAW.
AND I, SIR, AM NO GUNFIGHTER.
WE NEED HELP, MR BONIFACE.
YOUR MANNER OF HELP.
BRANDED, YOU SAID.
SHOW ME.
DARQUE.

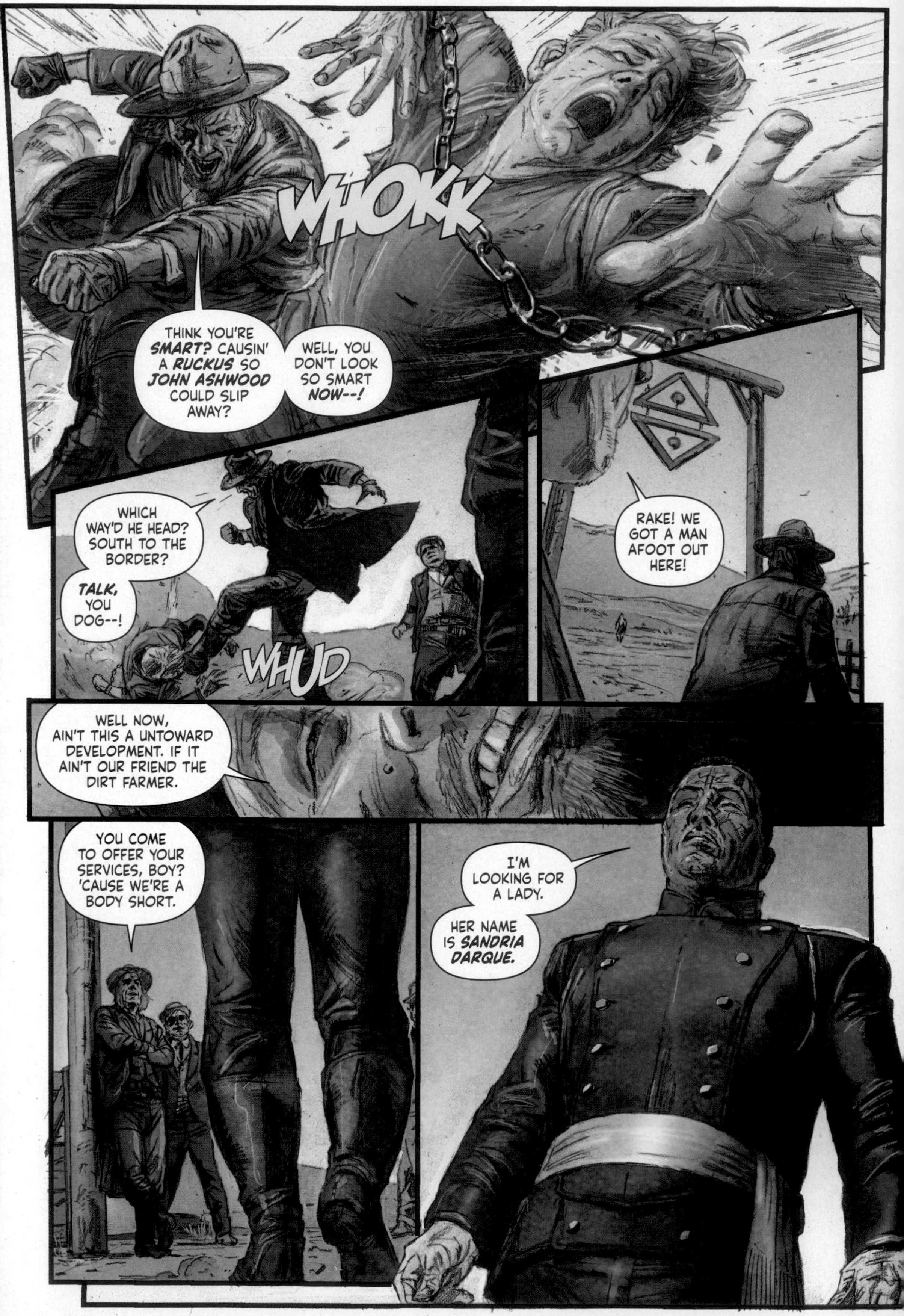
WHOKK
THINK YOU'RE SMART? CAUSIN' A RUCKUS SO JOHN ASHWOOD COULD SLIP AWAY?
WELL, YOU DON'T LOOK SO SMART NOW--!
WHICH WAY'D HE HEAD? SOUTH TO THE BORDER?
TALK, YOU DOG--!
WHUD
RAKE! WE GOT A MAN AFOOT OUT HERE!
WELL NOW, AIN'T THIS A UNTOWARD DEVELOPMENT. IF IT AIN'T OUR FRIEND THE DIRT FARMER.
YOU COME TO OFFER YOUR SERVICES, BOY? 'CAUSE WE'RE A BODY SHORT.
I'M LOOKING FOR A LADY.
HER NAME IS SANDRIA DARQUE.

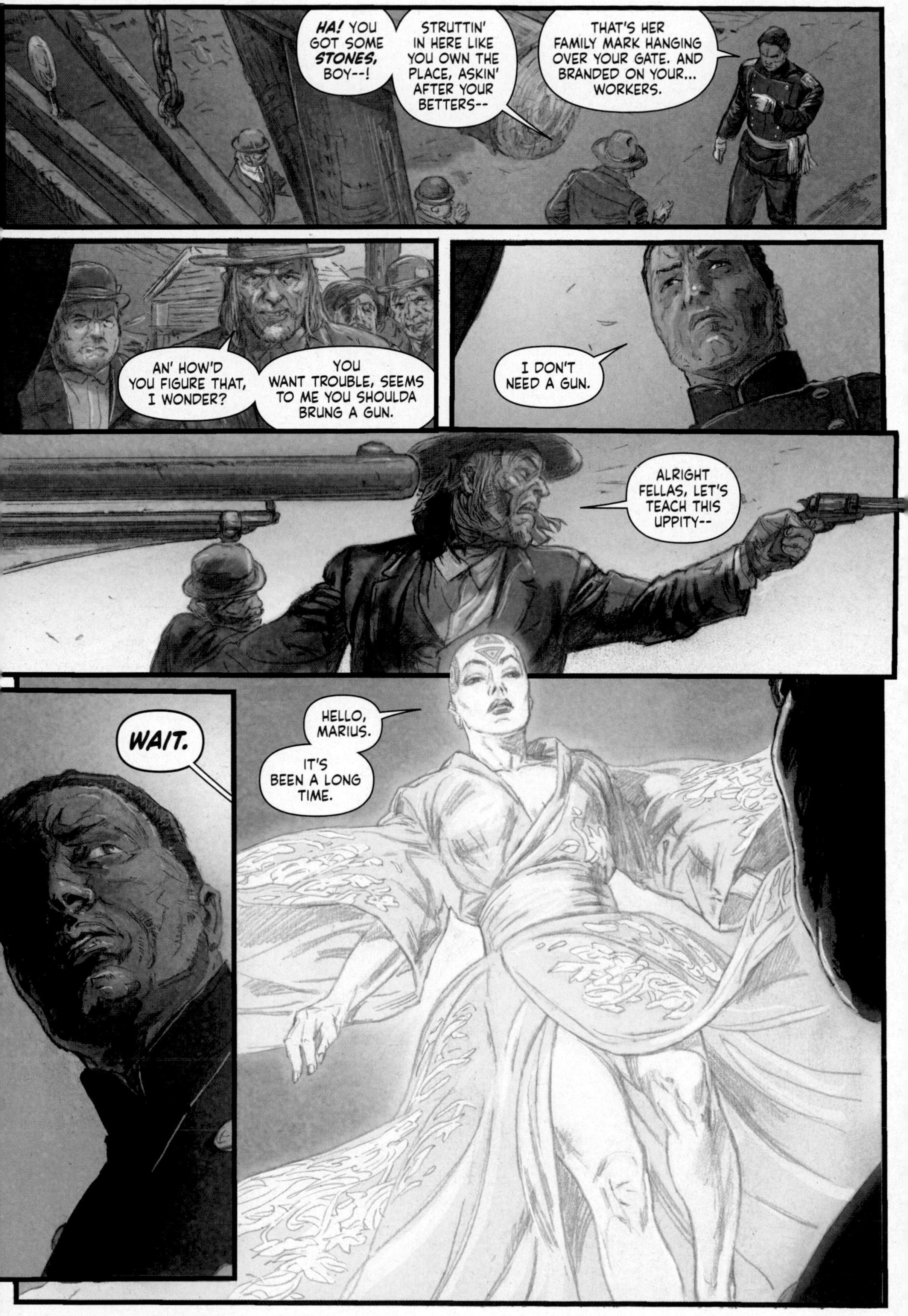
HA! YOU GOT SOME STONES, BOY--!
STRUTTIN' IN HERE LIKE YOU OWN THE PLACE, ASKIN' AFTER YOUR BETTERS--
THAT'S HER FAMILY MARK HANGING OVER YOUR GATE. AND BRANDED ON YOUR... WORKERS.
AN' HOW'D YOU FIGURE THAT, I WONDER?
YOU WANT TROUBLE, SEEMS TO ME YOU SHOULDA BRUNG A GUN.
I DON'T NEED A GUN.
ALRIGHT FELLAS, LET'S TEACH THIS UPPITY--
WAIT.
HELLO, MARIUS.
IT'S BEEN A LONG TIME.

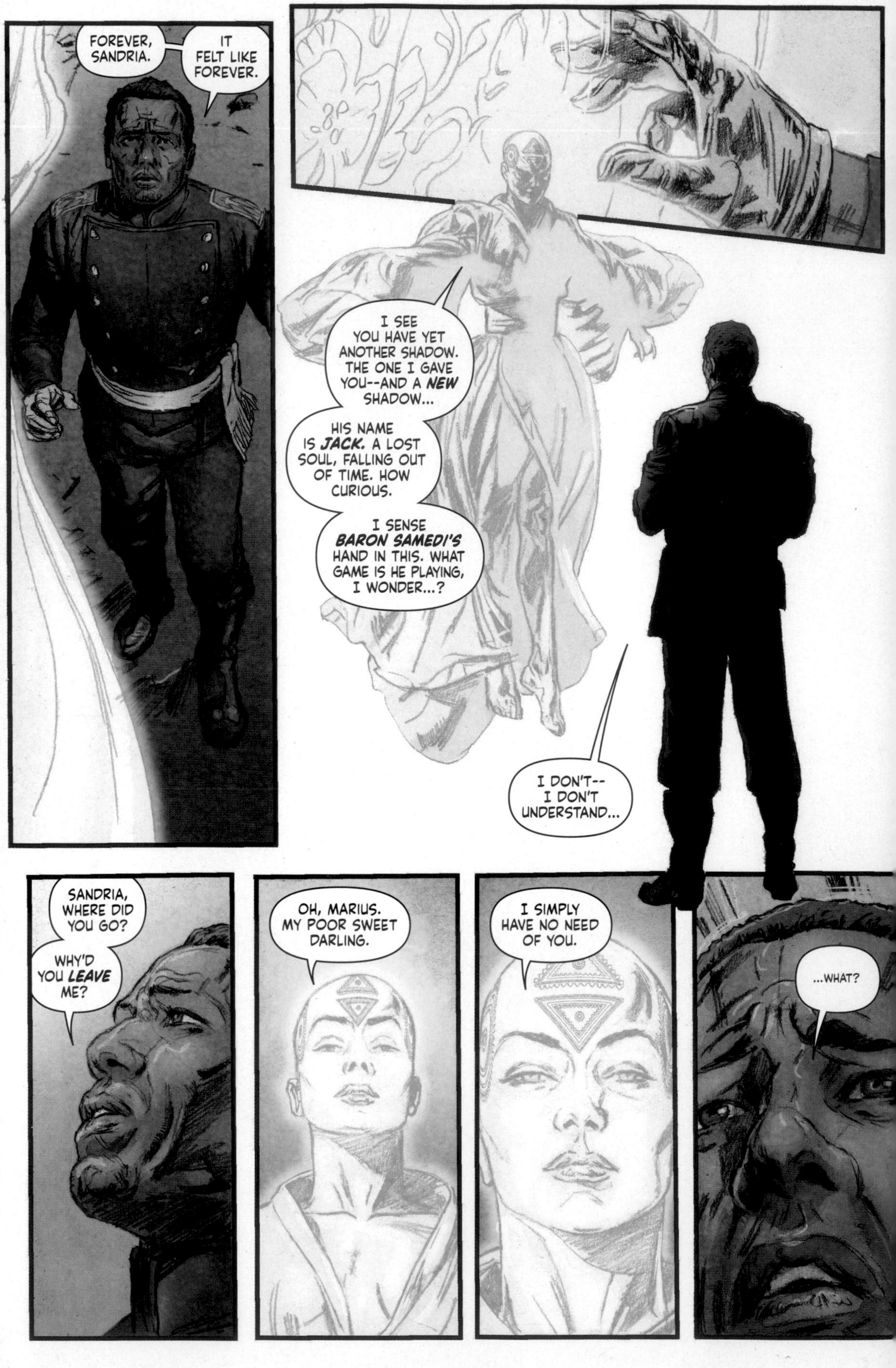
FOREVER, SANDRIA.
IT FELT LIKE FOREVER.
I SEE YOU HAVE YET ANOTHER SHADOW. THE ONE I GAVE YOU--AND A *NEW* SHADOW...
HIS NAME IS ***JACK.*** A LOST SOUL, FALLING OUT OF TIME. HOW CURIOUS.
I SENSE ***BARON SAMEDI'S*** HAND IN THIS. WHAT GAME IS HE PLAYING, I WONDER...?
I DON'T-- I DON'T UNDERSTAND...
SANDRIA, WHERE DID YOU GO?
WHY'D YOU ***LEAVE*** ME?
OH, MARIUS. MY POOR SWEET DARLING.
I SIMPLY HAVE NO NEED OF YOU.
...WHAT?

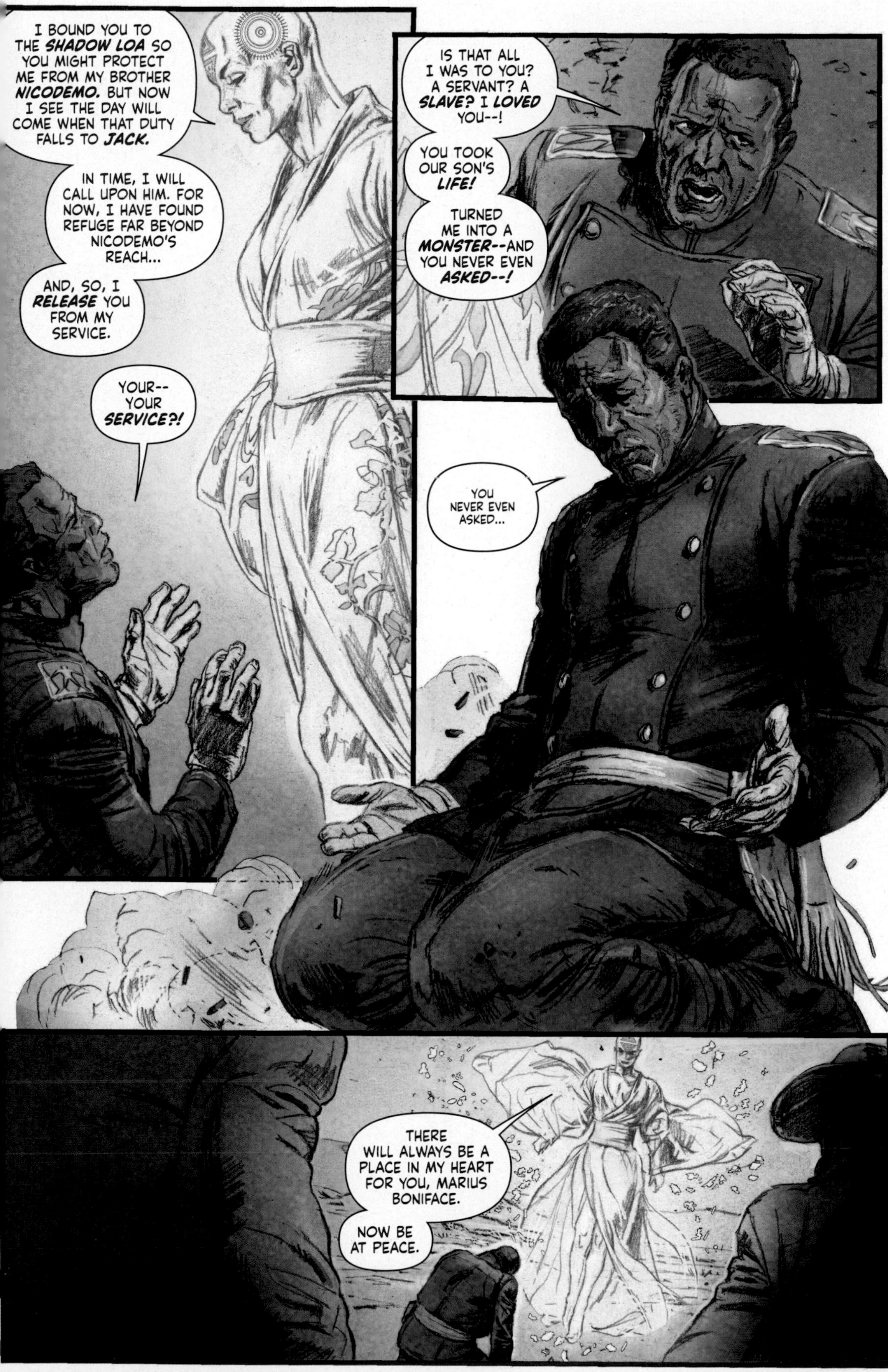
I BOUND YOU TO THE SHADOW LOA SO YOU MIGHT PROTECT ME FROM MY BROTHER NICODEMO. BUT NOW I SEE THE DAY WILL COME WHEN THAT DUTY FALLS TO JACK.
IN TIME, I WILL CALL UPON HIM. FOR NOW, I HAVE FOUND REFUGE FAR BEYOND NICODEMO'S REACH...
AND, SO, I RELEASE YOU FROM MY SERVICE.
YOUR--YOUR SERVICE?!
IS THAT ALL I WAS TO YOU? A SERVANT? A SLAVE? I LOVED YOU--!
YOU TOOK OUR SON'S LIFE!
TURNED ME INTO A MONSTER--AND YOU NEVER EVEN ASKED--!
YOU NEVER EVEN ASKED...
THERE WILL ALWAYS BE A PLACE IN MY HEART FOR YOU, MARIUS BONIFACE.
NOW BE AT PEACE.

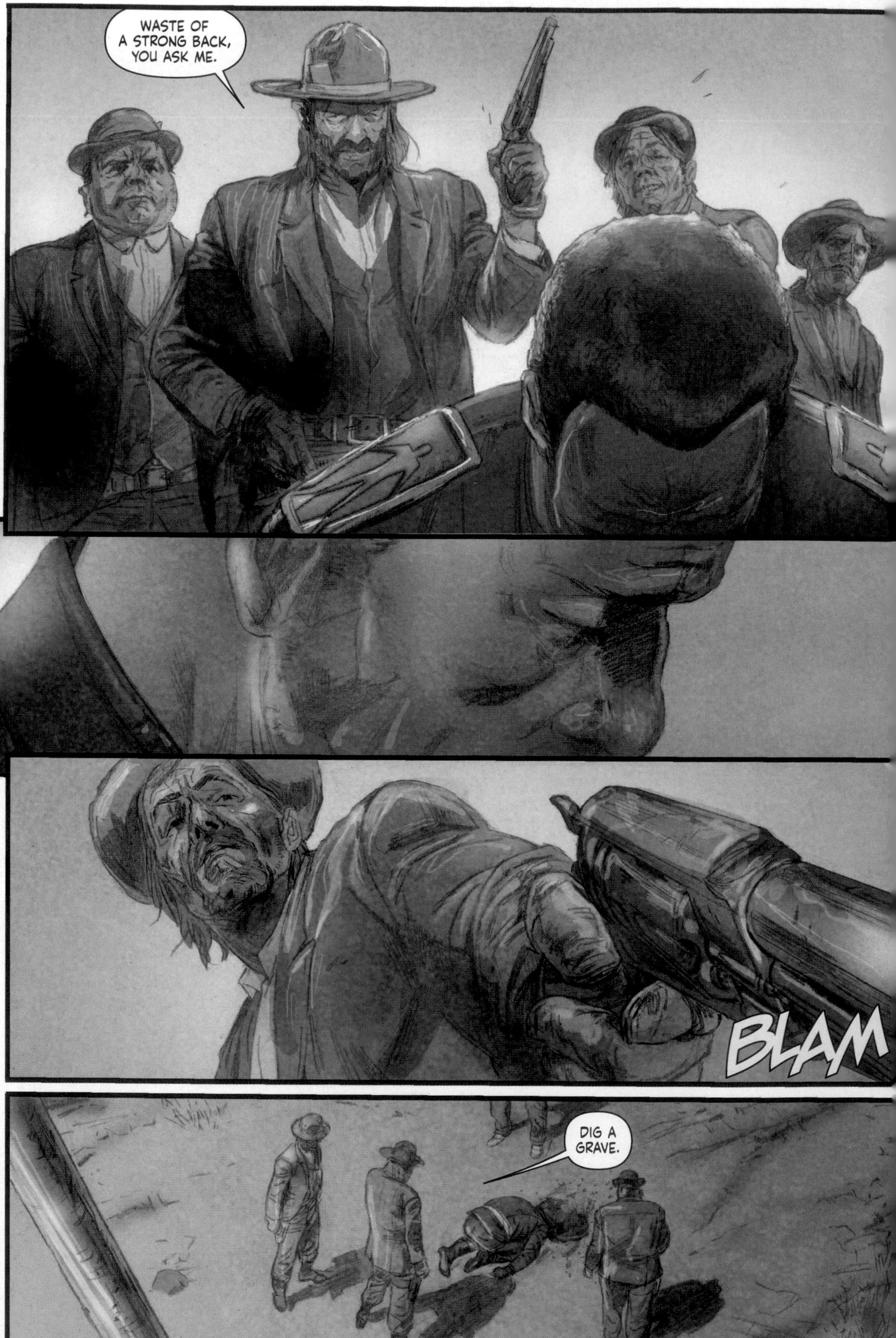
WASTE OF A STRONG BACK, YOU ASK ME.
BLAM
DIG A GRAVE.

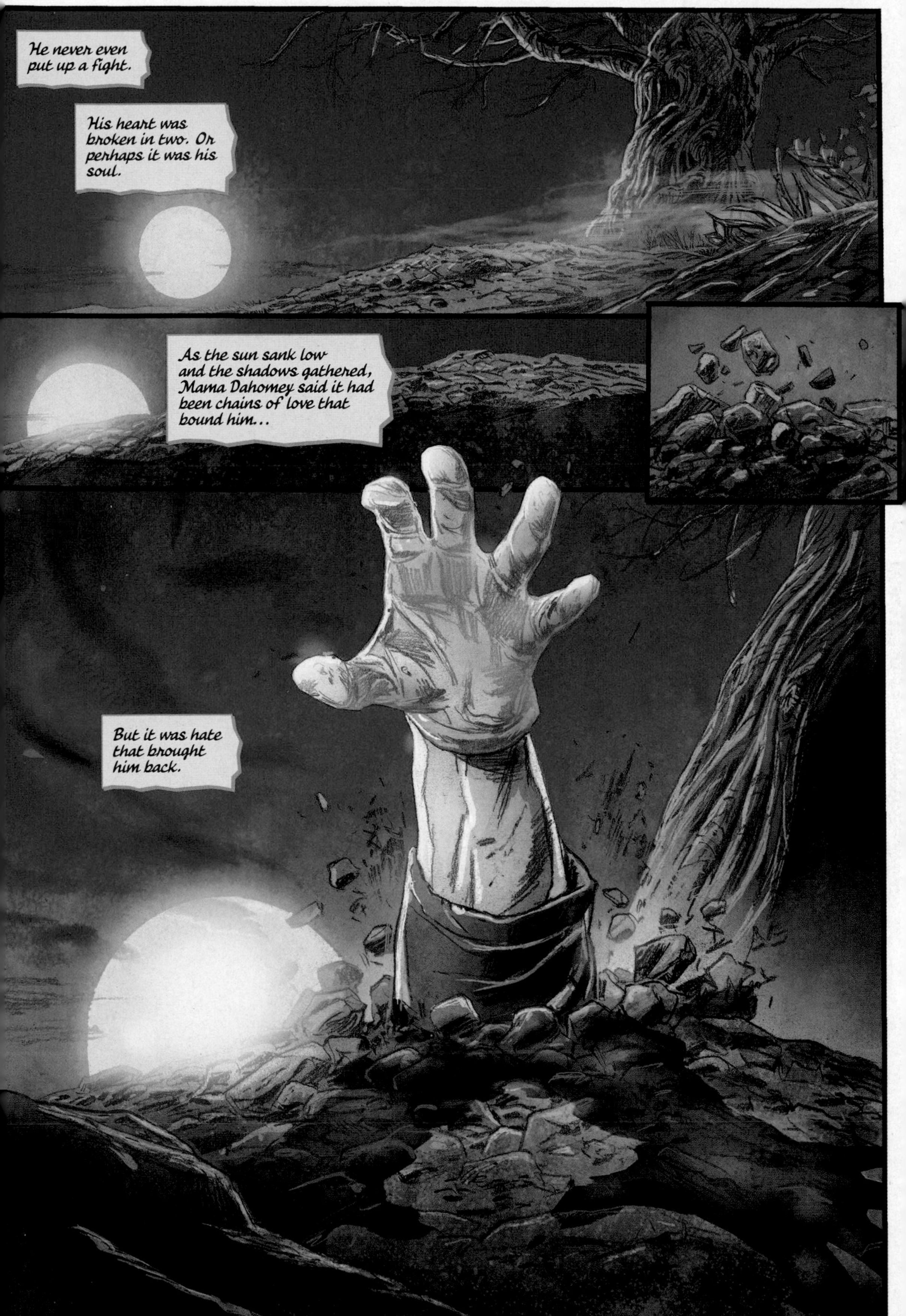
He never even put up a fight.
His heart was broken in two. Or perhaps it was his soul.
As the sun sank low and the shadows gathered, Mama Dahomey said it had been chains of love that bound him...
But it was hate that brought him back.

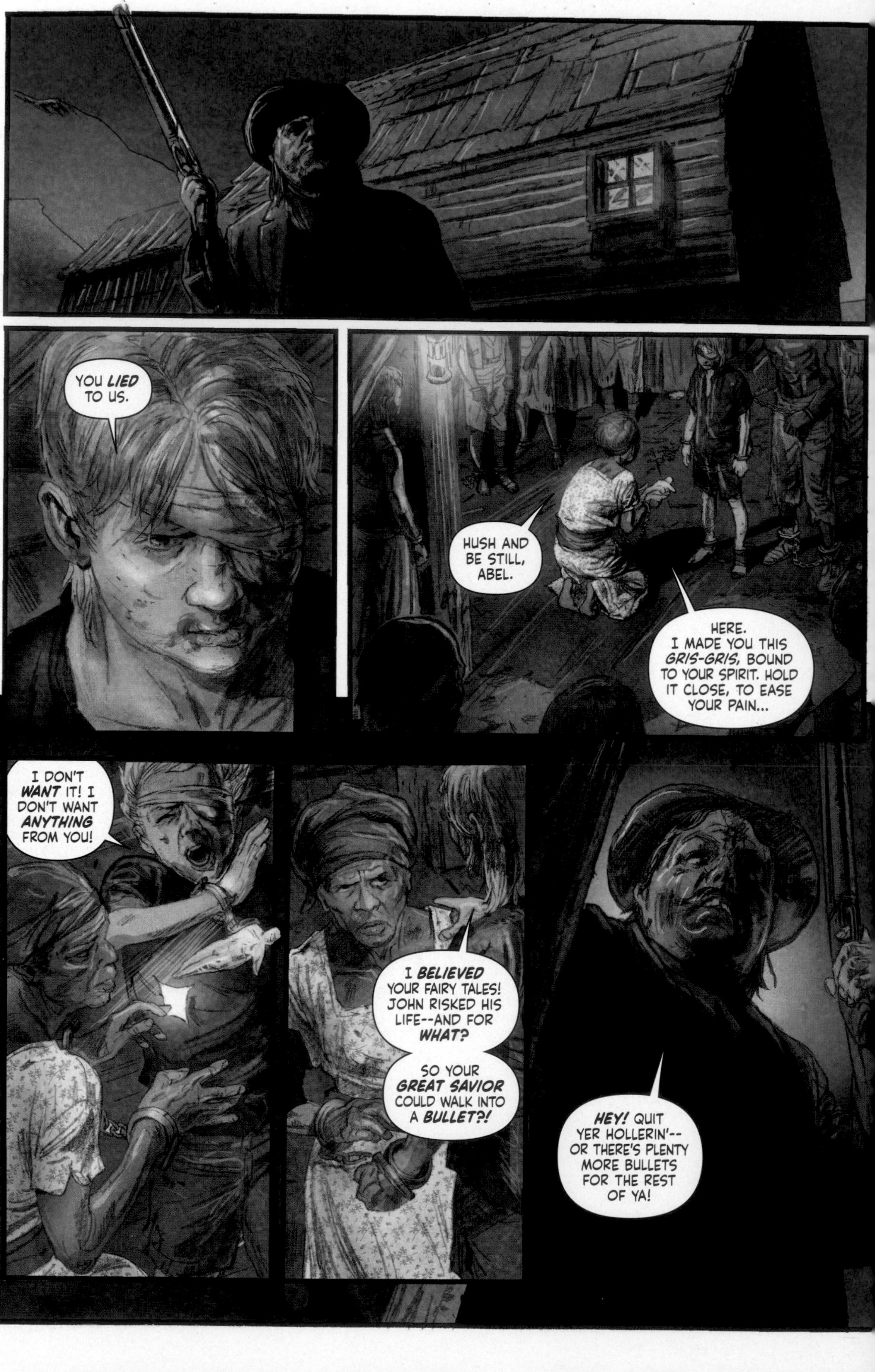
YOU LIED TO US.
HUSH AND BE STILL, ABEL.
HERE. I MADE YOU THIS GRIS-GRIS, BOUND TO YOUR SPIRIT. HOLD IT CLOSE, TO EASE YOUR PAIN...
I DON'T WANT IT! I DON'T WANT ANYTHING FROM YOU!
I BELIEVED YOUR FAIRY TALES! JOHN RISKED HIS LIFE--AND FOR WHAT?
SO YOUR GREAT SAVIOR COULD WALK INTO A BULLET?!
HEY! QUIT YER HOLLERIN'--OR THERE'S PLENTY MORE BULLETS FOR THE REST OF YA!

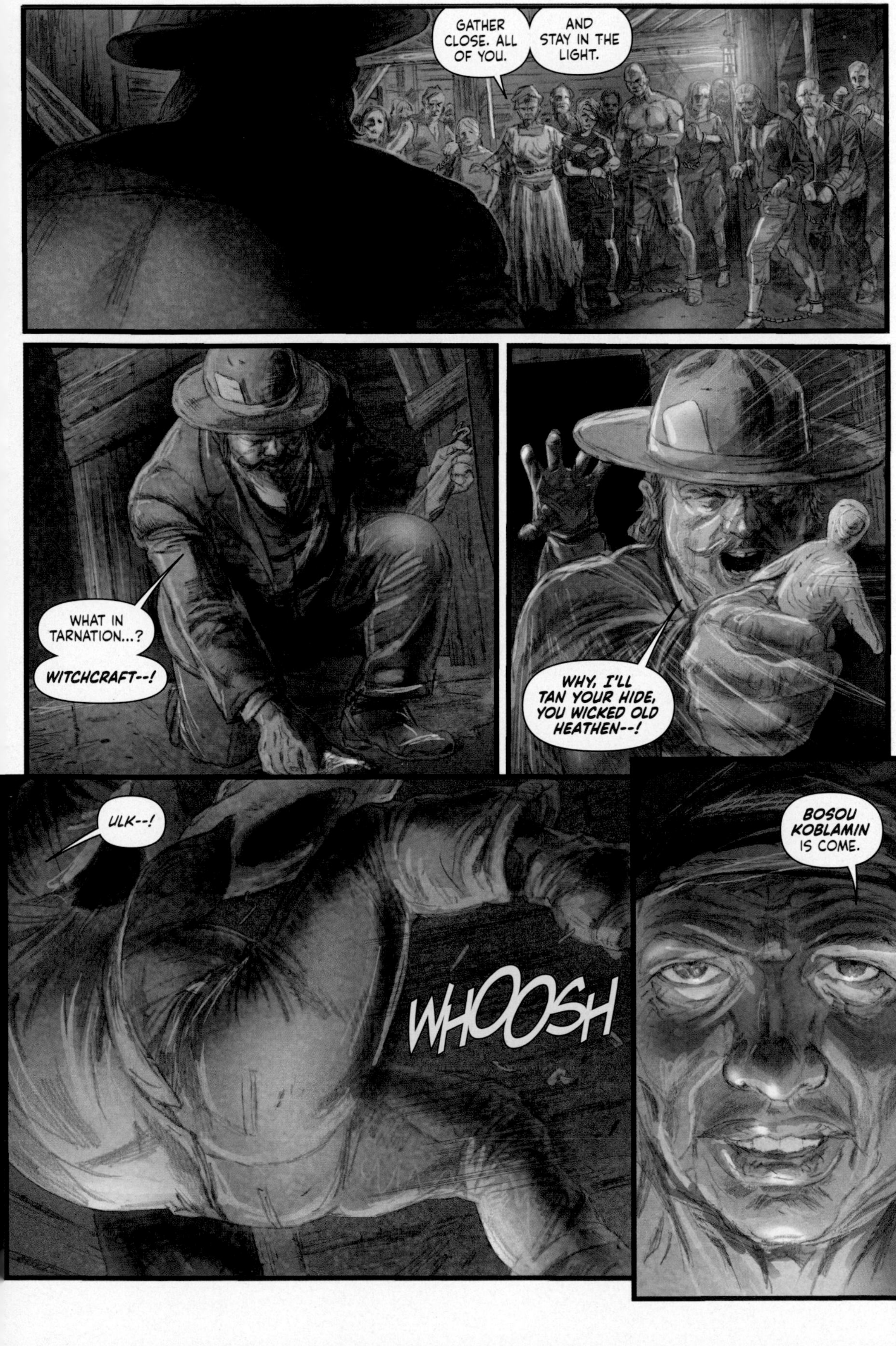

GATHER CLOSE. ALL OF YOU.
AND STAY IN THE LIGHT.
WHAT IN TARNATION...?
WITCHCRAFT--!
WHY, I'LL TAN YOUR HIDE, YOU WICKED OLD HEATHEN--!
ULK--!
WHOOSH
BOSOU KOBLAMIN IS COME.

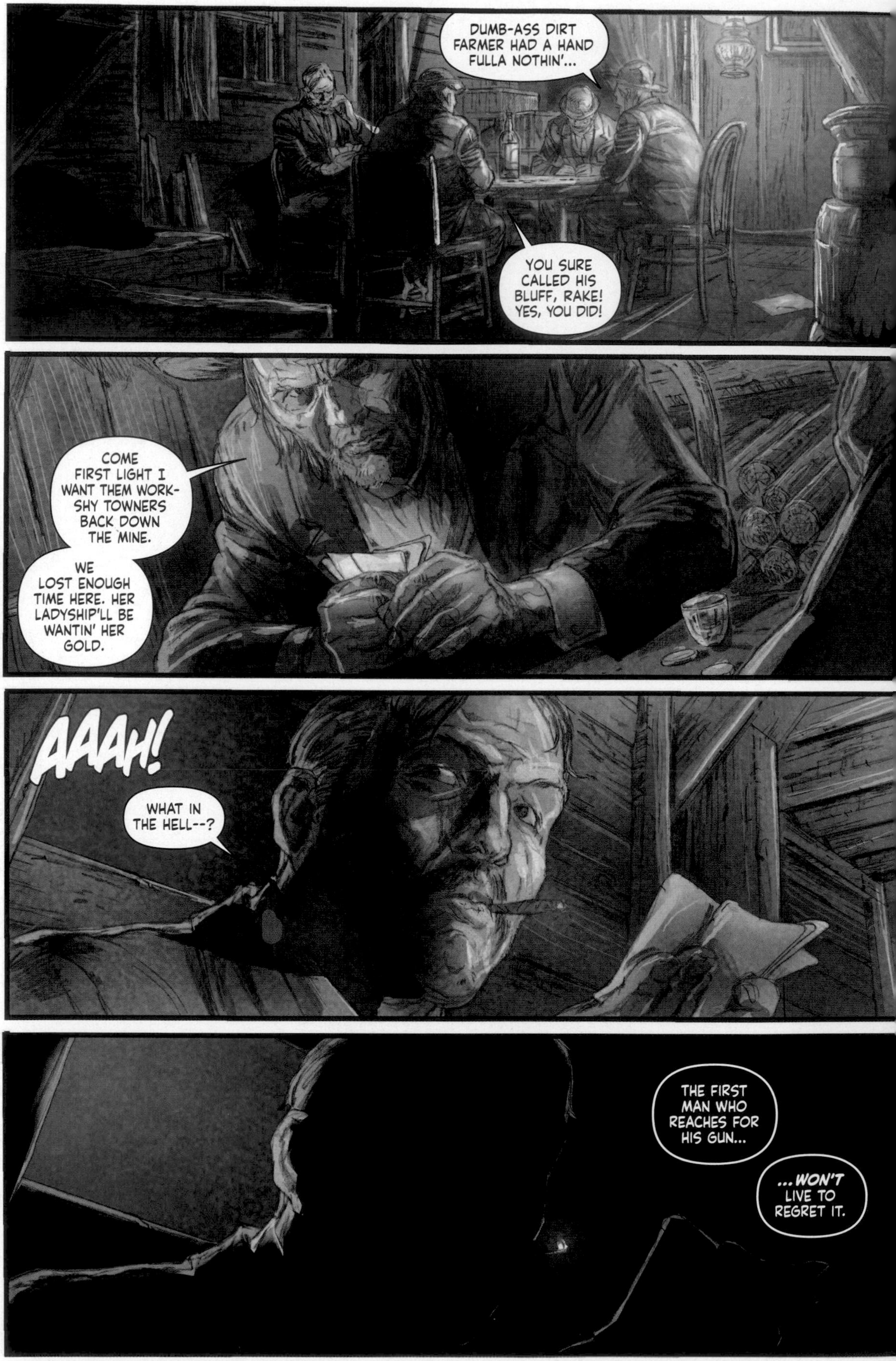
DUMB-ASS DIRT FARMER HAD A HAND FULLA NOTHIN'...
YOU SURE CALLED HIS BLUFF, RAKE! YES, YOU DID!
COME FIRST LIGHT I WANT THEM WORK-SHY TOWNERS BACK DOWN THE MINE.
WE LOST ENOUGH TIME HERE. HER LADYSHIP'LL BE WANTIN' HER GOLD.
AAAH!
WHAT IN THE HELL--?
THE FIRST MAN WHO REACHES FOR HIS GUN...
...WON'T LIVE TO REGRET IT.

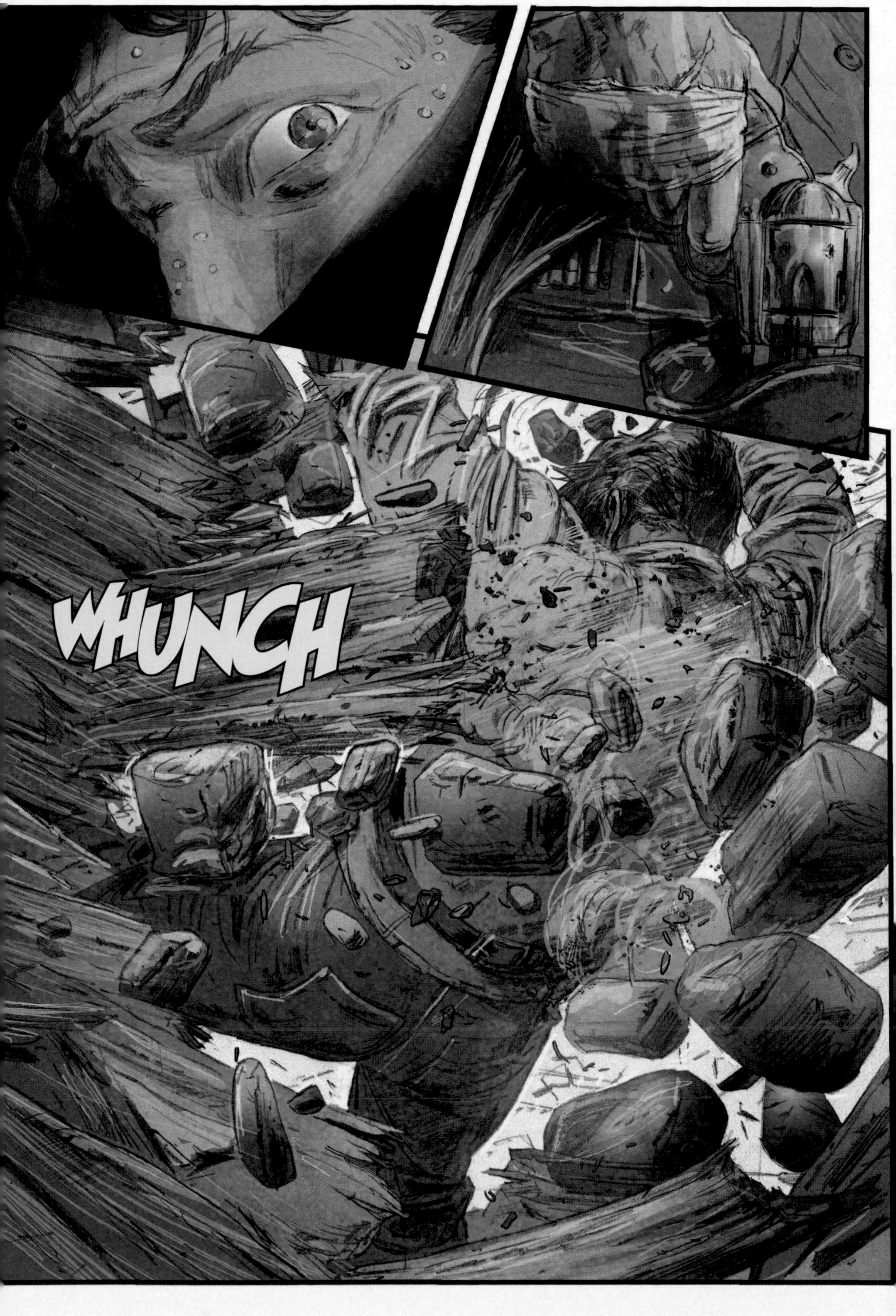
WHUNCH

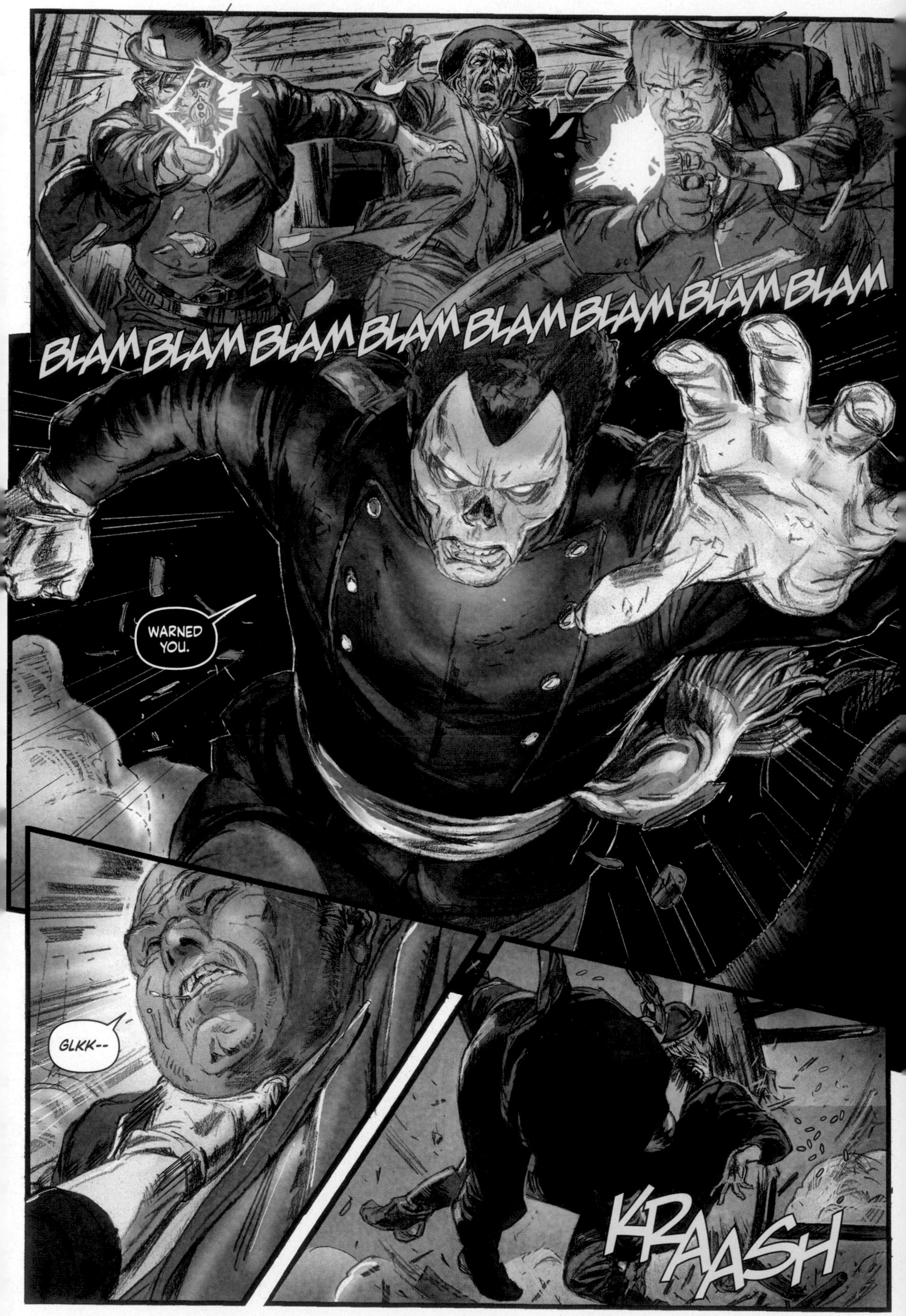
BLAM BLAM BLAM BLAM BLAM BLAM BLAM BLAM
WARNED YOU.
GLKK--
KRAASH

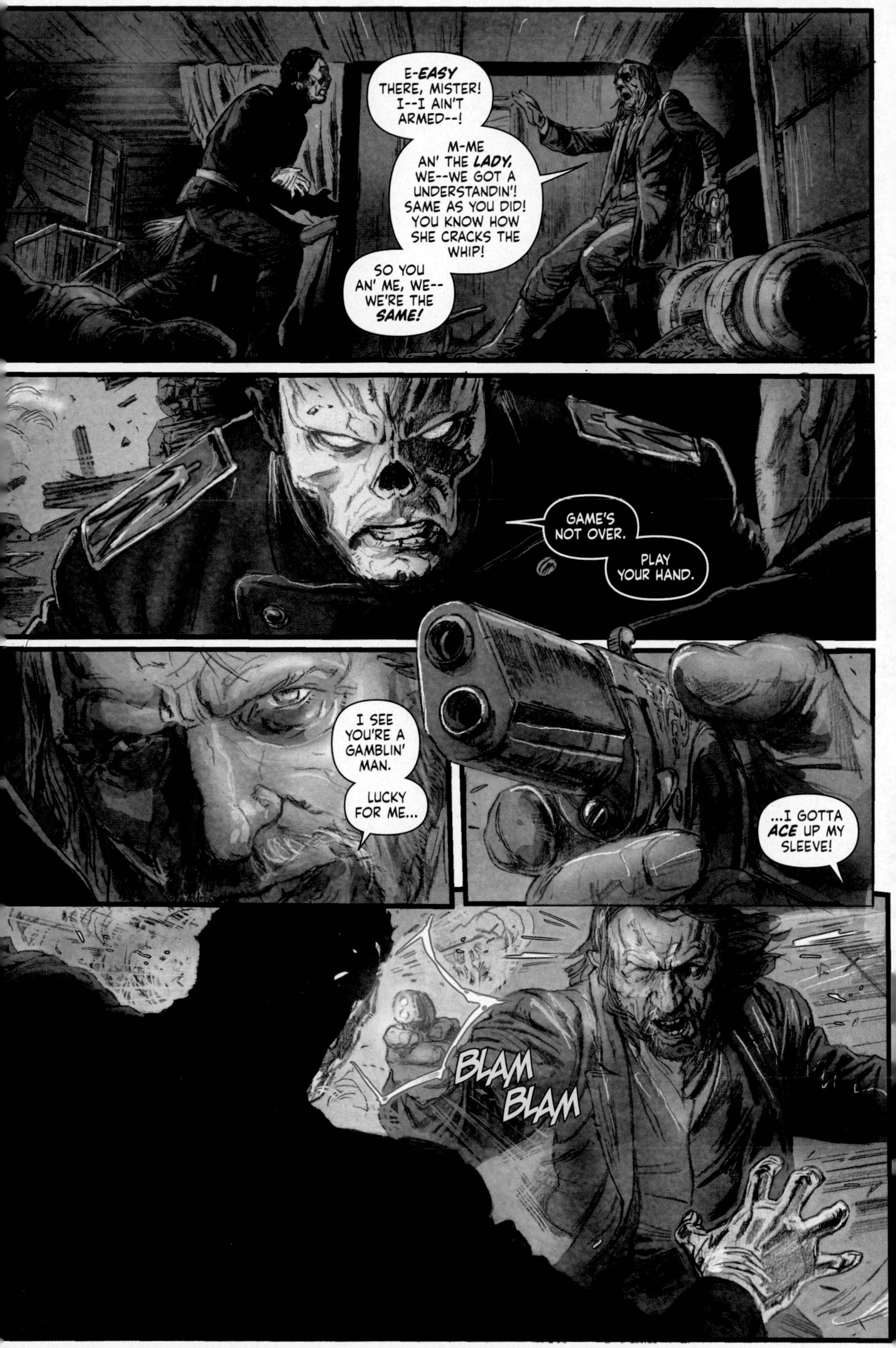
E-EASY THERE, MISTER! I--I AIN'T ARMED--!
M-ME AN' THE LADY, WE--WE GOT A UNDERSTANDIN'! SAME AS YOU DID! YOU KNOW HOW SHE CRACKS THE WHIP!
SO YOU AN' ME, WE--WE'RE THE SAME!
GAME'S NOT OVER.
PLAY YOUR HAND.
I SEE YOU'RE A GAMBLIN' MAN.
LUCKY FOR ME...
...I GOTTA ACE UP MY SLEEVE!
BLAM
BLAM

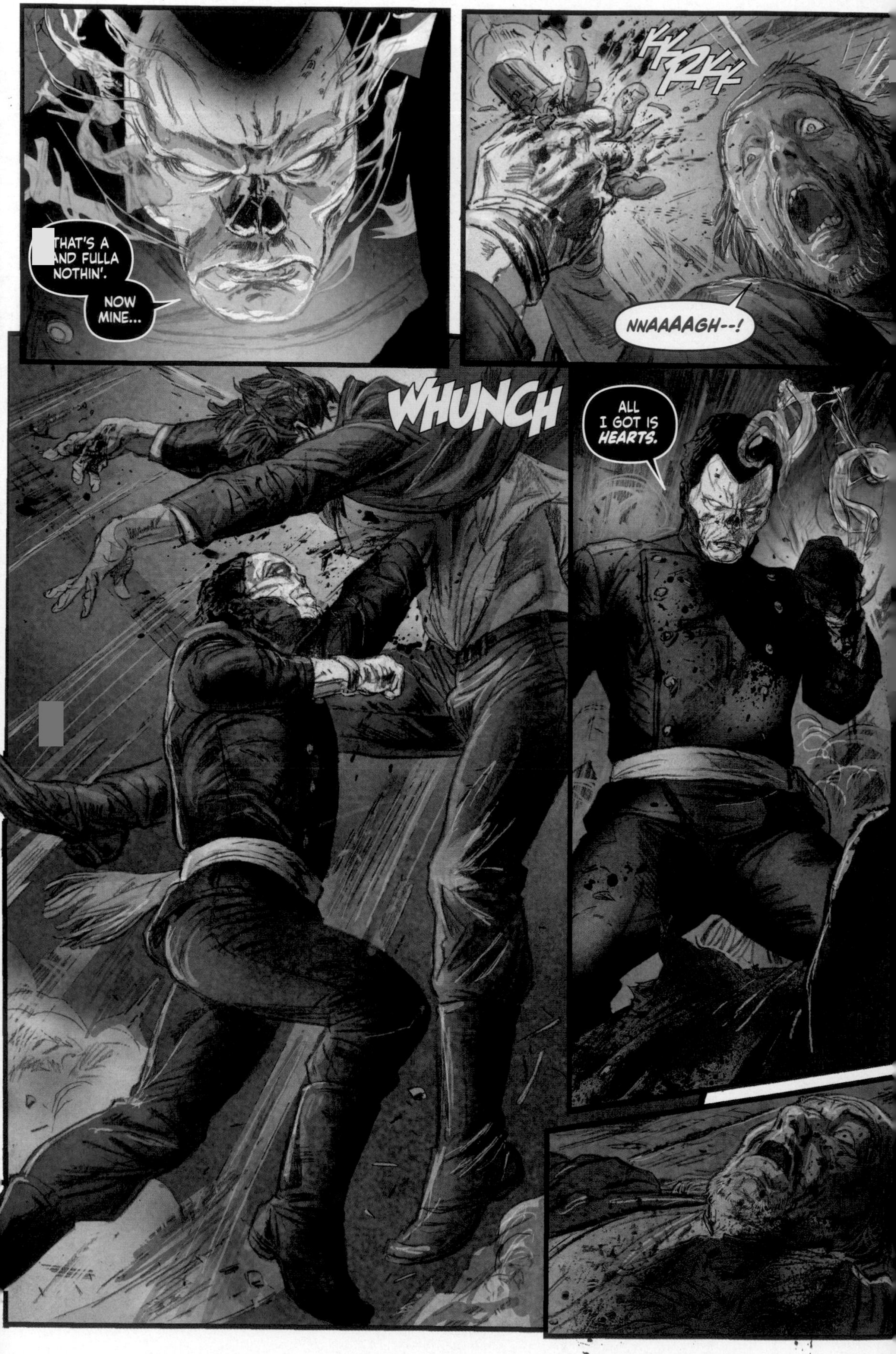
THAT'S A
AND FULLA
NOTHIN'.
NOW
MINE...
KKRKK
NNAAAAGH--!
WHUNCH
ALL
I GOT IS
HEARTS.

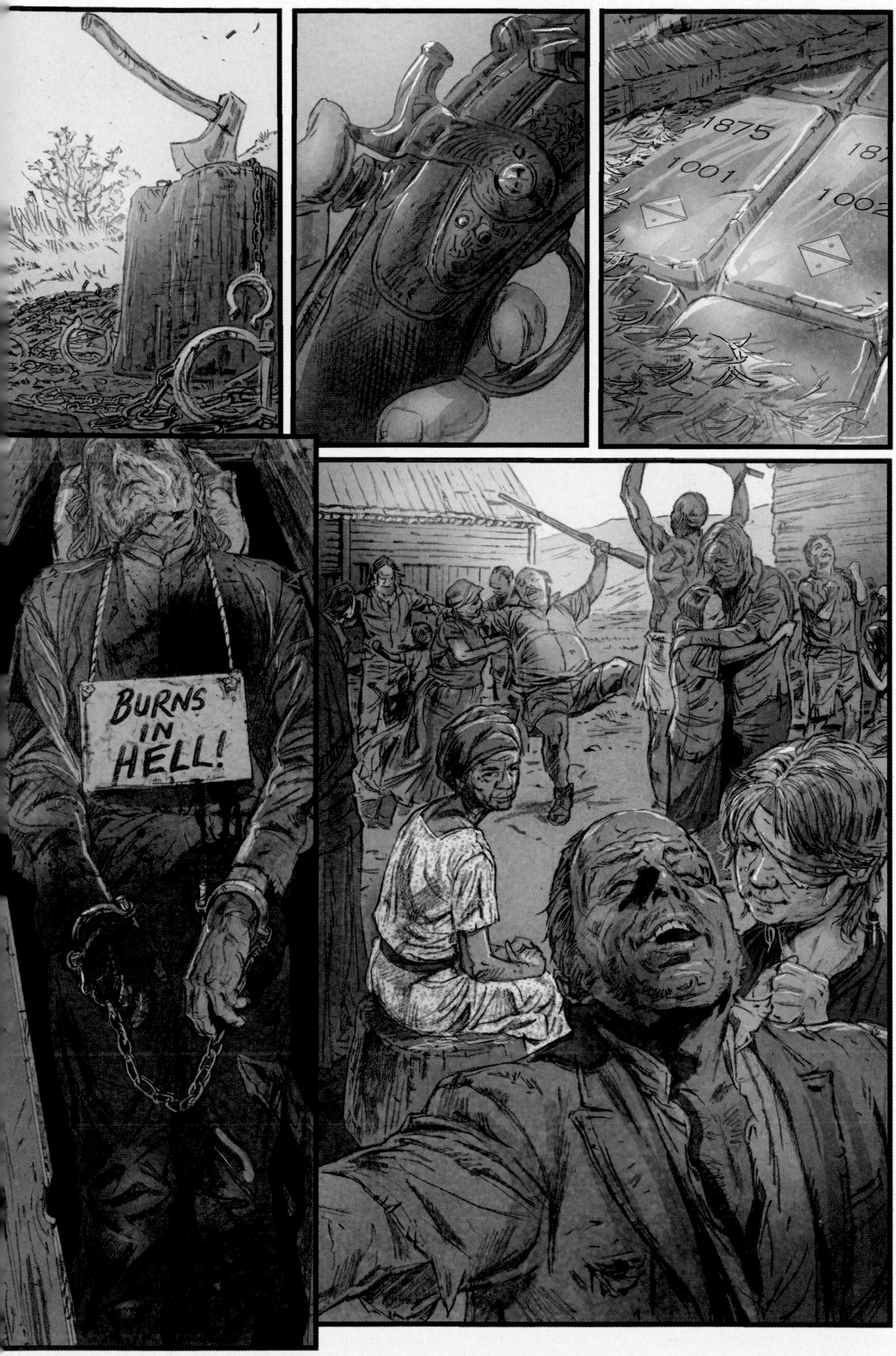
1875
1001
1002
BURNS IN HELL!

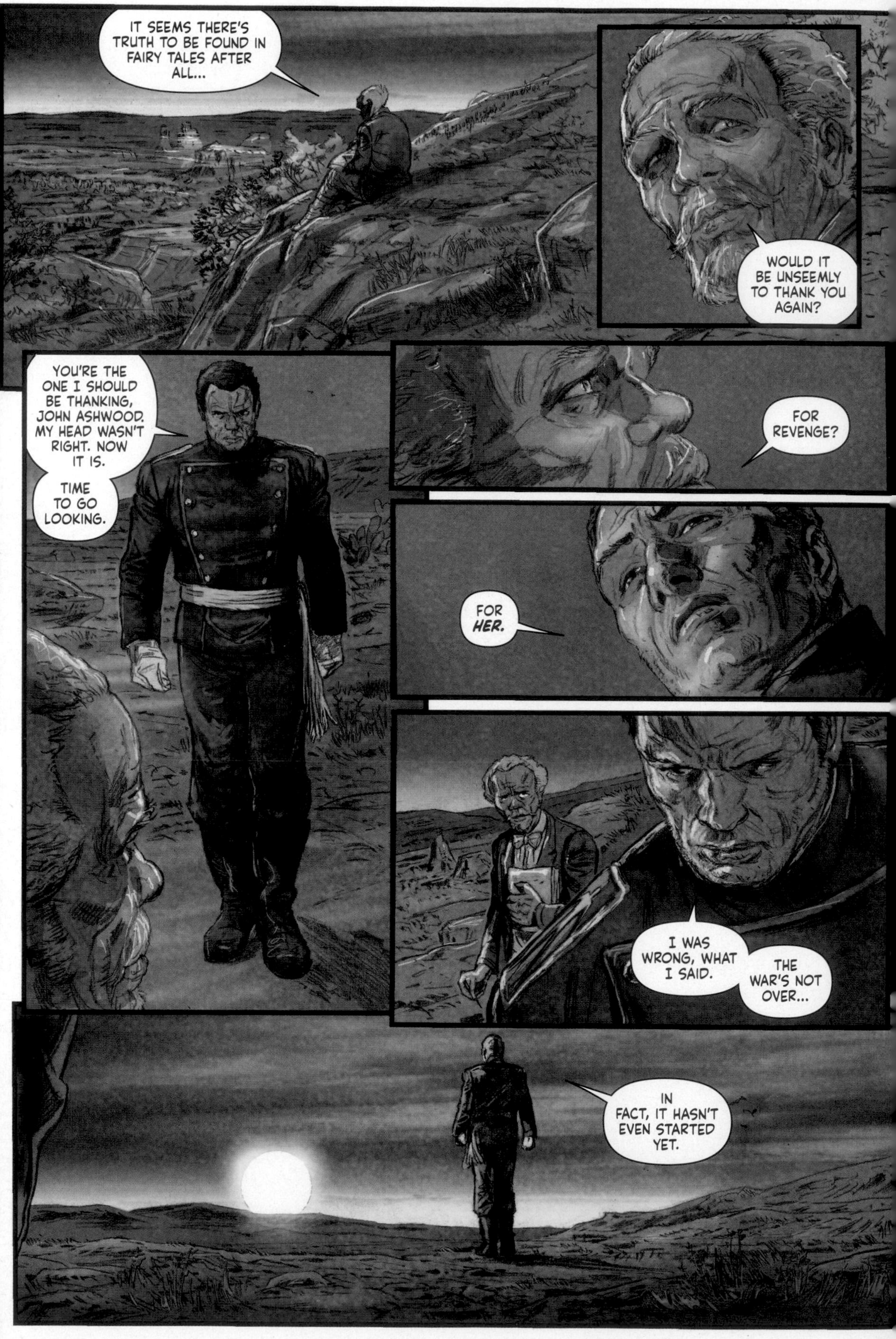
IT SEEMS THERE'S TRUTH TO BE FOUND IN FAIRY TALES AFTER ALL...
WOULD IT BE UNSEEMLY TO THANK YOU AGAIN?
YOU'RE THE ONE I SHOULD BE THANKING, JOHN ASHWOOD. MY HEAD WASN'T RIGHT. NOW IT IS.
TIME TO GO LOOKING.
FOR REVENGE?
FOR *HER.*
I WAS WRONG, WHAT I SAID.
THE WAR'S NOT OVER...
IN FACT, IT HASN'T EVEN STARTED YET.

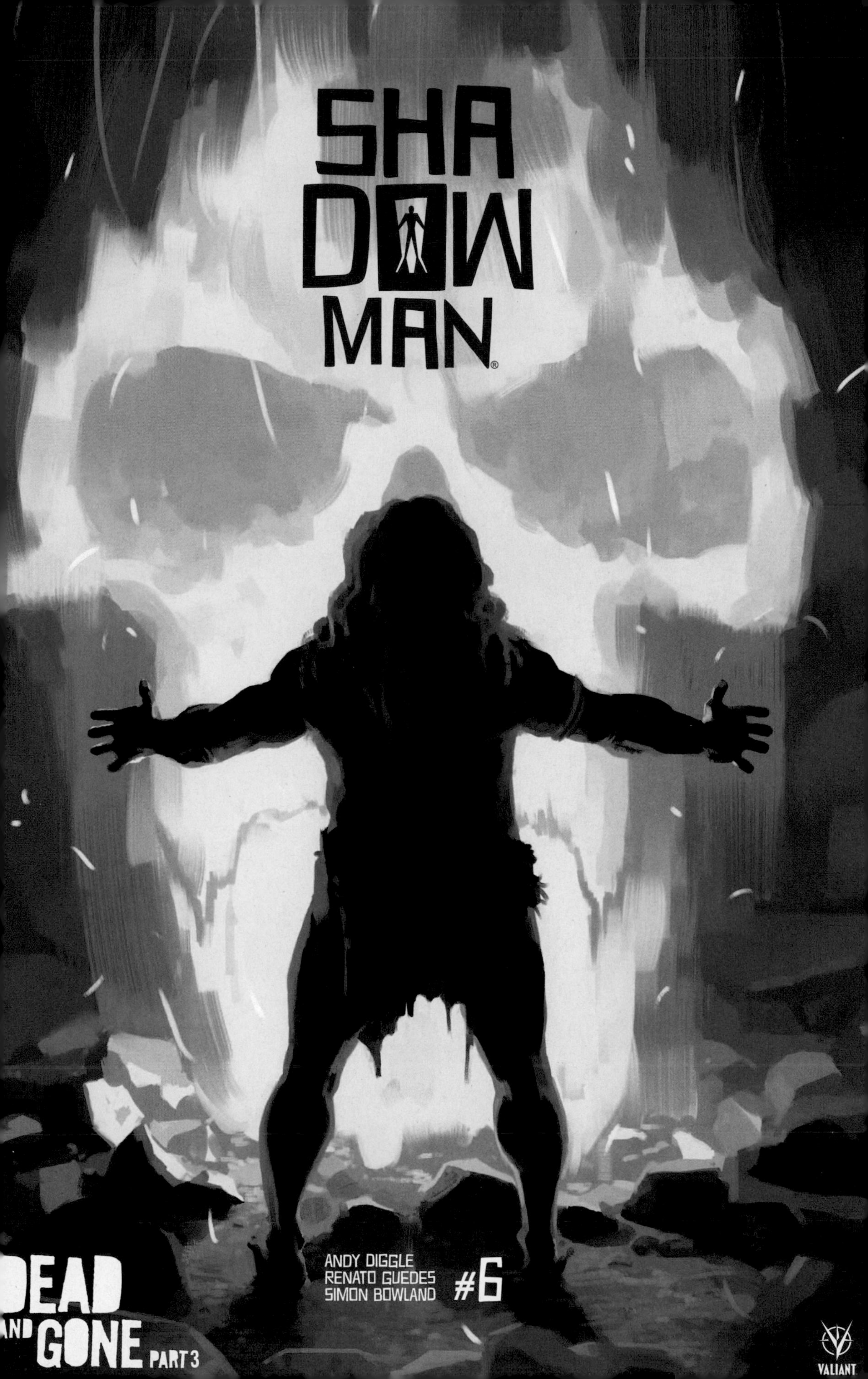
SHADOWMAN
DEAD AND GONE PART 3
ANDY DIGGLE
RENATO GUEDES
SIMON BOWLAND
#6
VALIANT

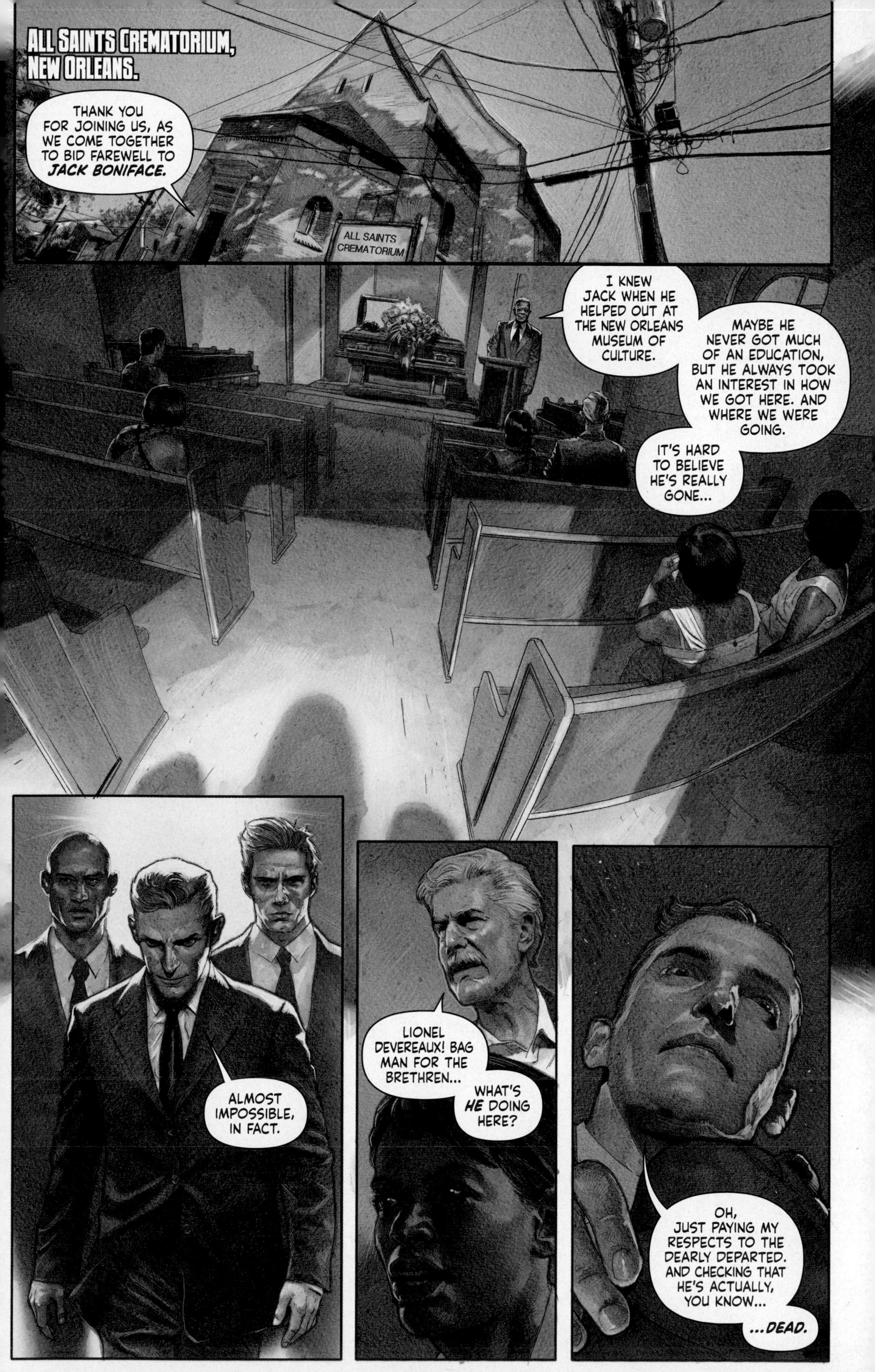
ALL SAINTS CREMATORIUM, NEW ORLEANS.
THANK YOU FOR JOINING US, AS WE COME TOGETHER TO BID FAREWELL TO JACK BONIFACE.
ALL SAINTS CREMATORIUM
I KNEW JACK WHEN HE HELPED OUT AT THE NEW ORLEANS MUSEUM OF CULTURE.
MAYBE HE NEVER GOT MUCH OF AN EDUCATION, BUT HE ALWAYS TOOK AN INTEREST IN HOW WE GOT HERE. AND WHERE WE WERE GOING.
IT'S HARD TO BELIEVE HE'S REALLY GONE...
ALMOST IMPOSSIBLE, IN FACT.
LIONEL DEVEREAUX! BAG MAN FOR THE BRETHREN...
WHAT'S HE DOING HERE?
OH, JUST PAYING MY RESPECTS TO THE DEARLY DEPARTED. AND CHECKING THAT HE'S ACTUALLY, YOU KNOW...
...DEAD.

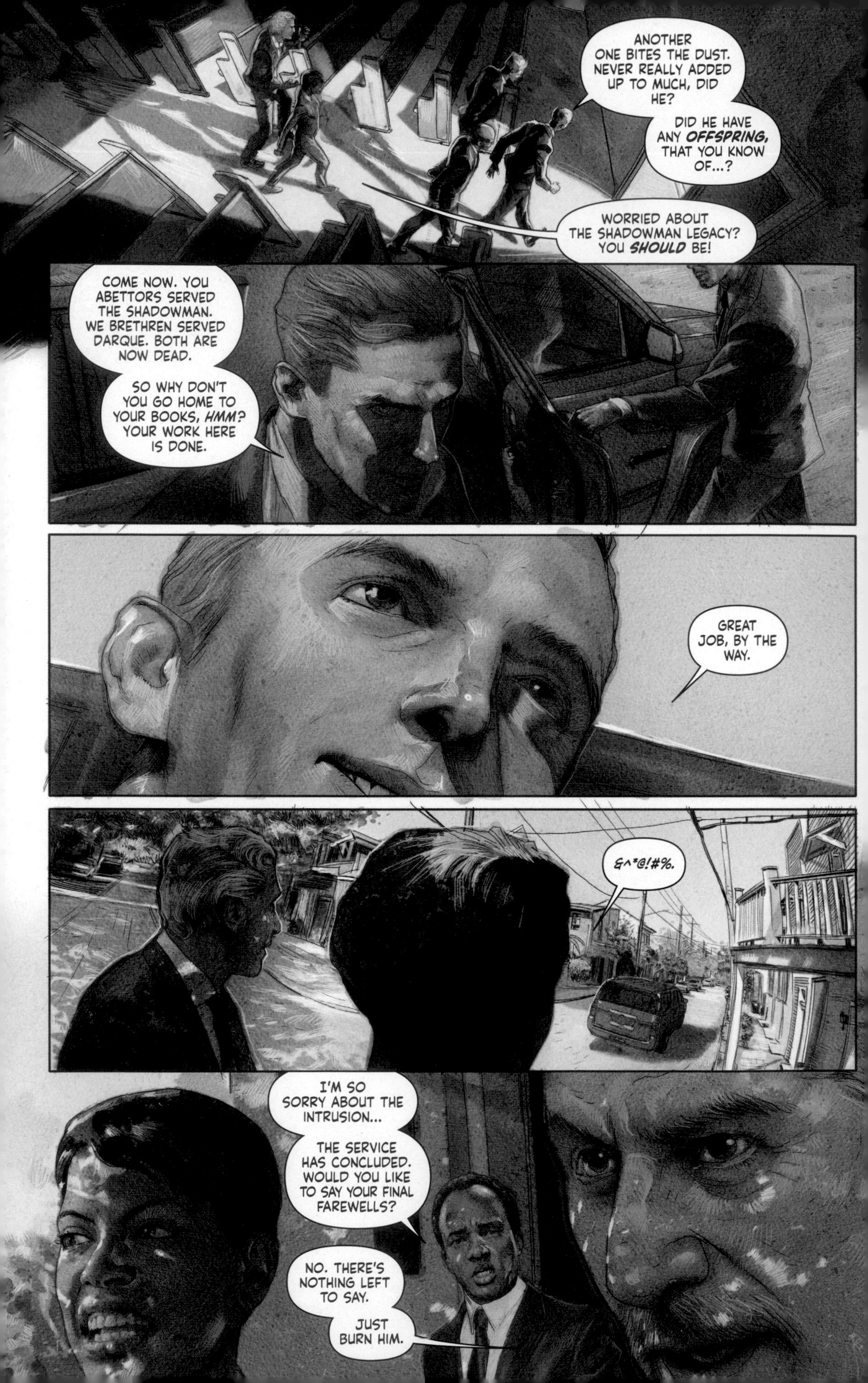

ANOTHER ONE BITES THE DUST. NEVER REALLY ADDED UP TO MUCH, DID HE?
DID HE HAVE ANY OFFSPRING, THAT YOU KNOW OF...?
WORRIED ABOUT THE SHADOWMAN LEGACY? YOU SHOULD BE!
COME NOW. YOU ABETTORS SERVED THE SHADOWMAN. WE BRETHREN SERVED DARQUE. BOTH ARE NOW DEAD.
SO WHY DON'T YOU GO HOME TO YOUR BOOKS, HMM? YOUR WORK HERE IS DONE.
GREAT JOB, BY THE WAY.
&^*@!#%.
I'M SO SORRY ABOUT THE INTRUSION...
THE SERVICE HAS CONCLUDED. WOULD YOU LIKE TO SAY YOUR FINAL FAREWELLS?
NO. THERE'S NOTHING LEFT TO SAY.
JUST BURN HIM.

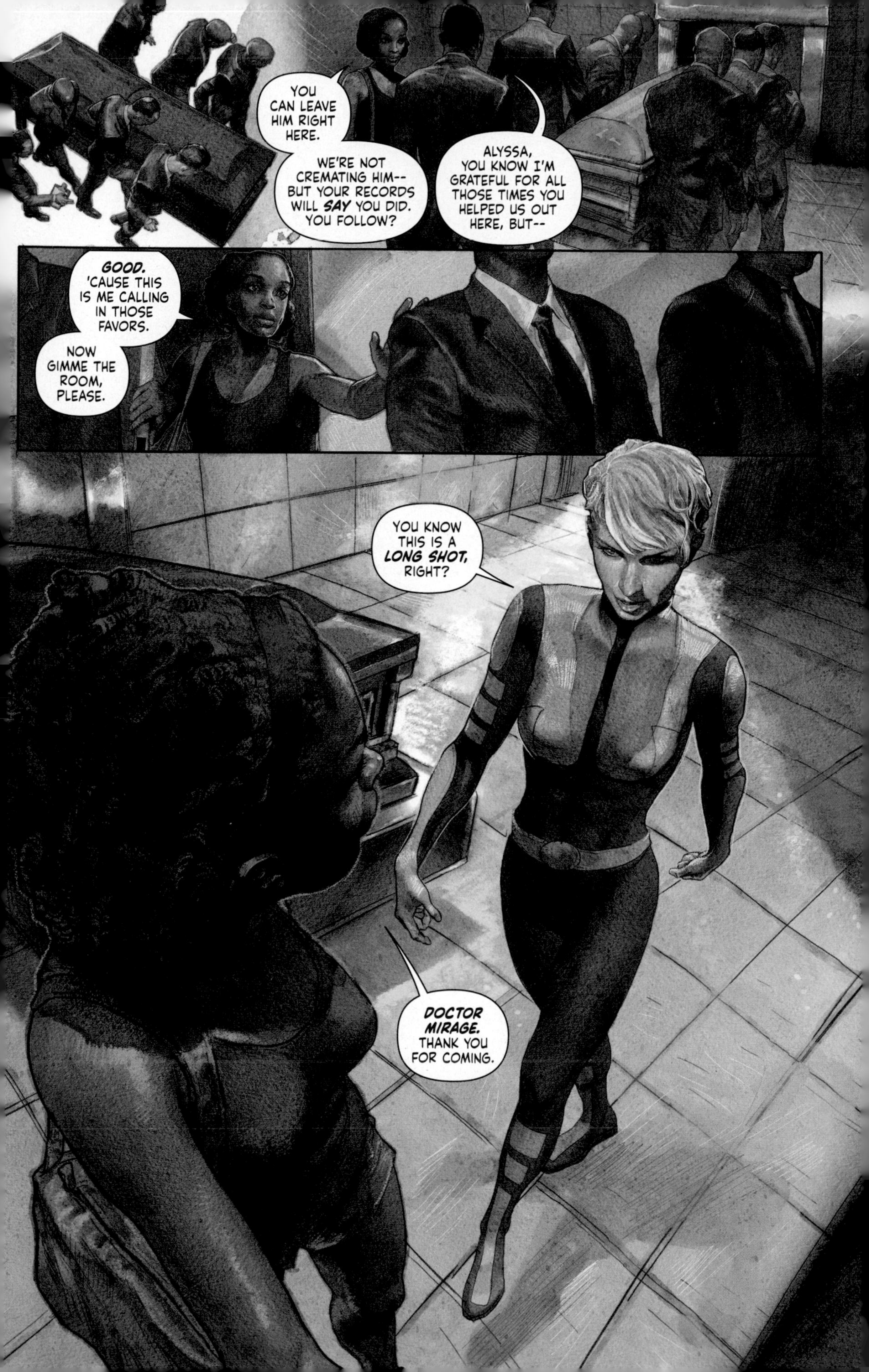
YOU CAN LEAVE HIM RIGHT HERE.
WE'RE NOT CREMATING HIM-- BUT YOUR RECORDS WILL SAY YOU DID. YOU FOLLOW?
ALYSSA, YOU KNOW I'M GRATEFUL FOR ALL THOSE TIMES YOU HELPED US OUT HERE, BUT--
GOOD. 'CAUSE THIS IS ME CALLING IN THOSE FAVORS.
NOW GIMME THE ROOM, PLEASE.
YOU KNOW THIS IS A LONG SHOT, RIGHT?
DOCTOR MIRAGE. THANK YOU FOR COMING.

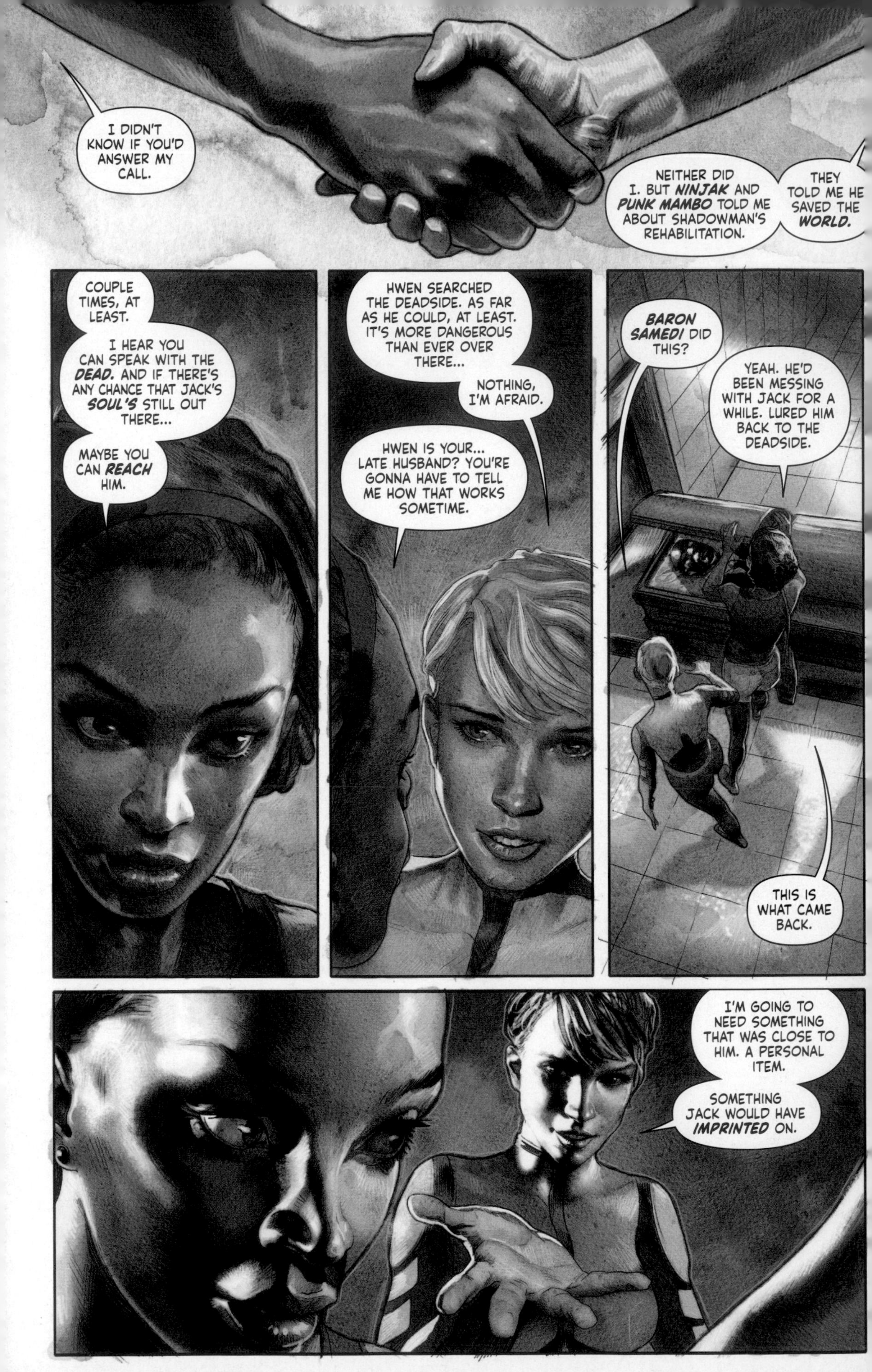
I DIDN'T KNOW IF YOU'D ANSWER MY CALL.
NEITHER DID I. BUT NINJAK AND PUNK MAMBO TOLD ME ABOUT SHADOWMAN'S REHABILITATION.
THEY TOLD ME HE SAVED THE WORLD.
COUPLE TIMES, AT LEAST.
I HEAR YOU CAN SPEAK WITH THE DEAD. AND IF THERE'S ANY CHANCE THAT JACK'S SOUL'S STILL OUT THERE...
MAYBE YOU CAN REACH HIM.
HWEN SEARCHED THE DEADSIDE. AS FAR AS HE COULD, AT LEAST. IT'S MORE DANGEROUS THAN EVER OVER THERE...
NOTHING, I'M AFRAID.
HWEN IS YOUR... LATE HUSBAND? YOU'RE GONNA HAVE TO TELL ME HOW THAT WORKS SOMETIME.
BARON SAMEDI DID THIS?
YEAH. HE'D BEEN MESSING WITH JACK FOR A WHILE. LURED HIM BACK TO THE DEADSIDE.
THIS IS WHAT CAME BACK.
I'M GOING TO NEED SOMETHING THAT WAS CLOSE TO HIM. A PERSONAL ITEM.
SOMETHING JACK WOULD HAVE IMPRINTED ON.

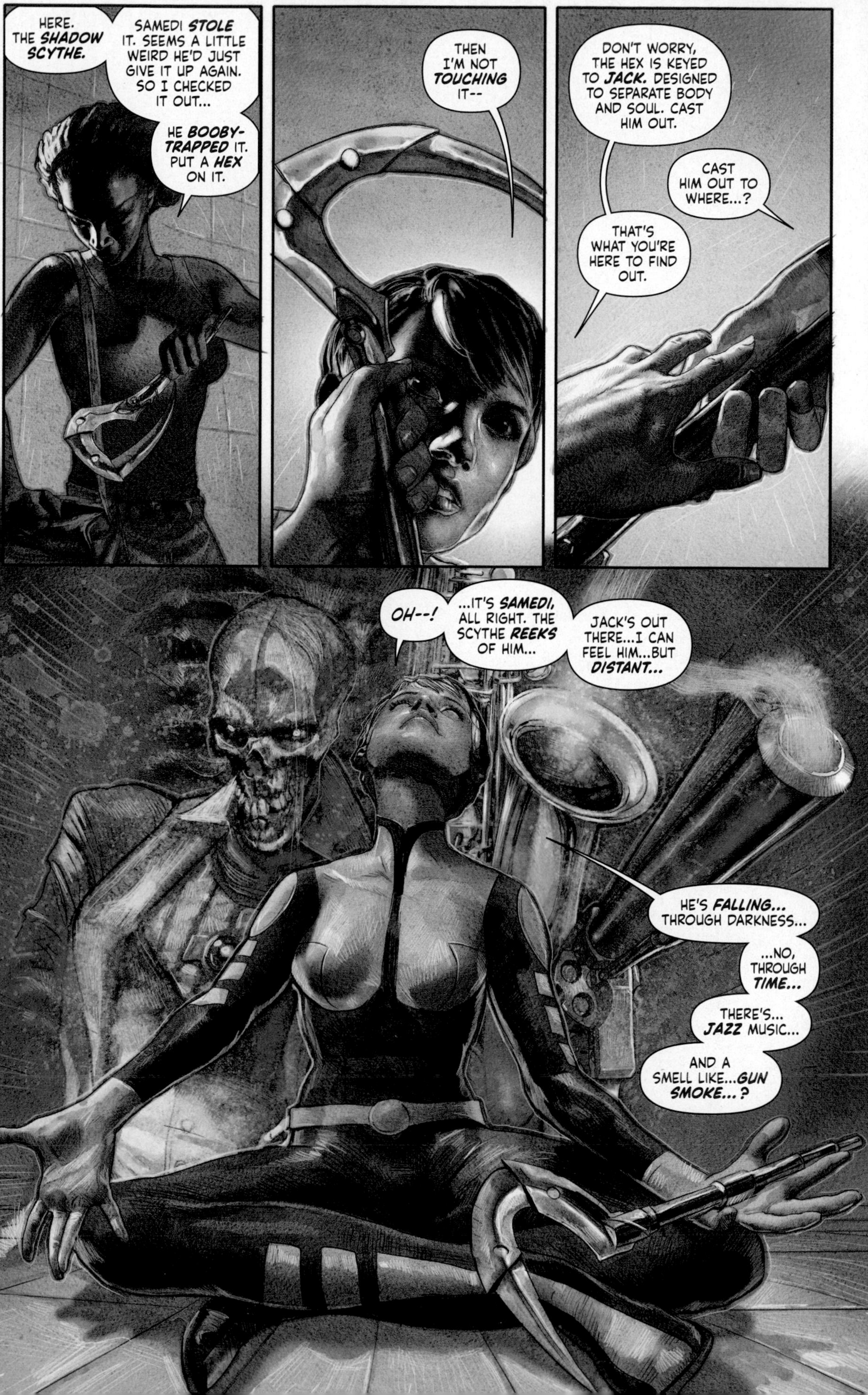
HERE. THE SHADOW SCYTHE.
SAMEDI STOLE IT. SEEMS A LITTLE WEIRD HE'D JUST GIVE IT UP AGAIN. SO I CHECKED IT OUT...
HE BOOBY-TRAPPED IT. PUT A HEX ON IT.
THEN I'M NOT TOUCHING IT--
DON'T WORRY, THE HEX IS KEYED TO JACK. DESIGNED TO SEPARATE BODY AND SOUL. CAST HIM OUT.
CAST HIM OUT TO WHERE...?
THAT'S WHAT YOU'RE HERE TO FIND OUT.
OH--!
...IT'S SAMEDI, ALL RIGHT. THE SCYTHE REEKS OF HIM...
JACK'S OUT THERE...I CAN FEEL HIM...BUT DISTANT...
HE'S FALLING... THROUGH DARKNESS...
...NO, THROUGH TIME...
THERE'S... JAZZ MUSIC...
AND A SMELL LIKE...GUN SMOKE...?

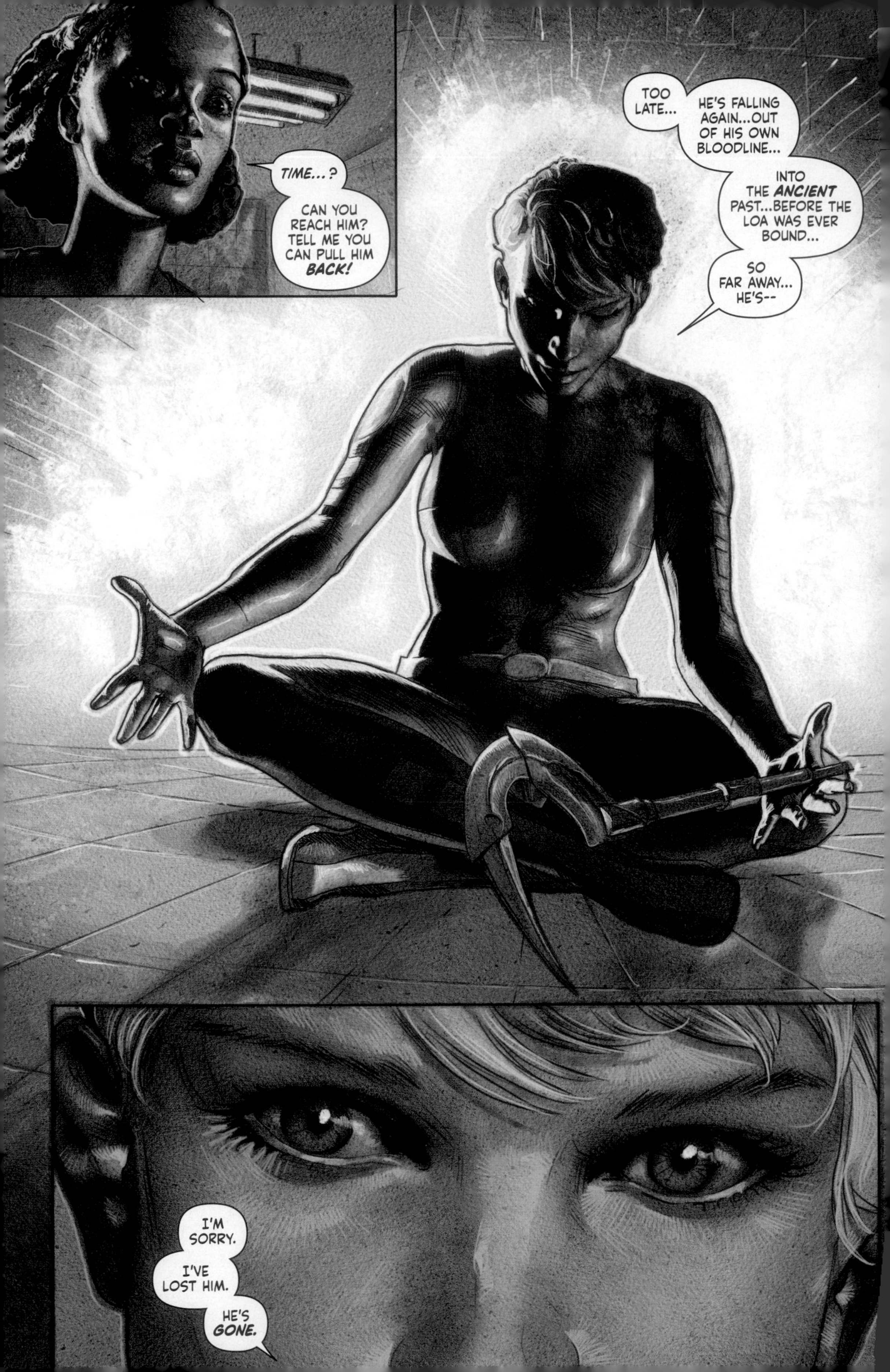
TIME...?
CAN YOU REACH HIM? TELL ME YOU CAN PULL HIM BACK!
TOO LATE...
HE'S FALLING AGAIN...OUT OF HIS OWN BLOODLINE...
INTO THE ANCIENT PAST...BEFORE THE LOA WAS EVER BOUND...
SO FAR AWAY... HE'S--
I'M SORRY.
I'VE LOST HIM.
HE'S GONE.

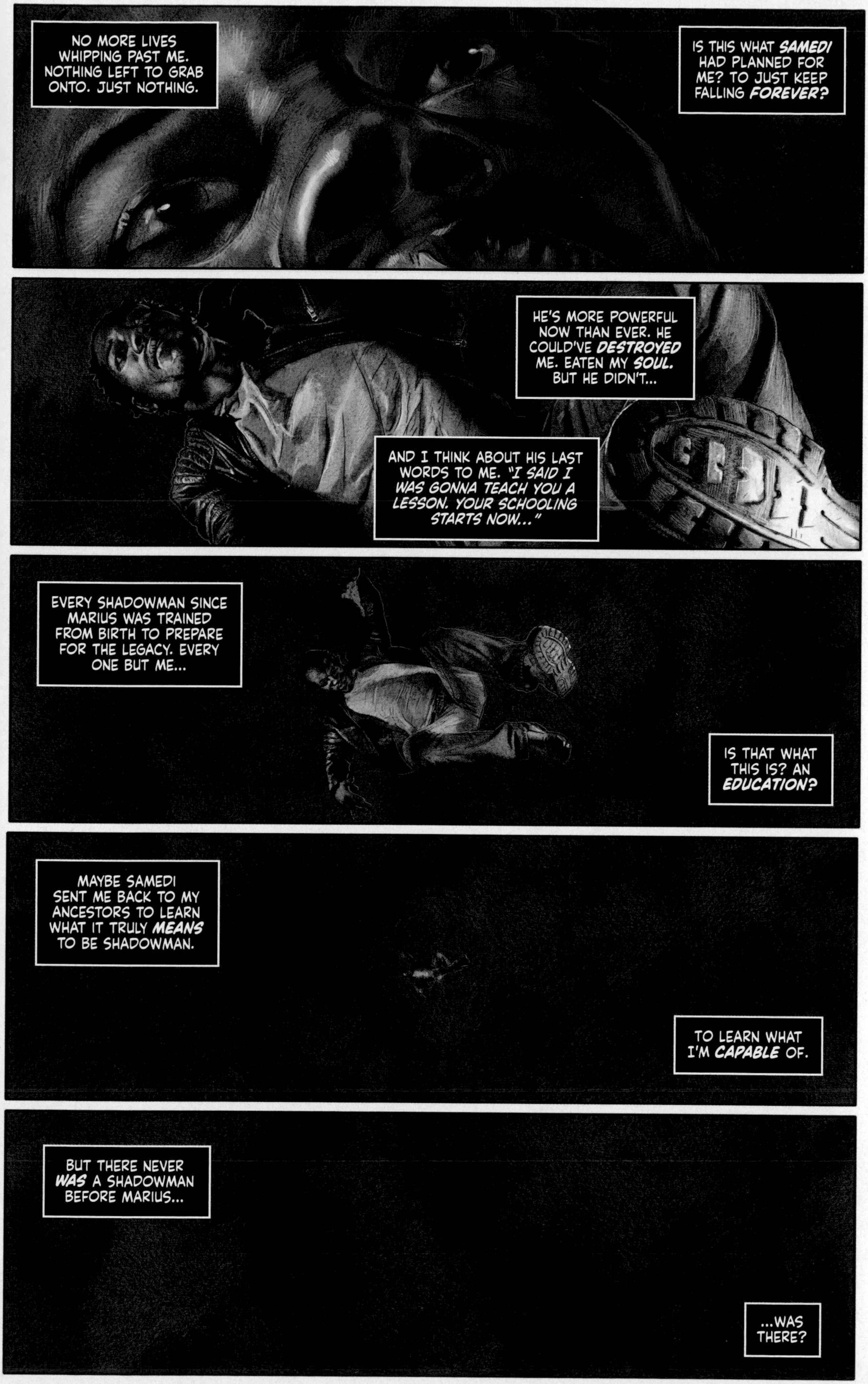
NO MORE LIVES WHIPPING PAST ME. NOTHING LEFT TO GRAB ONTO. JUST NOTHING.
IS THIS WHAT *SAMEDI* HAD PLANNED FOR ME? TO JUST KEEP FALLING *FOREVER?*
HE'S MORE POWERFUL NOW THAN EVER. HE COULD'VE *DESTROYED* ME. EATEN MY *SOUL.* BUT HE DIDN'T...
AND I THINK ABOUT HIS LAST WORDS TO ME. *"I SAID I WAS GONNA TEACH YOU A LESSON. YOUR SCHOOLING STARTS NOW..."*
EVERY SHADOWMAN SINCE MARIUS WAS TRAINED FROM BIRTH TO PREPARE FOR THE LEGACY. EVERY ONE BUT ME...
IS THAT WHAT THIS IS? AN *EDUCATION?*
MAYBE SAMEDI SENT ME BACK TO MY ANCESTORS TO LEARN WHAT IT TRULY *MEANS* TO BE SHADOWMAN.
TO LEARN WHAT I'M *CAPABLE* OF.
BUT THERE NEVER *WAS* A SHADOWMAN BEFORE MARIUS...
...WAS THERE?

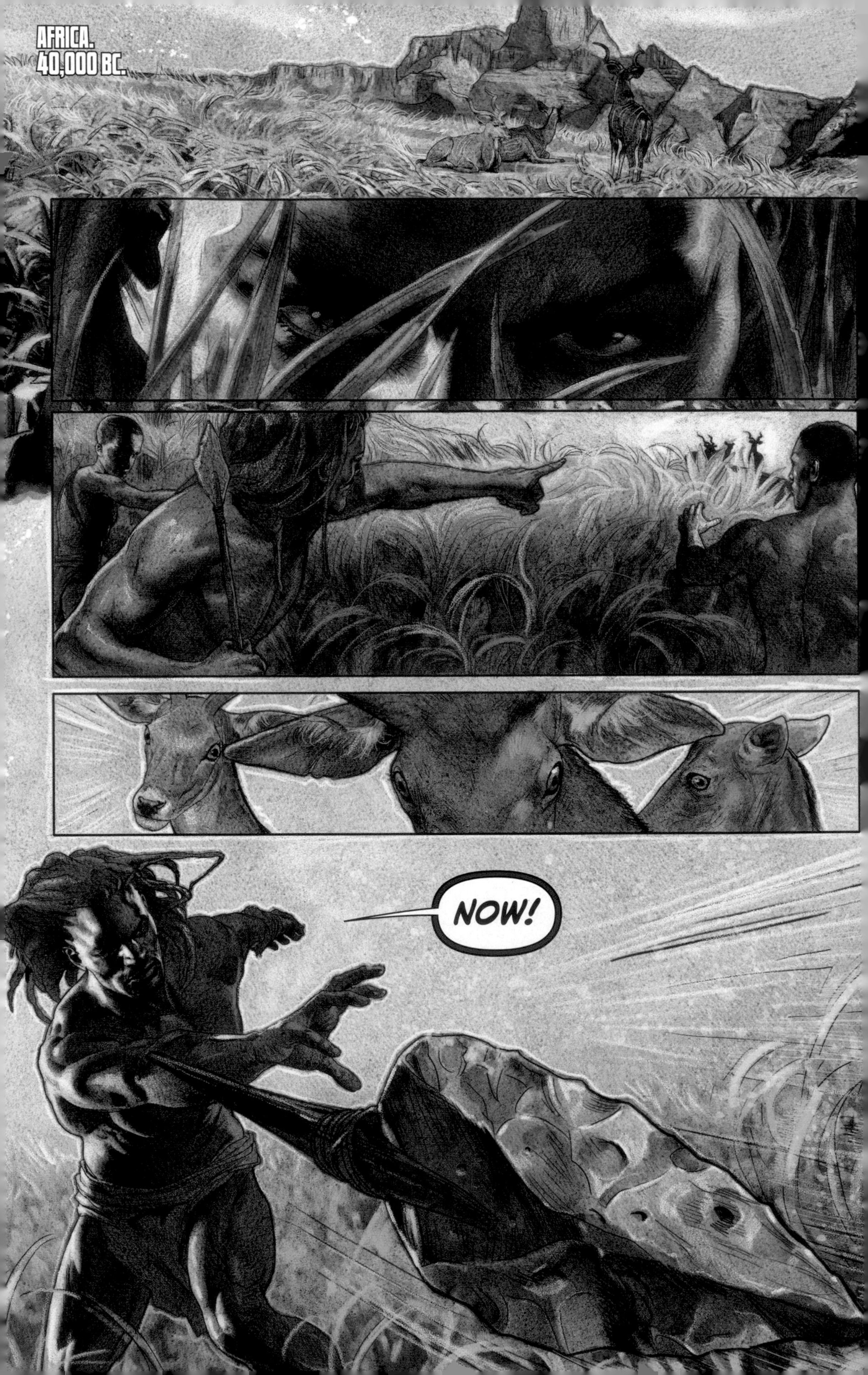
AFRICA.
40,000 BC.
NOW!

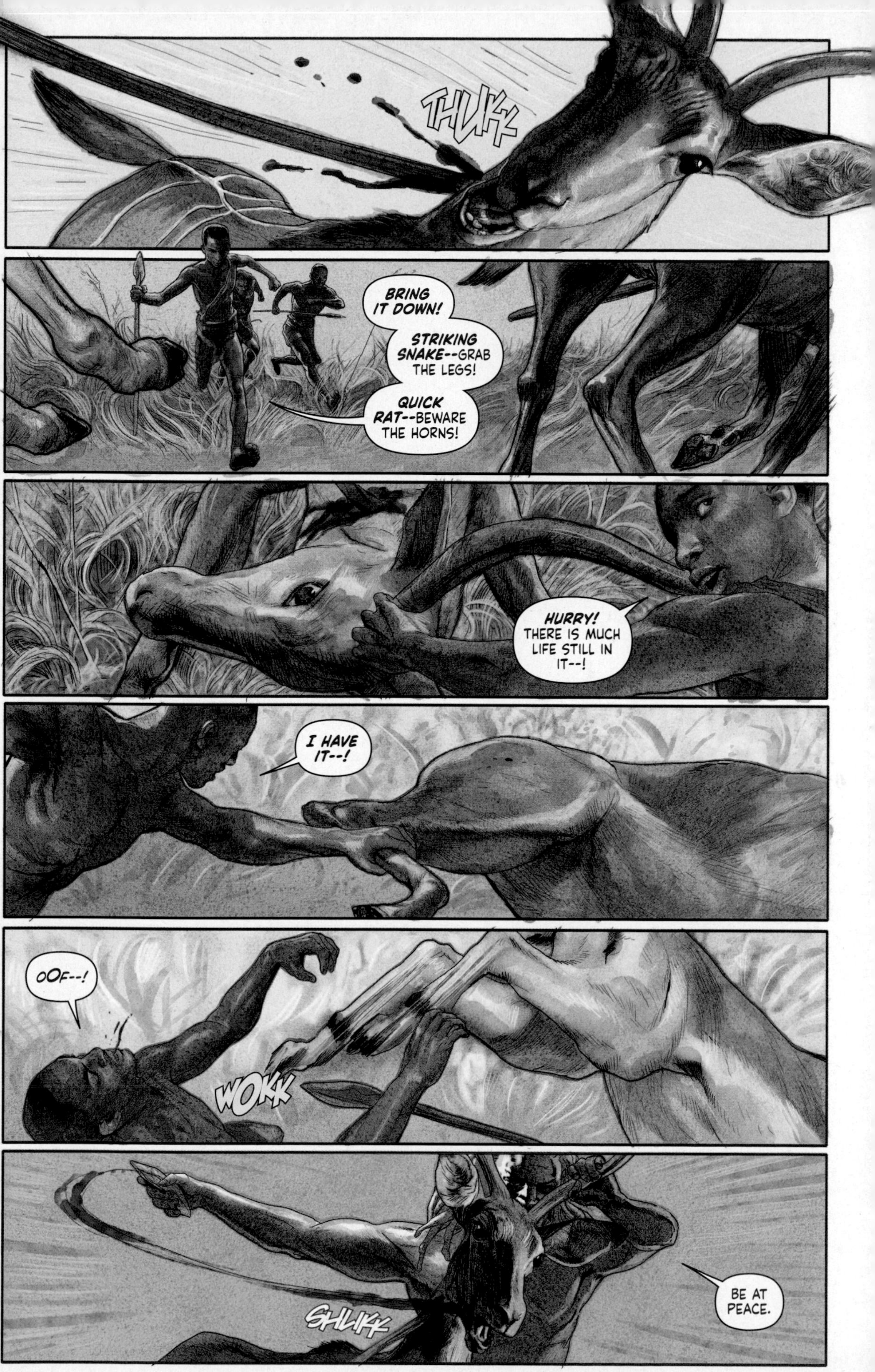
THUKK
BRING IT DOWN!
STRIKING SNAKE--GRAB THE LEGS!
QUICK RAT--BEWARE THE HORNS!
HURRY! THERE IS MUCH LIFE STILL IN IT--!
I HAVE IT--!
OOF--!
WOKK
BE AT PEACE.
SHLIKK

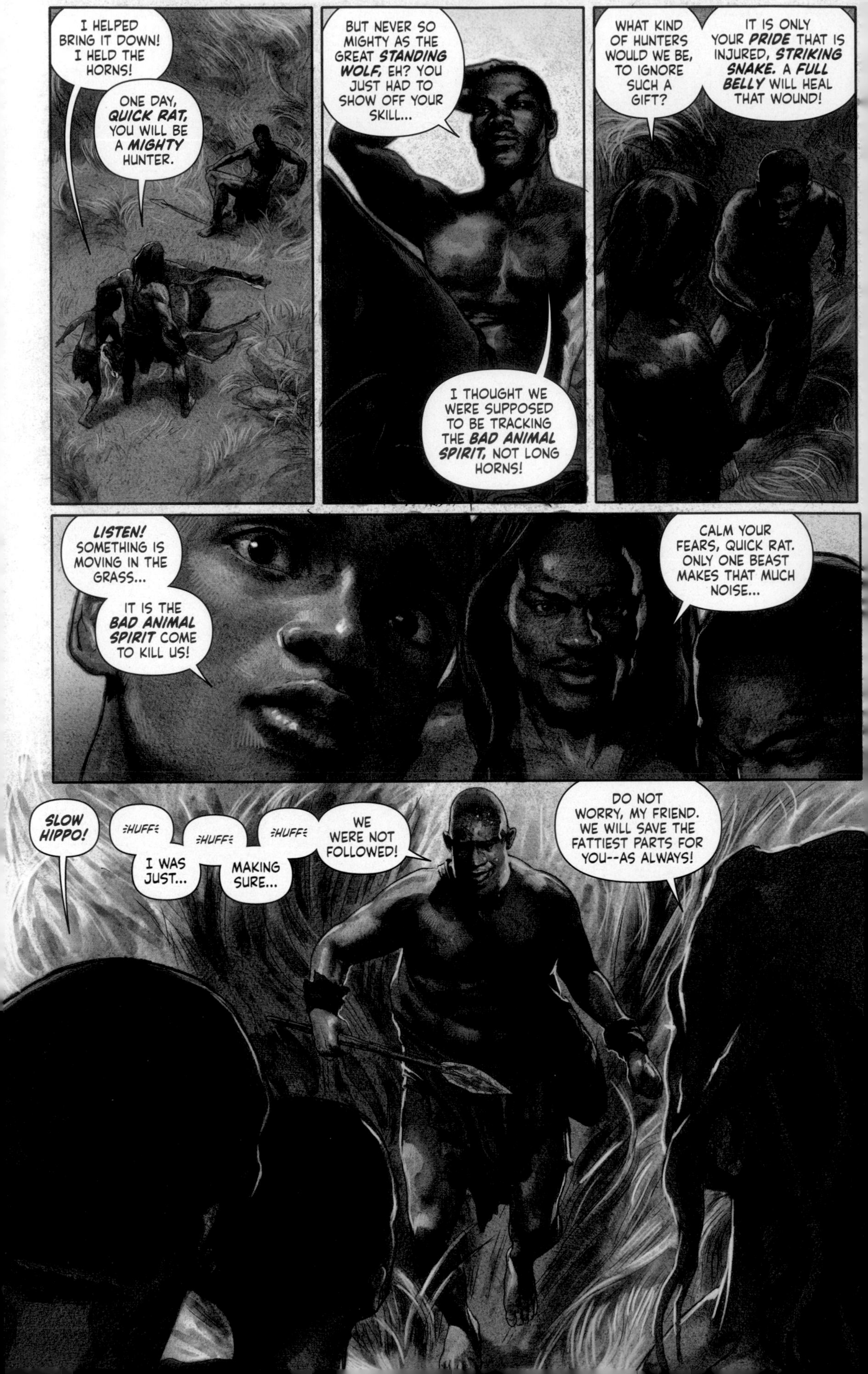
I HELPED BRING IT DOWN! I HELD THE HORNS!
ONE DAY, QUICK RAT, YOU WILL BE A MIGHTY HUNTER.
BUT NEVER SO MIGHTY AS THE GREAT STANDING WOLF, EH? YOU JUST HAD TO SHOW OFF YOUR SKILL...
I THOUGHT WE WERE SUPPOSED TO BE TRACKING THE BAD ANIMAL SPIRIT, NOT LONG HORNS!
WHAT KIND OF HUNTERS WOULD WE BE, TO IGNORE SUCH A GIFT?
IT IS ONLY YOUR PRIDE THAT IS INJURED, STRIKING SNAKE. A FULL BELLY WILL HEAL THAT WOUND!
LISTEN! SOMETHING IS MOVING IN THE GRASS...
IT IS THE BAD ANIMAL SPIRIT COME TO KILL US!
CALM YOUR FEARS, QUICK RAT. ONLY ONE BEAST MAKES THAT MUCH NOISE...
SLOW HIPPO!
HUFF
I WAS JUST...
HUFF
MAKING SURE...
HUFF
WE WERE NOT FOLLOWED!
DO NOT WORRY, MY FRIEND. WE WILL SAVE THE FATTIEST PARTS FOR YOU--AS ALWAYS!

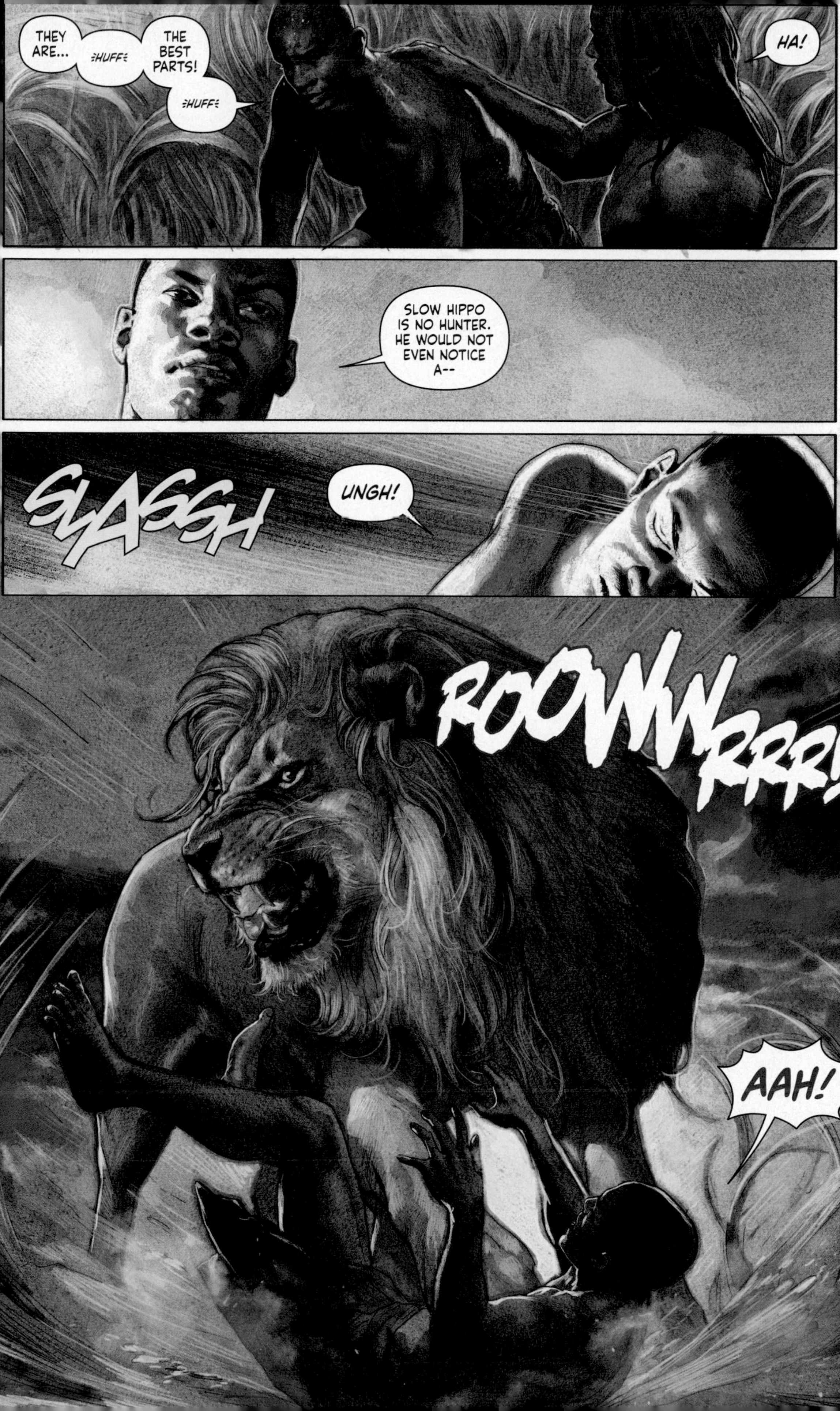
THEY ARE...
HUFF
THE BEST PARTS!
HUFF
HA!
SLOW HIPPO IS NO HUNTER. HE WOULD NOT EVEN NOTICE A--
SLASSH
UNGH!
ROOWWRRR!
AAH!

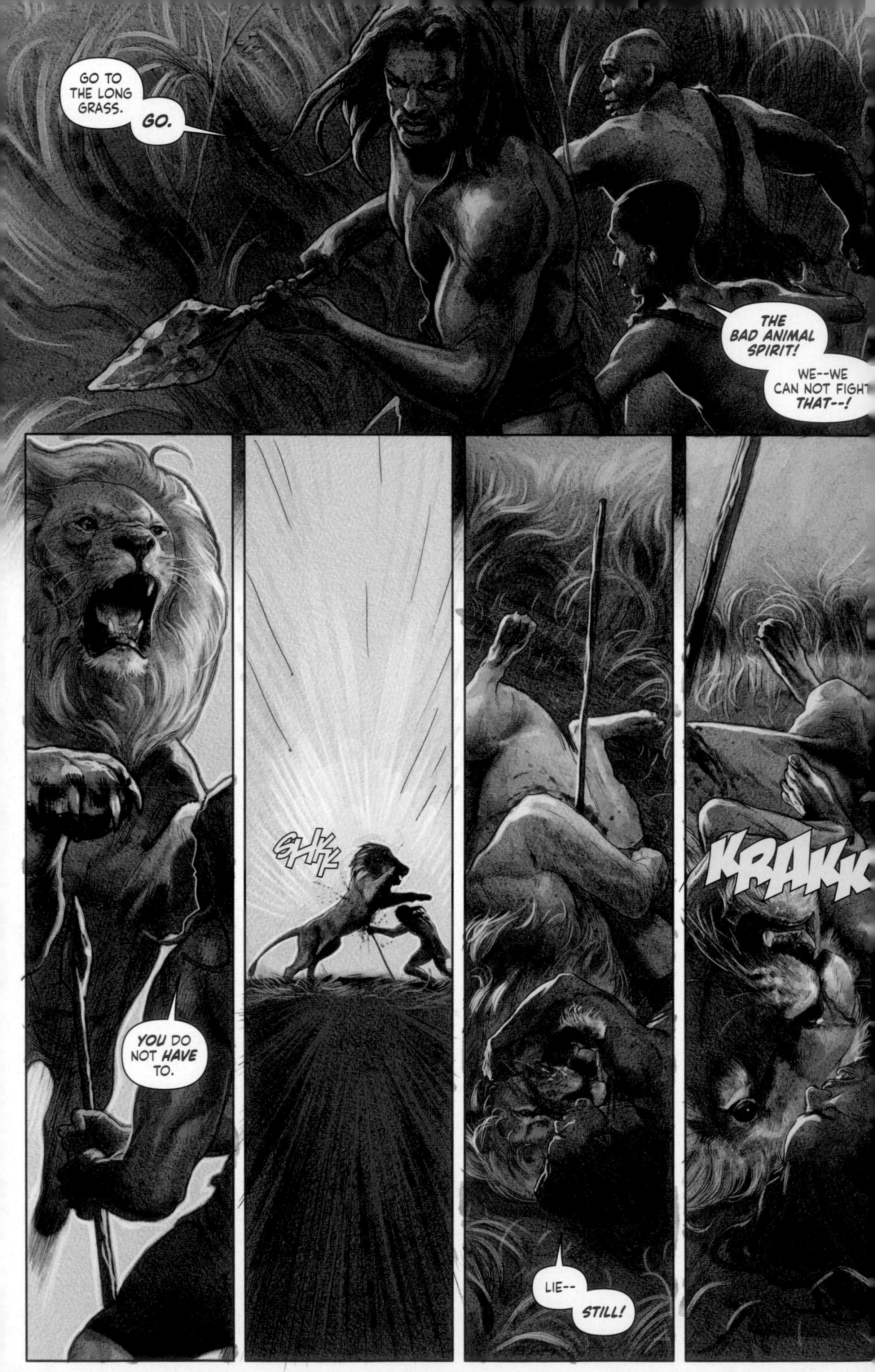
GO TO THE LONG GRASS.
GO.
THE BAD ANIMAL SPIRIT!
WE--WE CAN NOT FIGHT THAT--!
YOU DO NOT HAVE TO.
SHKK
LIE--
STILL!
KRAKK

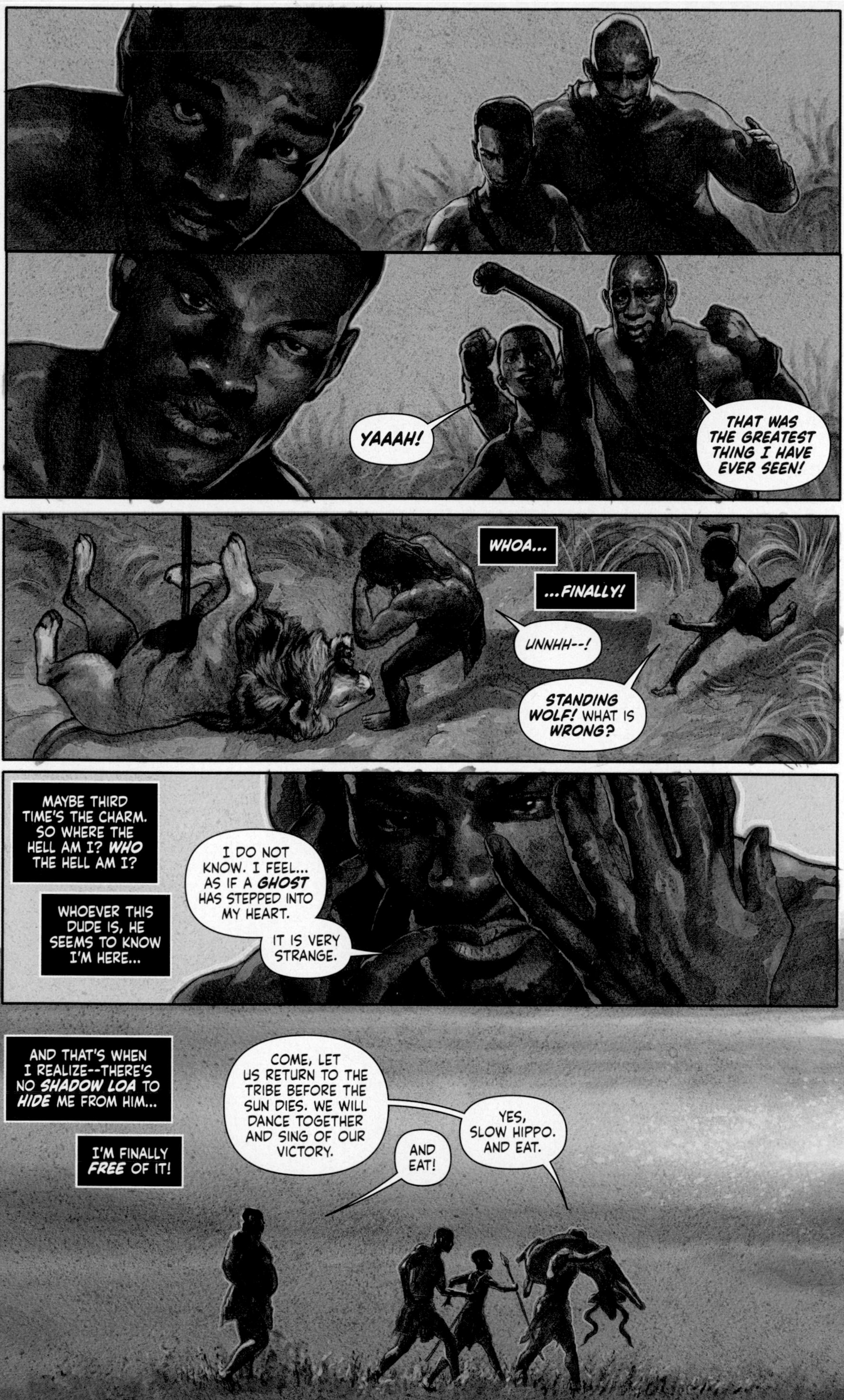
YAAAH!
THAT WAS THE GREATEST THING I HAVE EVER SEEN!
WHOA...
...FINALLY!
UNNHH--!
STANDING WOLF! WHAT IS WRONG?
MAYBE THIRD TIME'S THE CHARM. SO WHERE THE HELL AM I? WHO THE HELL AM I?
WHOEVER THIS DUDE IS, HE SEEMS TO KNOW I'M HERE...
I DO NOT KNOW. I FEEL... AS IF A GHOST HAS STEPPED INTO MY HEART.
IT IS VERY STRANGE.
AND THAT'S WHEN I REALIZE--THERE'S NO SHADOW LOA TO HIDE ME FROM HIM...
I'M FINALLY FREE OF IT!
COME, LET US RETURN TO THE TRIBE BEFORE THE SUN DIES. WE WILL DANCE TOGETHER AND SING OF OUR VICTORY.
AND EAT!
YES, SLOW HIPPO. AND EAT.

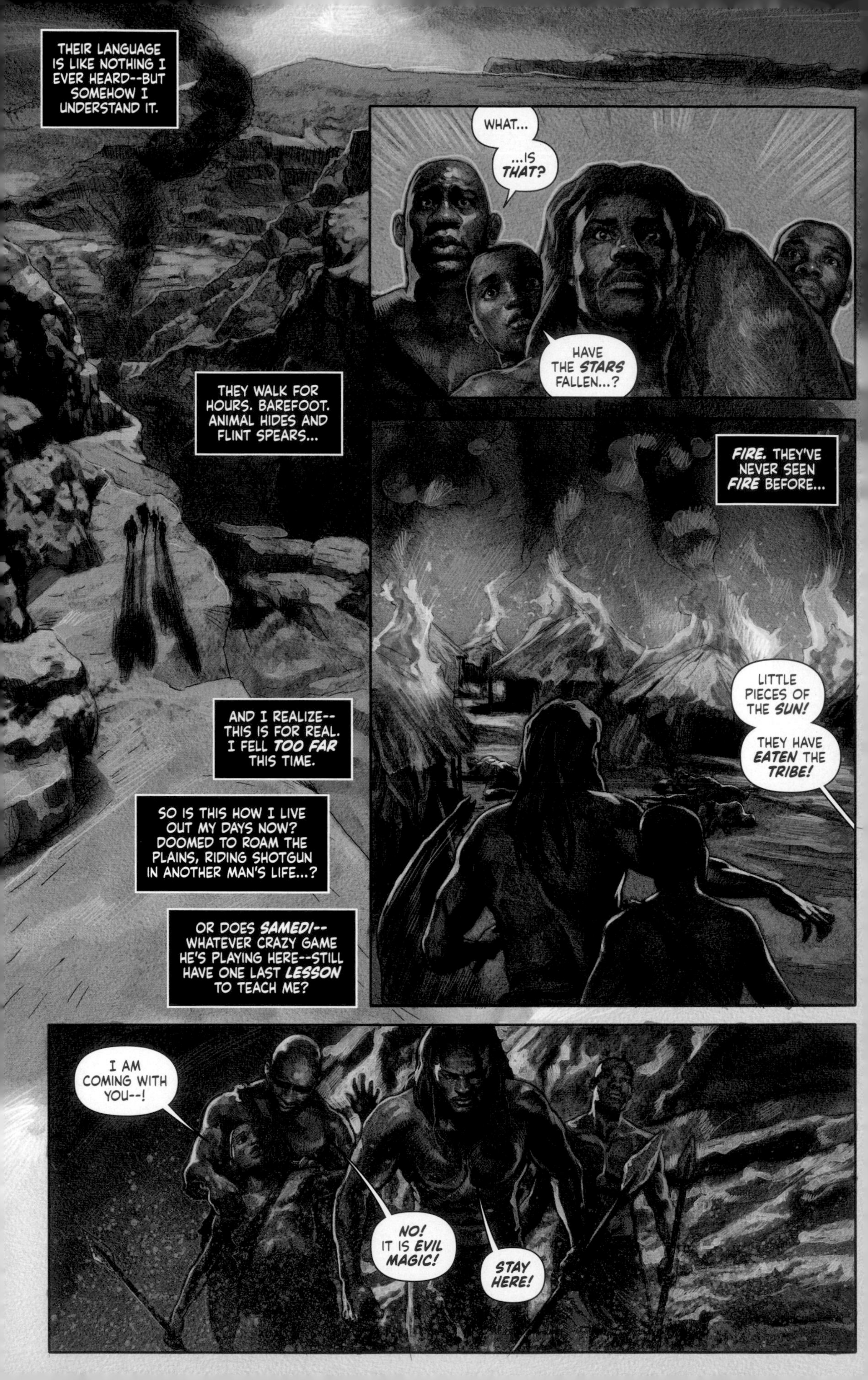
THEIR LANGUAGE IS LIKE NOTHING I EVER HEARD--BUT SOMEHOW I UNDERSTAND IT.
WHAT...
...IS *THAT?*
HAVE THE *STARS* FALLEN...?
THEY WALK FOR HOURS. BAREFOOT. ANIMAL HIDES AND FLINT SPEARS...
FIRE. THEY'VE NEVER SEEN *FIRE* BEFORE...
LITTLE PIECES OF THE *SUN!*
THEY HAVE *EATEN* THE *TRIBE!*
AND I REALIZE-- THIS IS FOR REAL. I FELL *TOO FAR* THIS TIME.
SO IS THIS HOW I LIVE OUT MY DAYS NOW? DOOMED TO ROAM THE PLAINS, RIDING SHOTGUN IN ANOTHER MAN'S LIFE...?
OR DOES *SAMEDI*-- WHATEVER CRAZY GAME HE'S PLAYING HERE--STILL HAVE ONE LAST *LESSON* TO TEACH ME?
I AM COMING WITH YOU--!
NO! IT IS *EVIL MAGIC!*
STAY HERE!

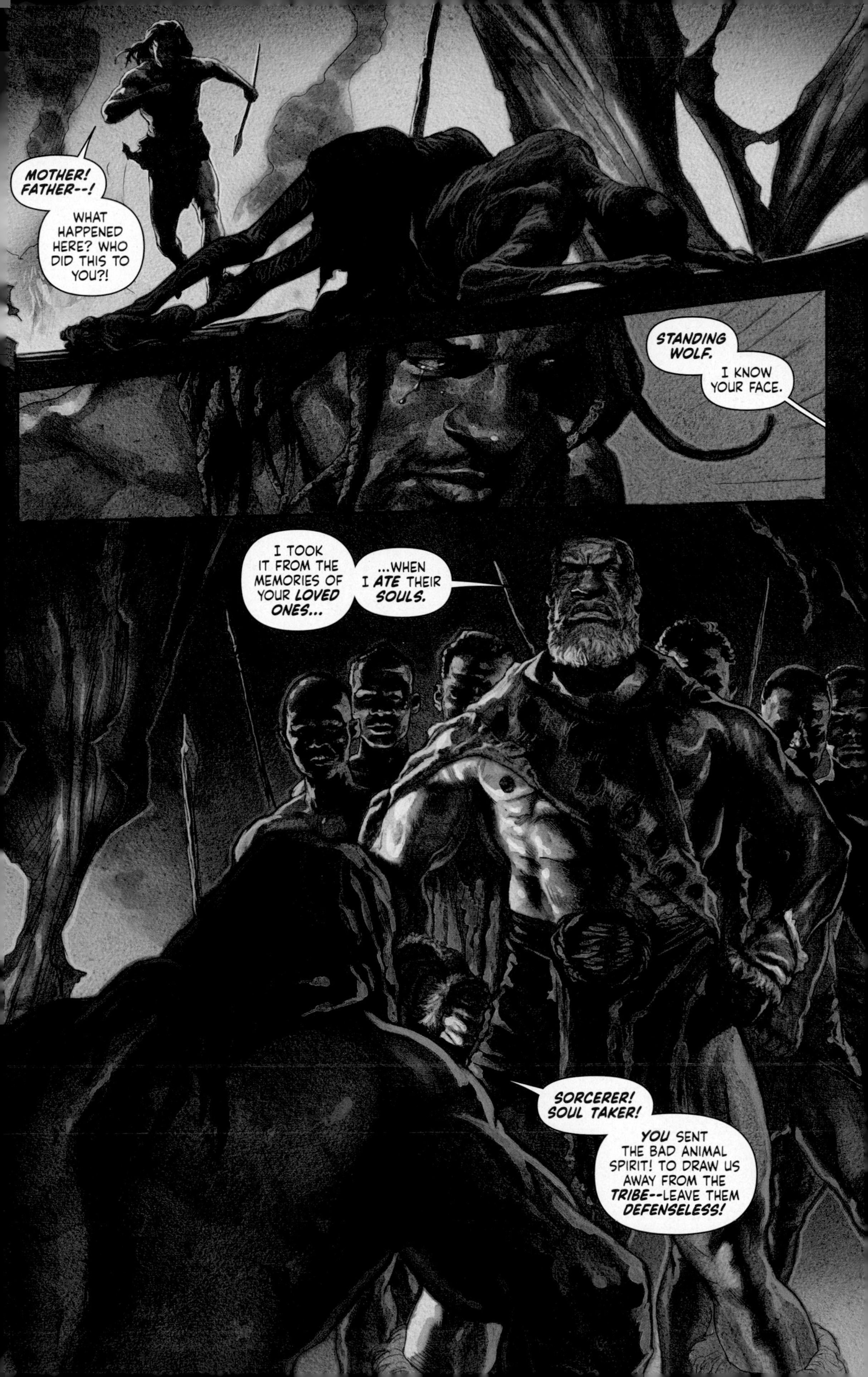
MOTHER! FATHER--!
WHAT HAPPENED HERE? WHO DID THIS TO YOU?!
STANDING WOLF.
I KNOW YOUR FACE.
I TOOK IT FROM THE MEMORIES OF YOUR LOVED ONES...
...WHEN I ATE THEIR SOULS.
SORCERER! SOUL TAKER!
YOU SENT THE BAD ANIMAL SPIRIT! TO DRAW US AWAY FROM THE TRIBE--LEAVE THEM DEFENSELESS!

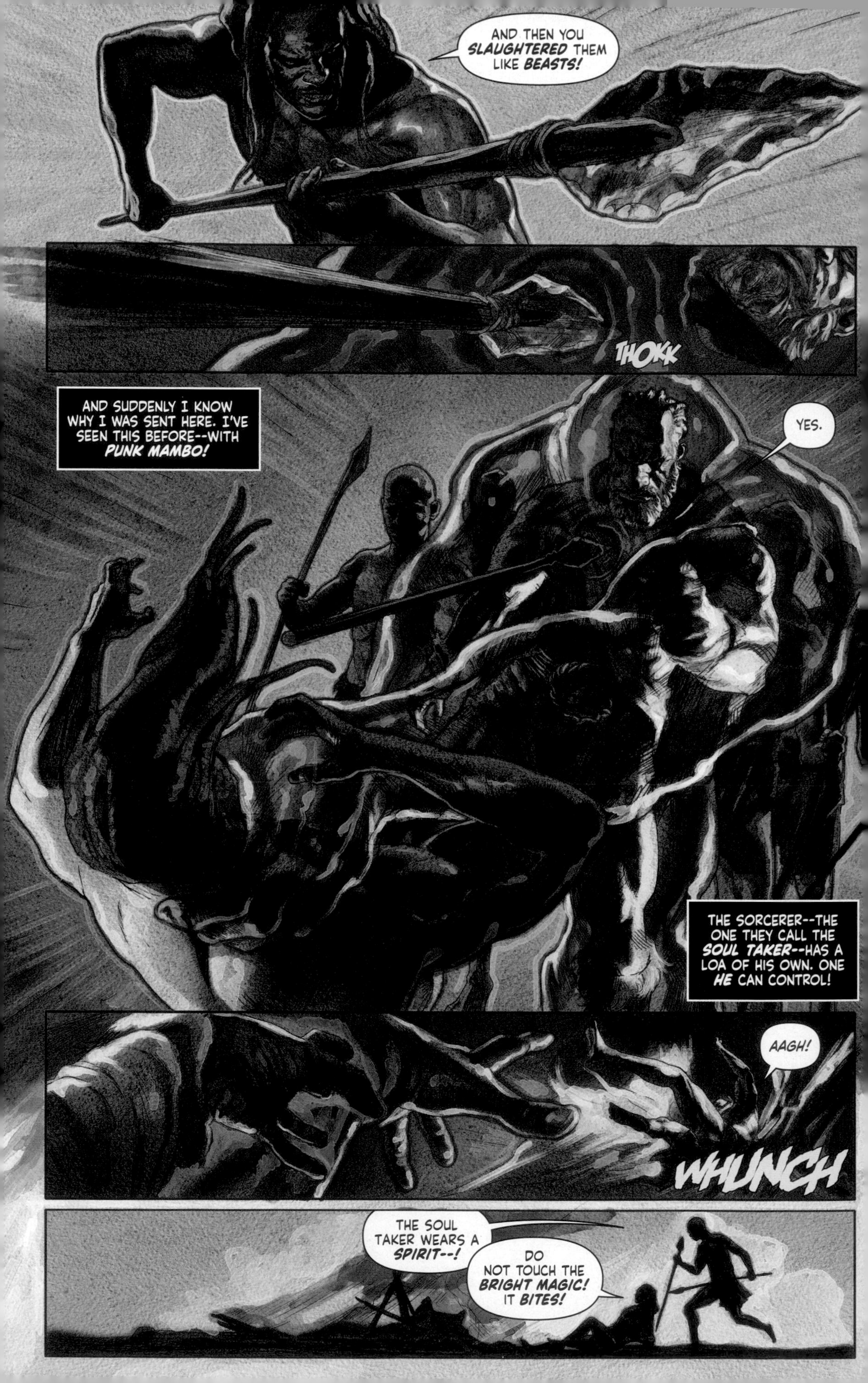
AND THEN YOU SLAUGHTERED THEM LIKE BEASTS!
THOKK
AND SUDDENLY I KNOW WHY I WAS SENT HERE. I'VE SEEN THIS BEFORE--WITH PUNK MAMBO!
YES.
THE SORCERER--THE ONE THEY CALL THE SOUL TAKER--HAS A LOA OF HIS OWN. ONE HE CAN CONTROL!
AAGH!
WHUNCH
THE SOUL TAKER WEARS A SPIRIT--!
DO NOT TOUCH THE BRIGHT MAGIC! IT BITES!

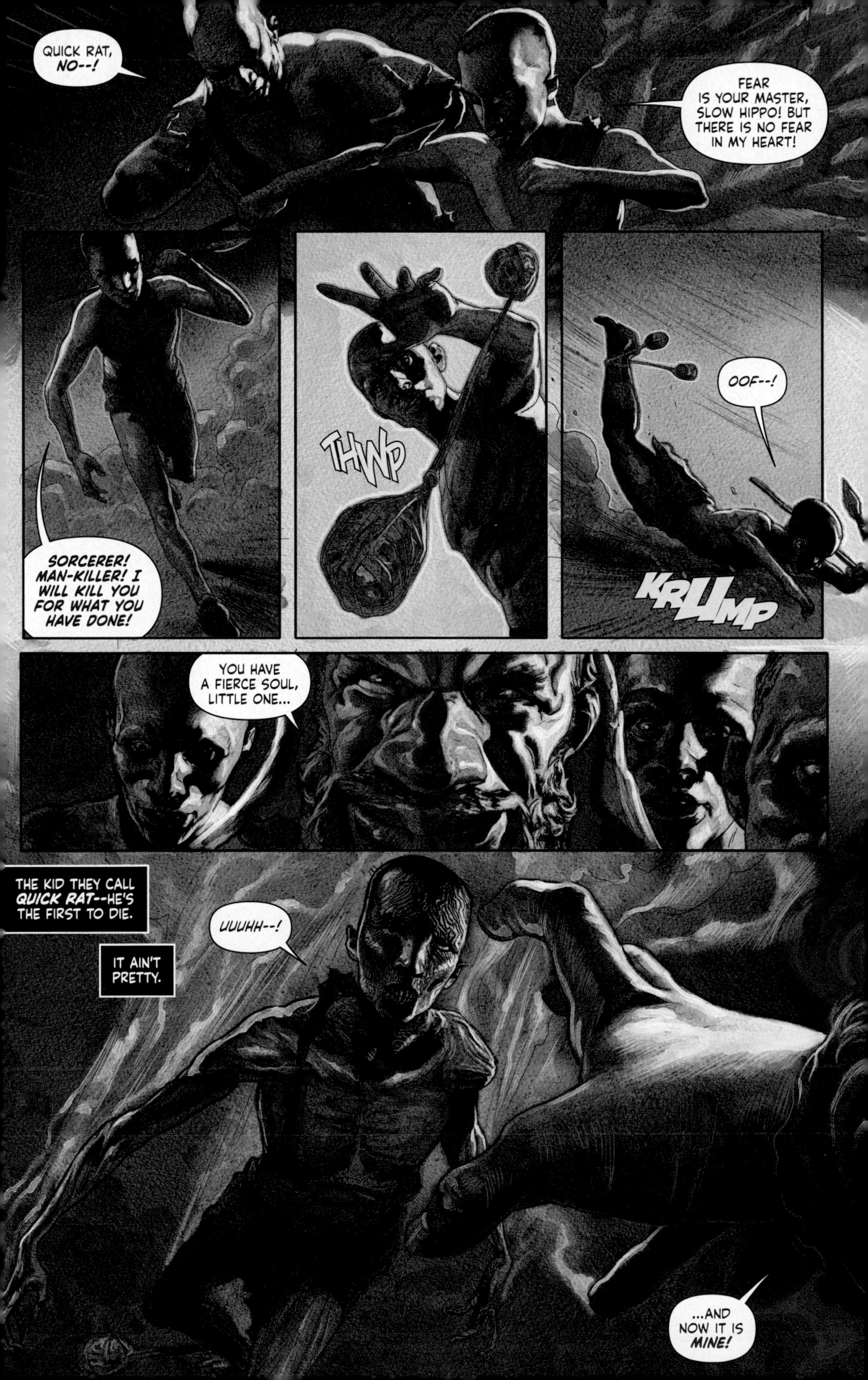
QUICK RAT, NO--!
FEAR IS YOUR MASTER, SLOW HIPPO! BUT THERE IS NO FEAR IN MY HEART!
SORCERER! MAN-KILLER! I WILL KILL YOU FOR WHAT YOU HAVE DONE!
THWP
OOF--!
KRUMP
YOU HAVE A FIERCE SOUL, LITTLE ONE...
THE KID THEY CALL QUICK RAT--HE'S THE FIRST TO DIE.
IT AIN'T PRETTY.
UUUHH--!
...AND NOW IT IS MINE!

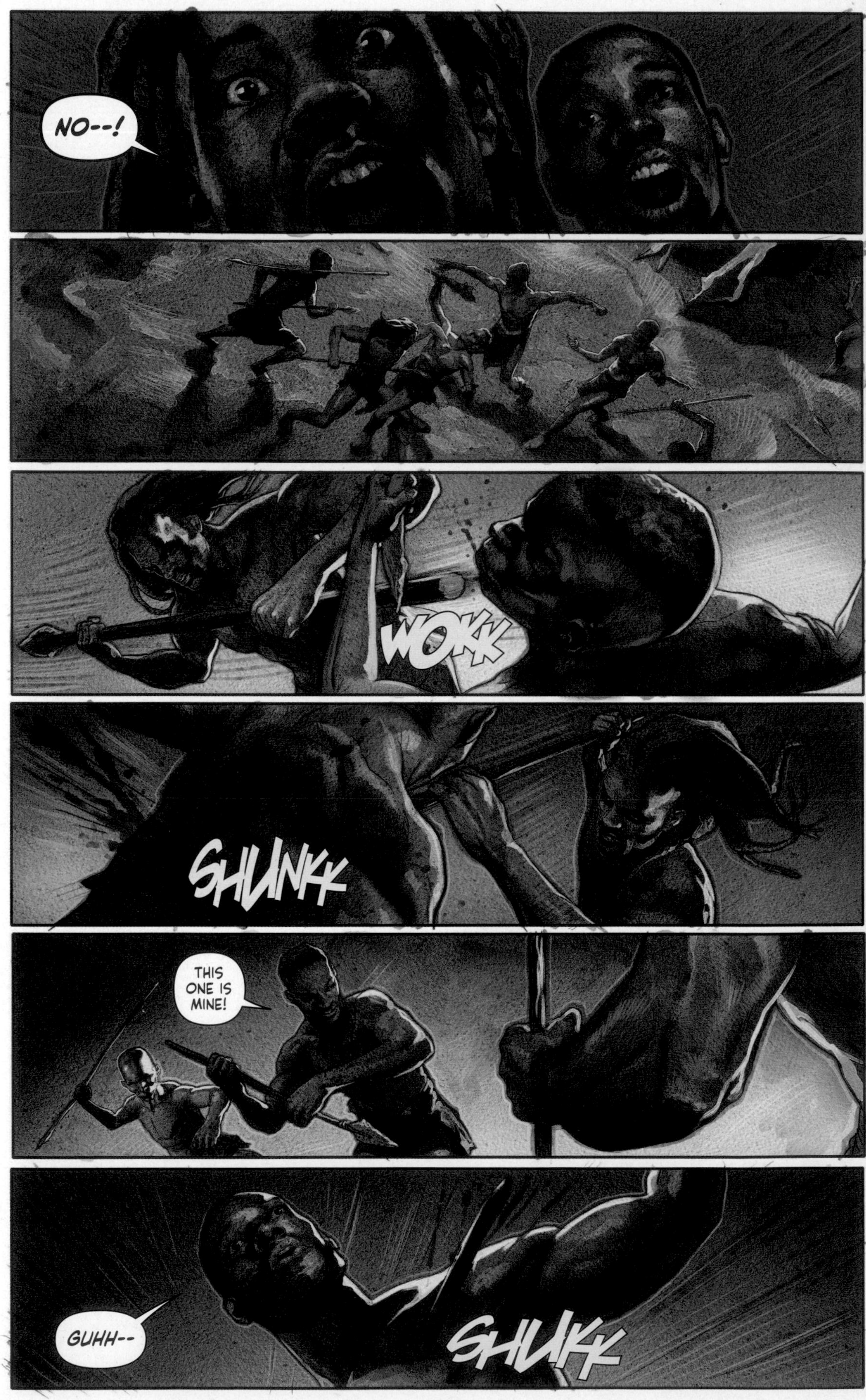
NO--!
WOKK
SHUNKK
THIS ONE IS MINE!
GUHH--
SHUKK

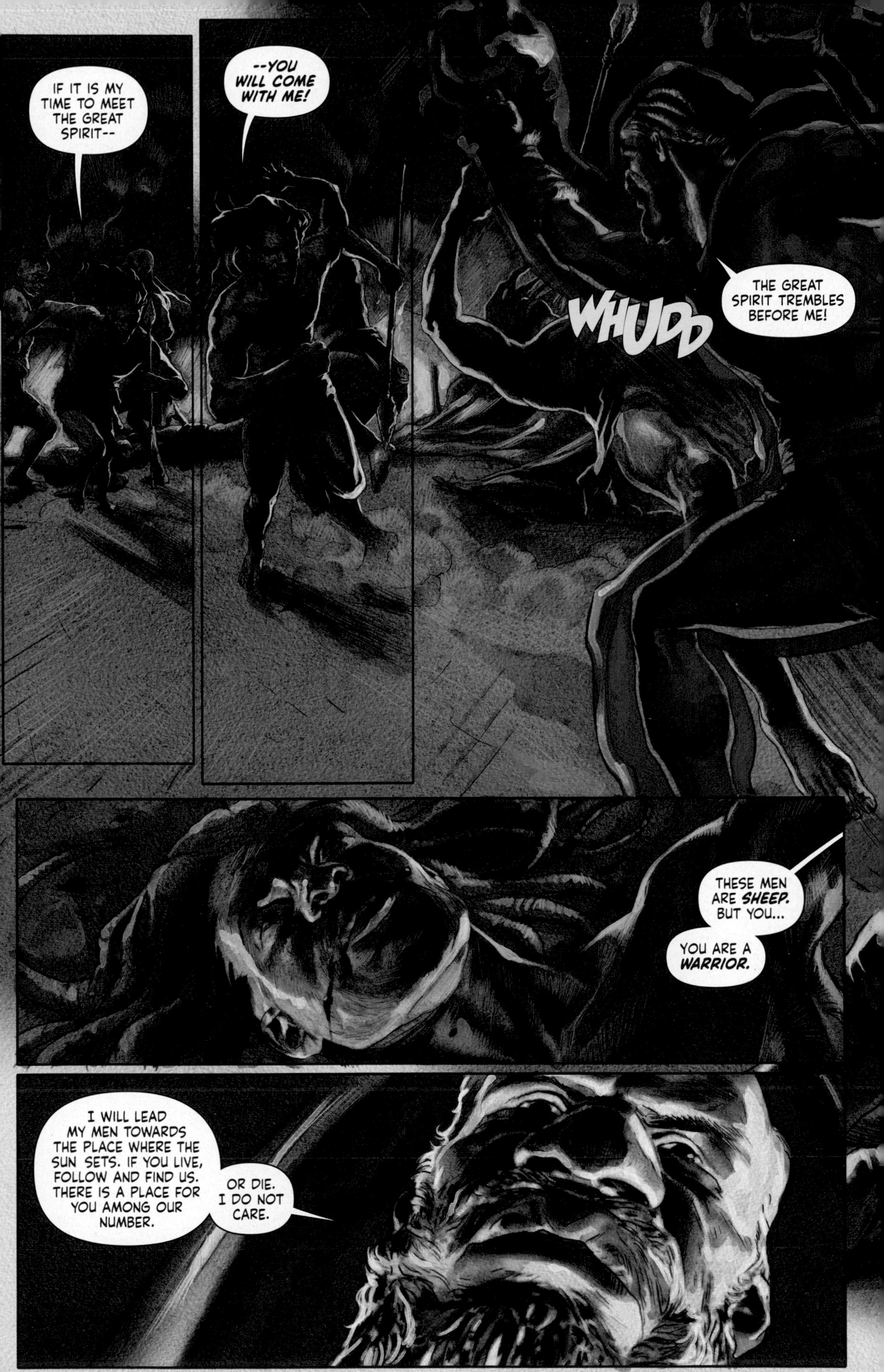
IF IT IS MY TIME TO MEET THE GREAT SPIRIT--
--YOU WILL COME WITH ME!
WHUDD
THE GREAT SPIRIT TREMBLES BEFORE ME!
THESE MEN ARE **SHEEP.** BUT YOU...
YOU ARE A **WARRIOR.**
I WILL LEAD MY MEN TOWARDS THE PLACE WHERE THE SUN SETS. IF YOU LIVE, FOLLOW AND FIND US. THERE IS A PLACE FOR YOU AMONG OUR NUMBER.
OR DIE. I DO NOT CARE.

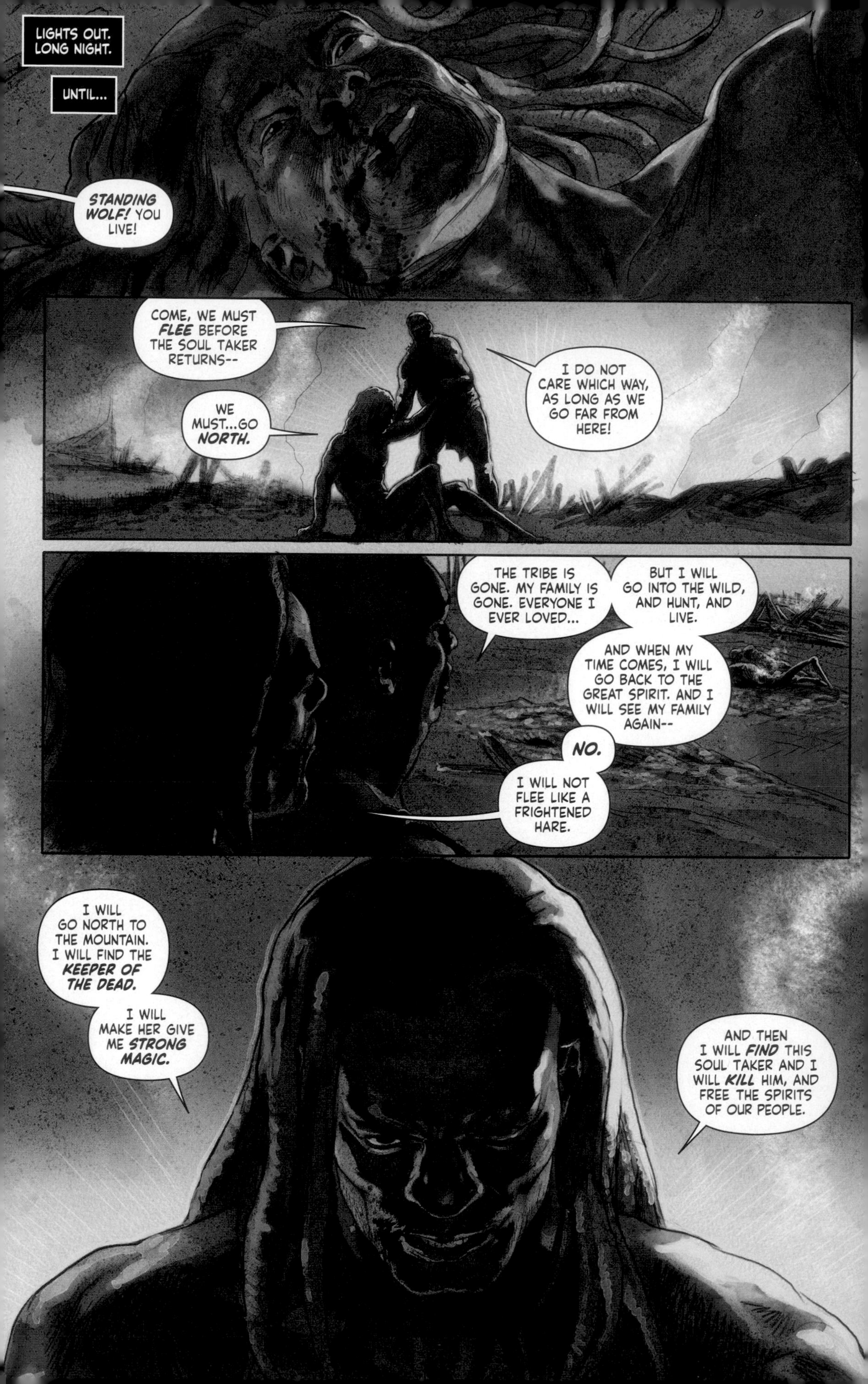
LIGHTS OUT. LONG NIGHT.
UNTIL...
STANDING WOLF! YOU LIVE!
COME, WE MUST FLEE BEFORE THE SOUL TAKER RETURNS--
WE MUST...GO NORTH.
I DO NOT CARE WHICH WAY, AS LONG AS WE GO FAR FROM HERE!
THE TRIBE IS GONE. MY FAMILY IS GONE. EVERYONE I EVER LOVED...
BUT I WILL GO INTO THE WILD, AND HUNT, AND LIVE.
AND WHEN MY TIME COMES, I WILL GO BACK TO THE GREAT SPIRIT. AND I WILL SEE MY FAMILY AGAIN--
NO.
I WILL NOT FLEE LIKE A FRIGHTENED HARE.
I WILL GO NORTH TO THE MOUNTAIN. I WILL FIND THE KEEPER OF THE DEAD.
I WILL MAKE HER GIVE ME STRONG MAGIC.
AND THEN I WILL FIND THIS SOUL TAKER AND I WILL KILL HIM, AND FREE THE SPIRITS OF OUR PEOPLE.

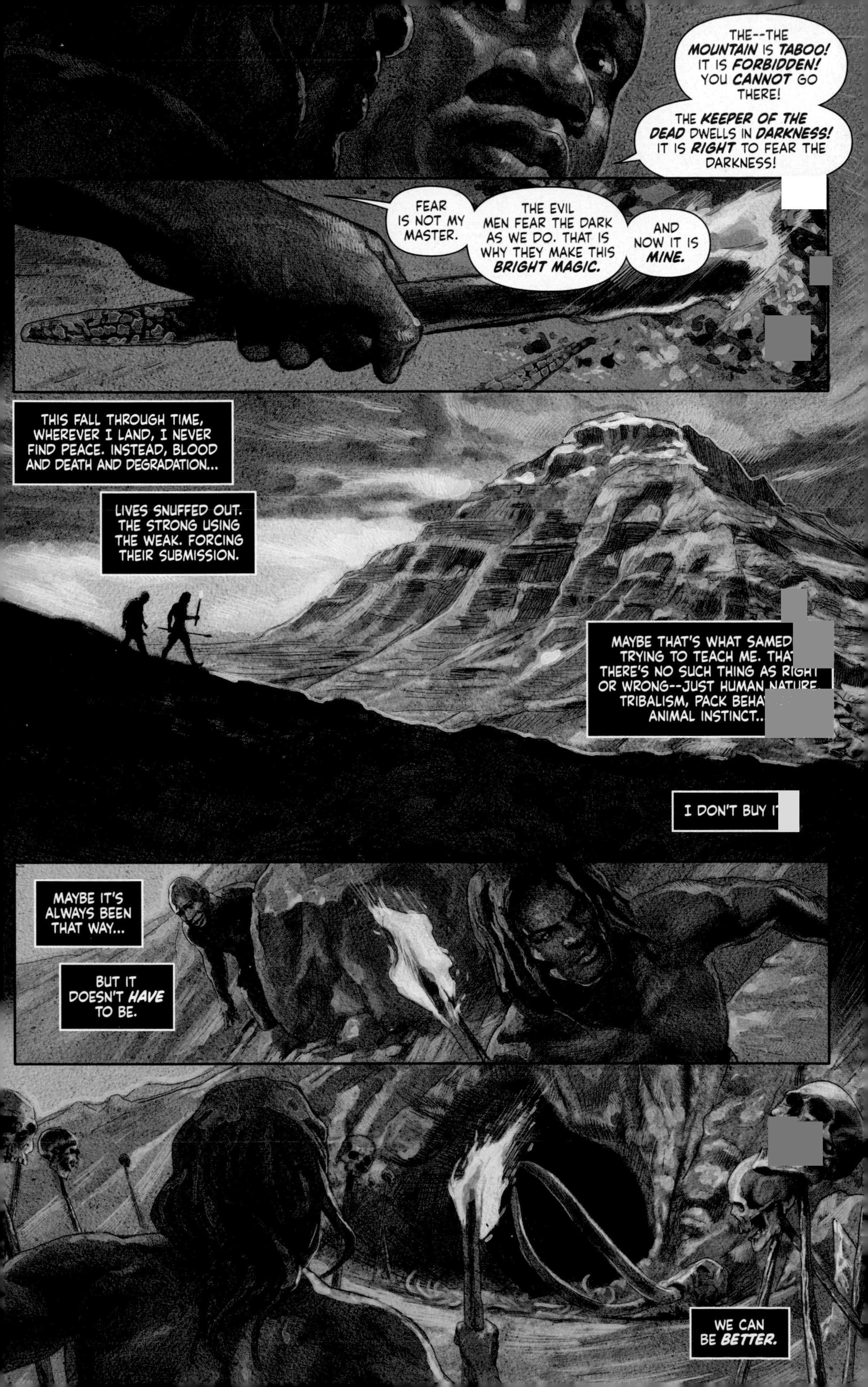
THE--THE MOUNTAIN IS TABOO! IT IS FORBIDDEN! YOU CANNOT GO THERE!
THE KEEPER OF THE DEAD DWELLS IN DARKNESS! IT IS RIGHT TO FEAR THE DARKNESS!
FEAR IS NOT MY MASTER.
THE EVIL MEN FEAR THE DARK AS WE DO. THAT IS WHY THEY MAKE THIS BRIGHT MAGIC.
AND NOW IT IS MINE.
THIS FALL THROUGH TIME, WHEREVER I LAND, I NEVER FIND PEACE. INSTEAD, BLOOD AND DEATH AND DEGRADATION...
LIVES SNUFFED OUT. THE STRONG USING THE WEAK. FORCING THEIR SUBMISSION.
MAYBE THAT'S WHAT SAMED
TRYING TO TEACH ME. THAT
THERE'S NO SUCH THING AS RIGHT
OR WRONG--JUST HUMAN NATURE
TRIBALISM, PACK BEHA
ANIMAL INSTINCT..
I DON'T BUY I
MAYBE IT'S ALWAYS BEEN THAT WAY...
BUT IT DOESN'T HAVE TO BE.
WE CAN BE BETTER.

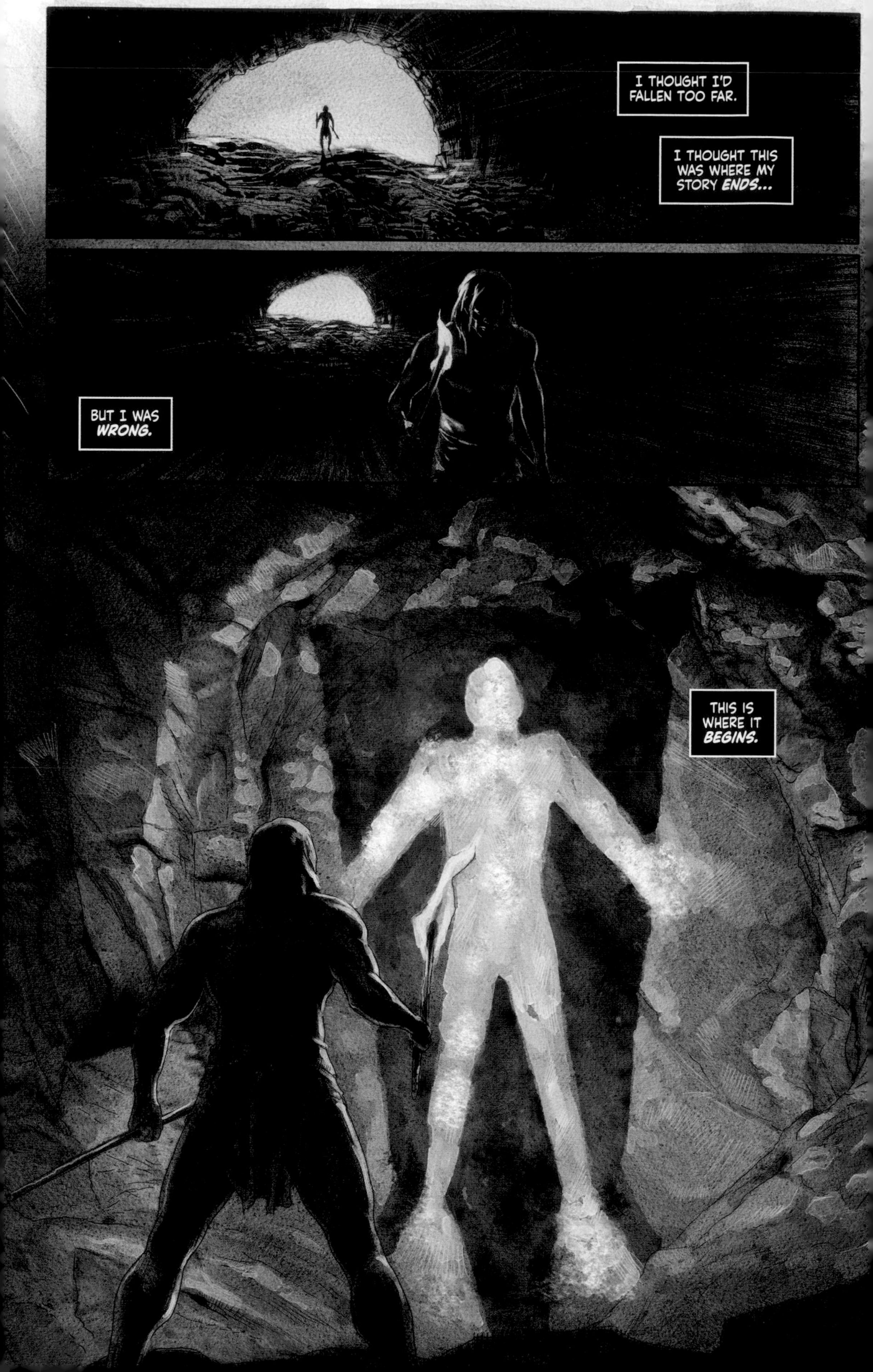
I THOUGHT I'D FALLEN TOO FAR.
I THOUGHT THIS WAS WHERE MY STORY *ENDS...*
BUT I WAS *WRONG.*
THIS IS WHERE IT *BEGINS.*

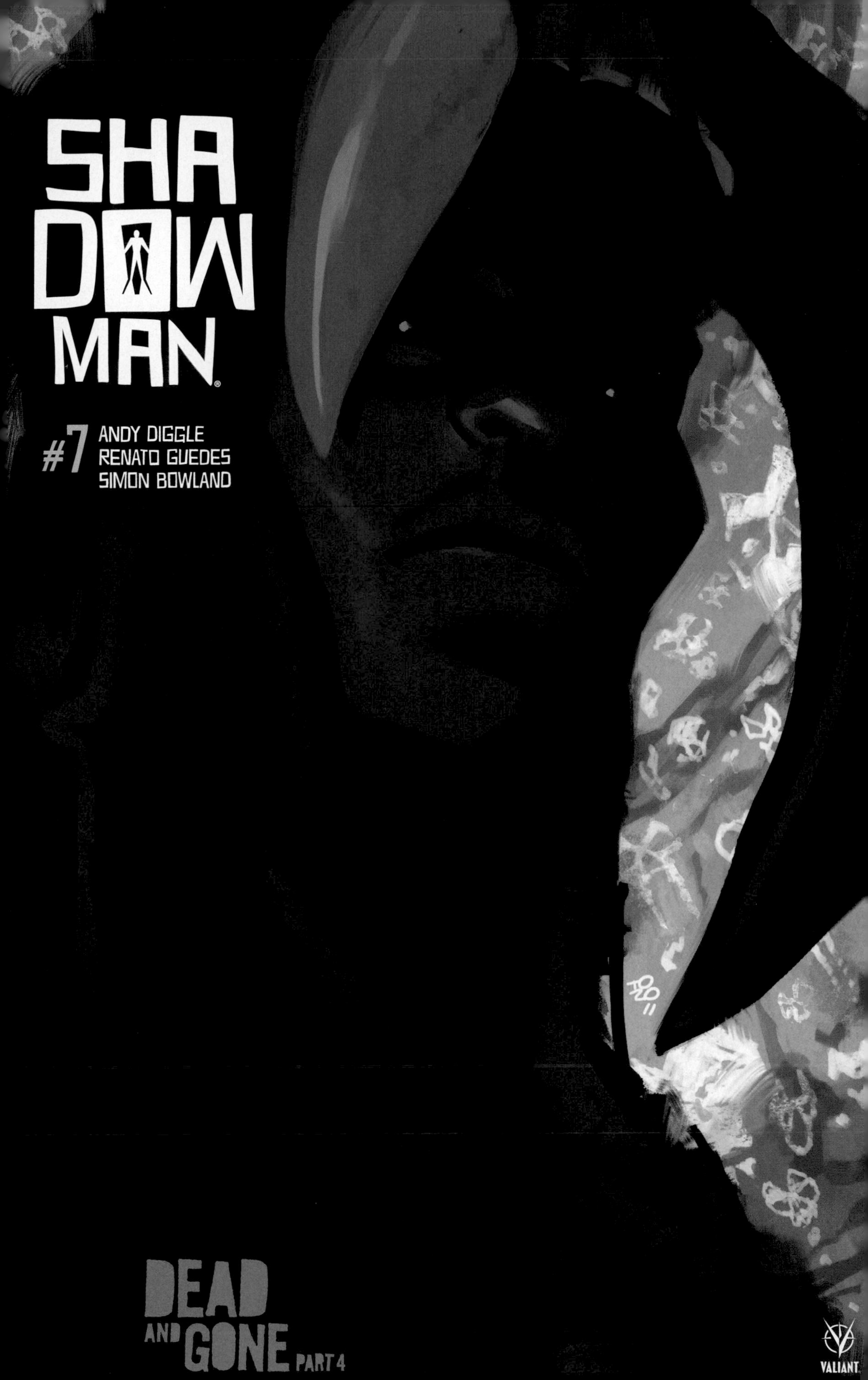

SHADOWMAN®
#7
ANDY DIGGLE
RENATO GUEDES
SIMON BOWLAND
DEAD AND GONE PART 4
VALIANT

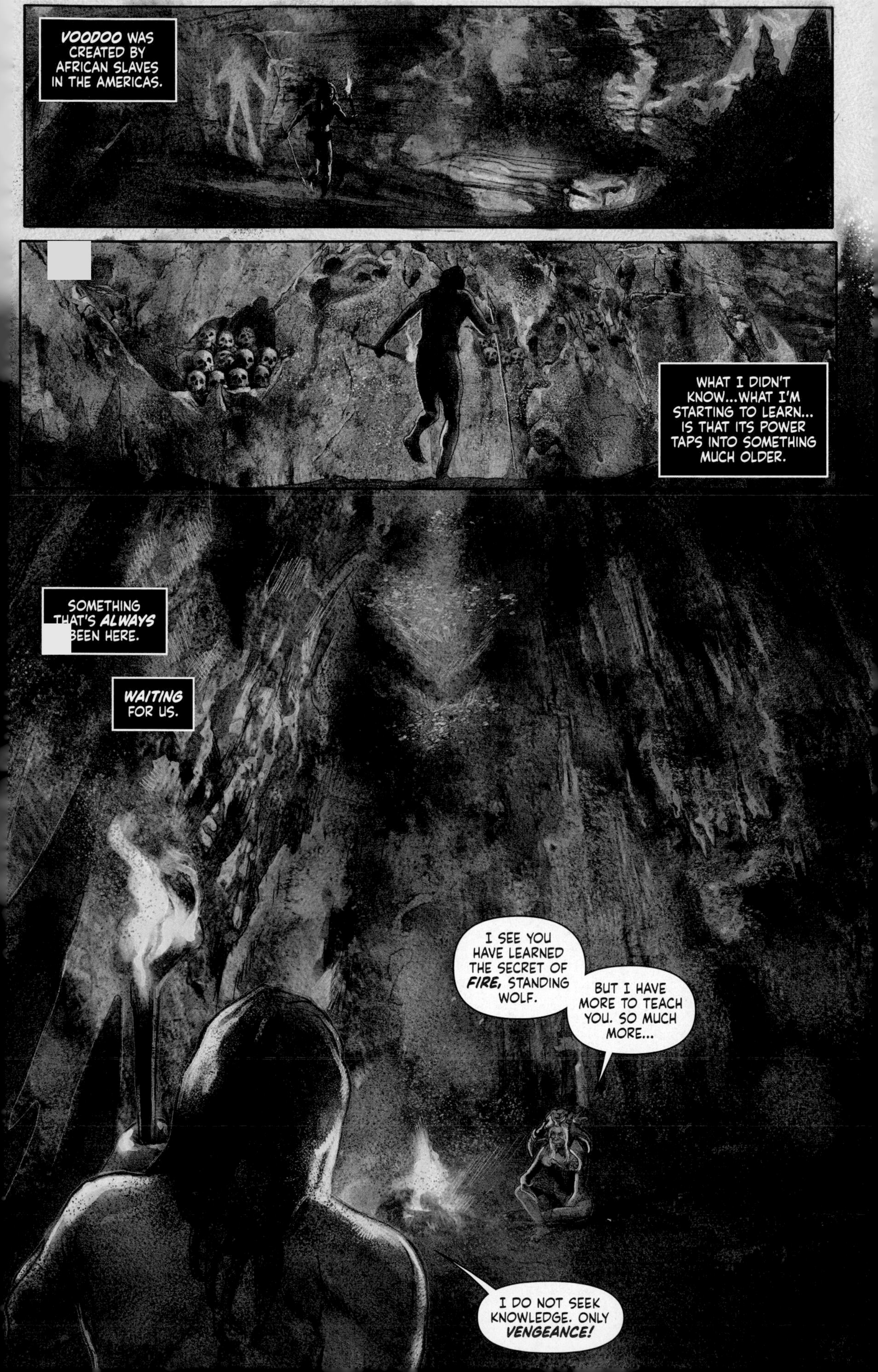
VOODOO WAS CREATED BY AFRICAN SLAVES IN THE AMERICAS.
WHAT I DIDN'T KNOW...WHAT I'M STARTING TO LEARN... IS THAT ITS POWER TAPS INTO SOMETHING MUCH OLDER.
SOMETHING THAT'S ALWAYS BEEN HERE.
WAITING FOR US.
I SEE YOU HAVE LEARNED THE SECRET OF FIRE, STANDING WOLF.
BUT I HAVE MORE TO TEACH YOU. SO MUCH MORE...
I DO NOT SEEK KNOWLEDGE. ONLY VENGEANCE!

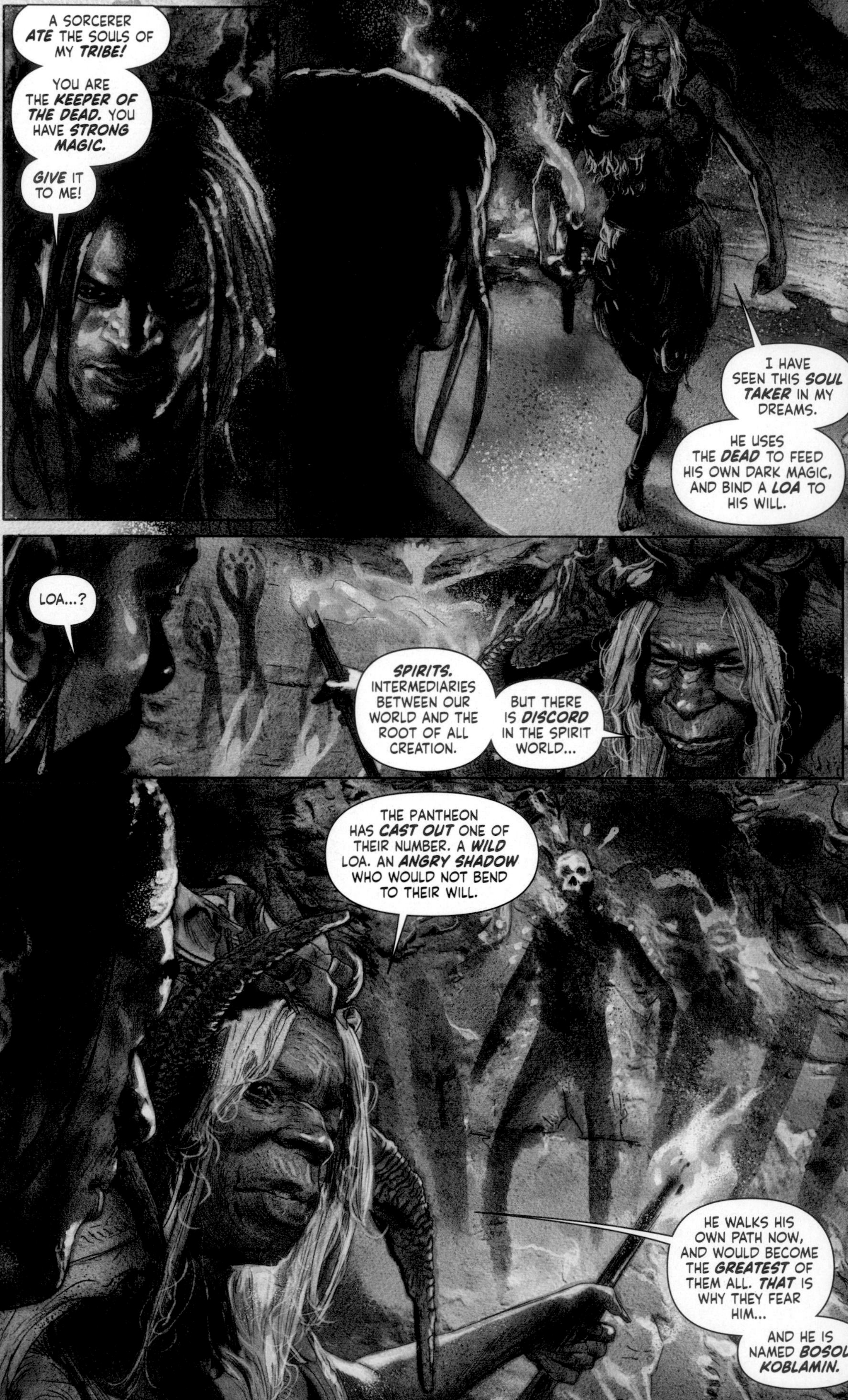
A SORCERER ATE THE SOULS OF MY TRIBE!
YOU ARE THE KEEPER OF THE DEAD. YOU HAVE STRONG MAGIC.
GIVE IT TO ME!
I HAVE SEEN THIS SOUL TAKER IN MY DREAMS.
HE USES THE DEAD TO FEED HIS OWN DARK MAGIC, AND BIND A LOA TO HIS WILL.
LOA...?
SPIRITS. INTERMEDIARIES BETWEEN OUR WORLD AND THE ROOT OF ALL CREATION.
BUT THERE IS DISCORD IN THE SPIRIT WORLD...
THE PANTHEON HAS CAST OUT ONE OF THEIR NUMBER. A WILD LOA. AN ANGRY SHADOW WHO WOULD NOT BEND TO THEIR WILL.
HE WALKS HIS OWN PATH NOW, AND WOULD BECOME THE GREATEST OF THEM ALL. THAT IS WHY THEY FEAR HIM...
AND HE IS NAMED BOSOU KOBLAMIN.

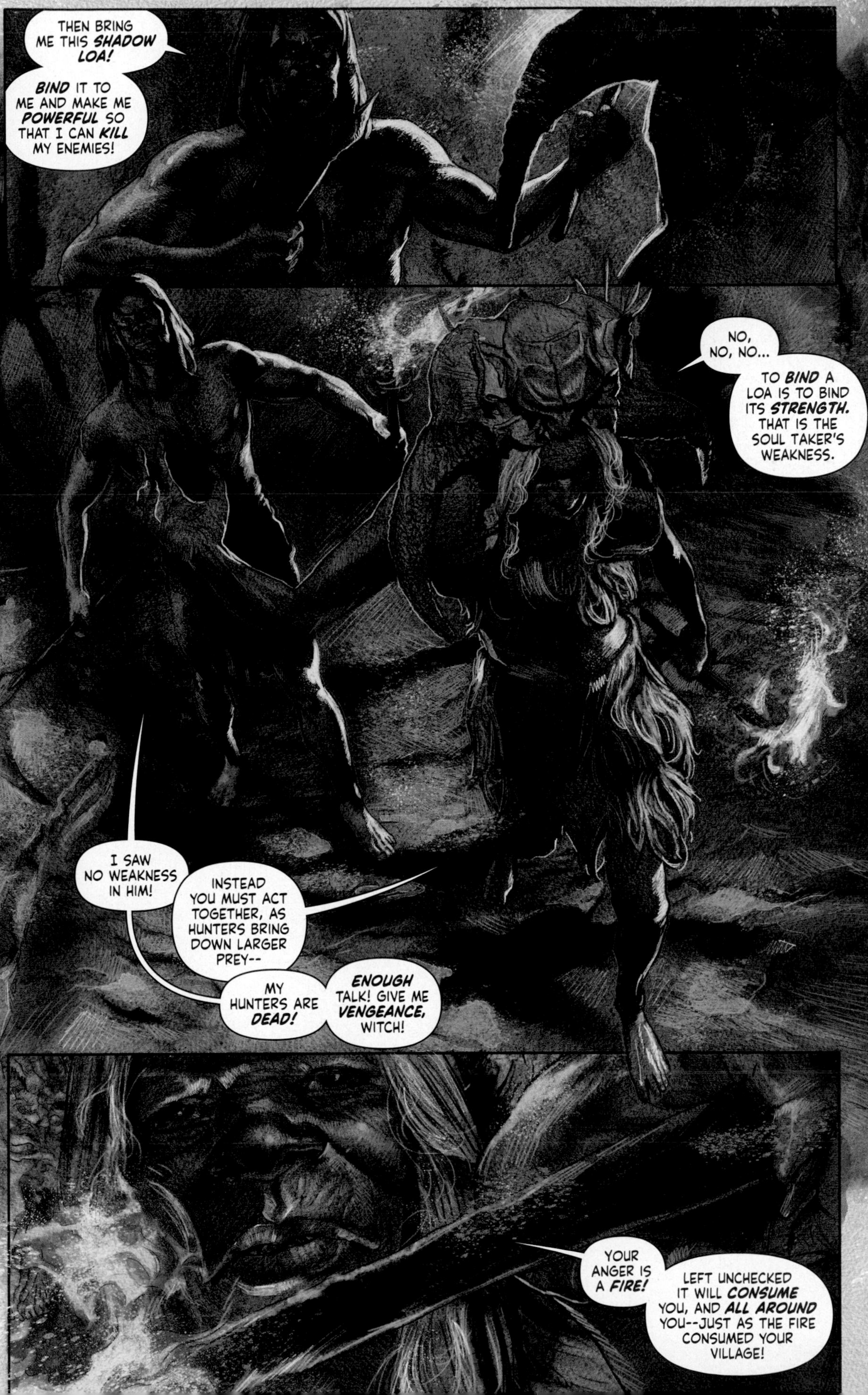
THEN BRING ME THIS SHADOW LOA!
BIND IT TO ME AND MAKE ME POWERFUL SO THAT I CAN KILL MY ENEMIES!
NO, NO, NO...
TO BIND A LOA IS TO BIND ITS STRENGTH. THAT IS THE SOUL TAKER'S WEAKNESS.
I SAW NO WEAKNESS IN HIM!
INSTEAD YOU MUST ACT TOGETHER, AS HUNTERS BRING DOWN LARGER PREY--
MY HUNTERS ARE DEAD!
ENOUGH TALK! GIVE ME VENGEANCE, WITCH!
YOUR ANGER IS A FIRE!
LEFT UNCHECKED IT WILL CONSUME YOU, AND ALL AROUND YOU--JUST AS THE FIRE CONSUMED YOUR VILLAGE!

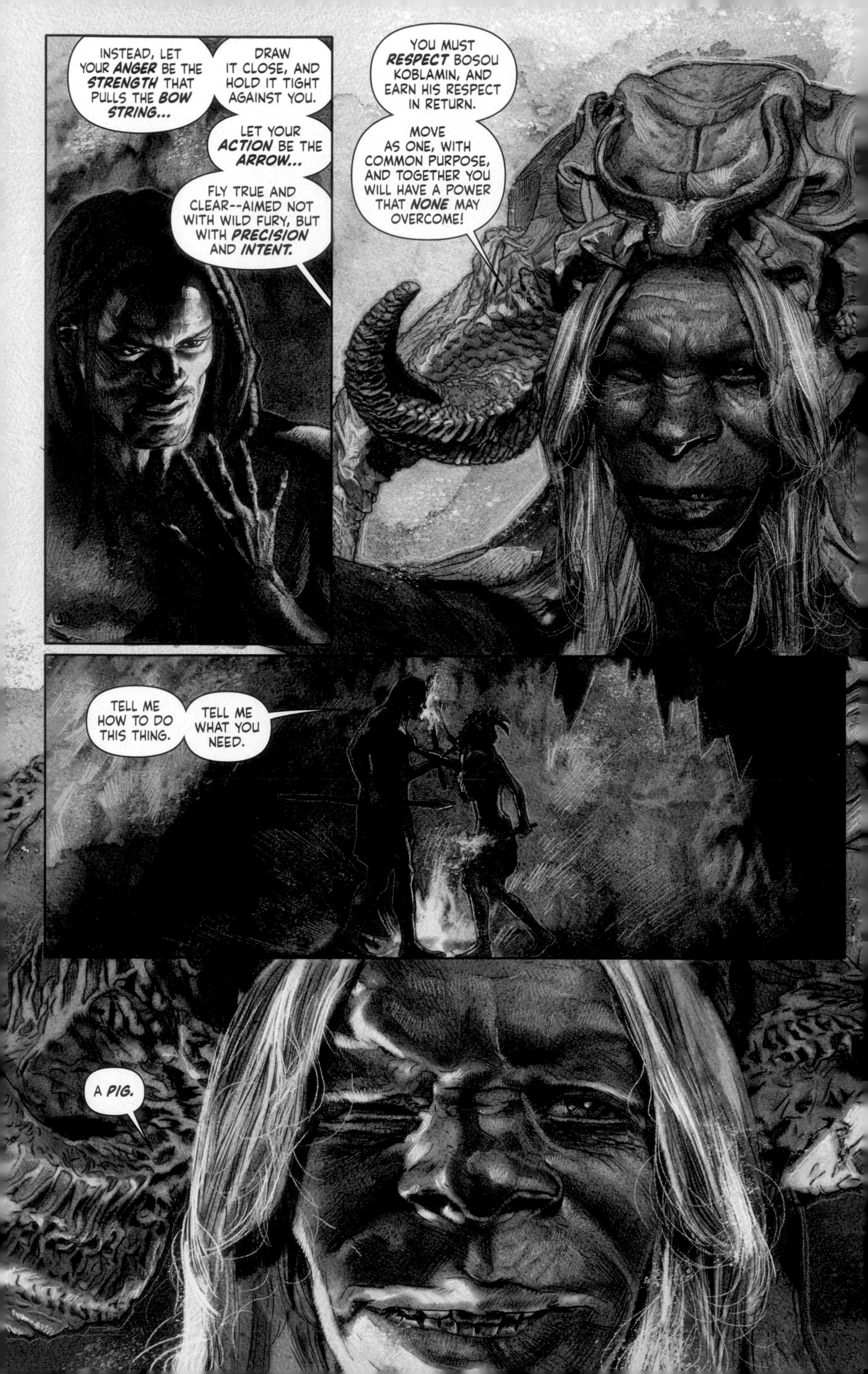

INSTEAD, LET YOUR ANGER BE THE STRENGTH THAT PULLS THE BOW STRING...
DRAW IT CLOSE, AND HOLD IT TIGHT AGAINST YOU.
LET YOUR ACTION BE THE ARROW...
FLY TRUE AND CLEAR--AIMED NOT WITH WILD FURY, BUT WITH PRECISION AND INTENT.
YOU MUST RESPECT BOSOU KOBLAMIN, AND EARN HIS RESPECT IN RETURN.
MOVE AS ONE, WITH COMMON PURPOSE, AND TOGETHER YOU WILL HAVE A POWER THAT NONE MAY OVERCOME!
TELL ME HOW TO DO THIS THING.
TELL ME WHAT YOU NEED.
A PIG.

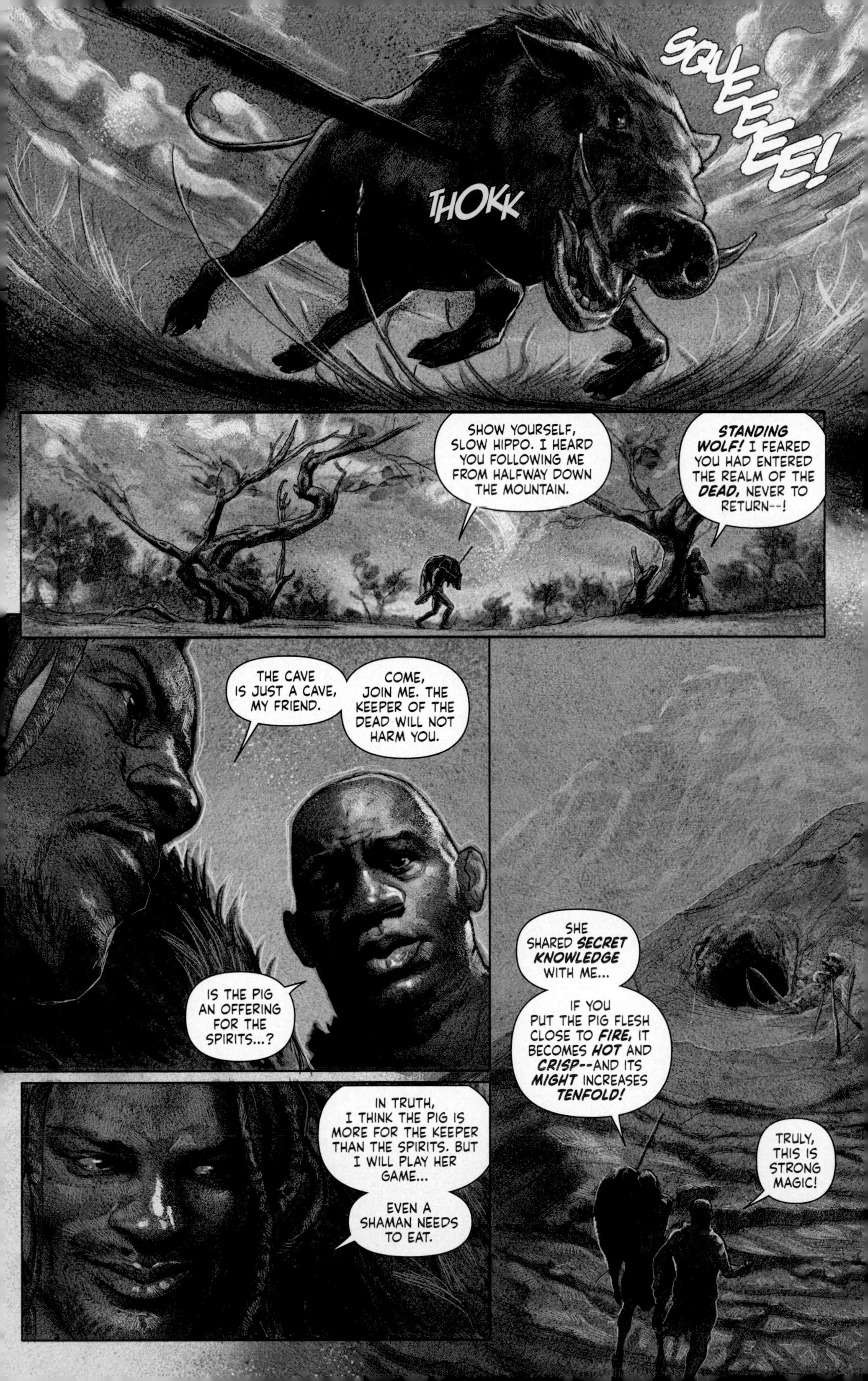
THOKK
SQUEEEEEE!
SHOW YOURSELF, SLOW HIPPO. I HEARD YOU FOLLOWING ME FROM HALFWAY DOWN THE MOUNTAIN.
STANDING WOLF! I FEARED YOU HAD ENTERED THE REALM OF THE DEAD, NEVER TO RETURN--!
THE CAVE IS JUST A CAVE, MY FRIEND.
COME, JOIN ME. THE KEEPER OF THE DEAD WILL NOT HARM YOU.
IS THE PIG AN OFFERING FOR THE SPIRITS...?
IN TRUTH, I THINK THE PIG IS MORE FOR THE KEEPER THAN THE SPIRITS. BUT I WILL PLAY HER GAME...
EVEN A SHAMAN NEEDS TO EAT.
SHE SHARED SECRET KNOWLEDGE WITH ME...
IF YOU PUT THE PIG FLESH CLOSE TO FIRE, IT BECOMES HOT AND CRISP--AND ITS MIGHT INCREASES TENFOLD!
TRULY, THIS IS STRONG MAGIC!

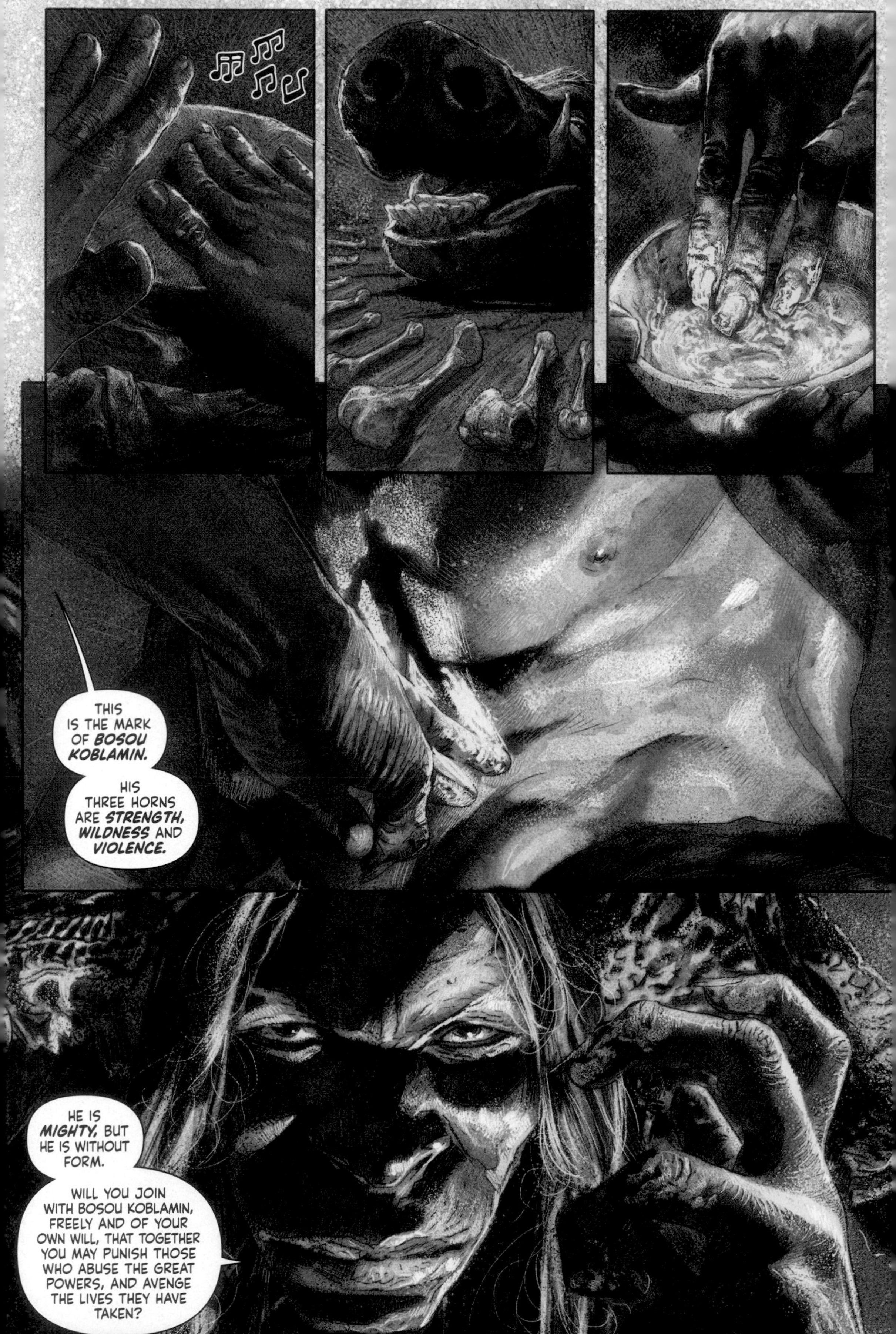
THIS IS THE MARK OF BOSOU KOBLAMIN.
HIS THREE HORNS ARE STRENGTH, WILDNESS AND VIOLENCE.
HE IS MIGHTY, BUT HE IS WITHOUT FORM.
WILL YOU JOIN WITH BOSOU KOBLAMIN, FREELY AND OF YOUR OWN WILL, THAT TOGETHER YOU MAY PUNISH THOSE WHO ABUSE THE GREAT POWERS, AND AVENGE THE LIVES THEY HAVE TAKEN?

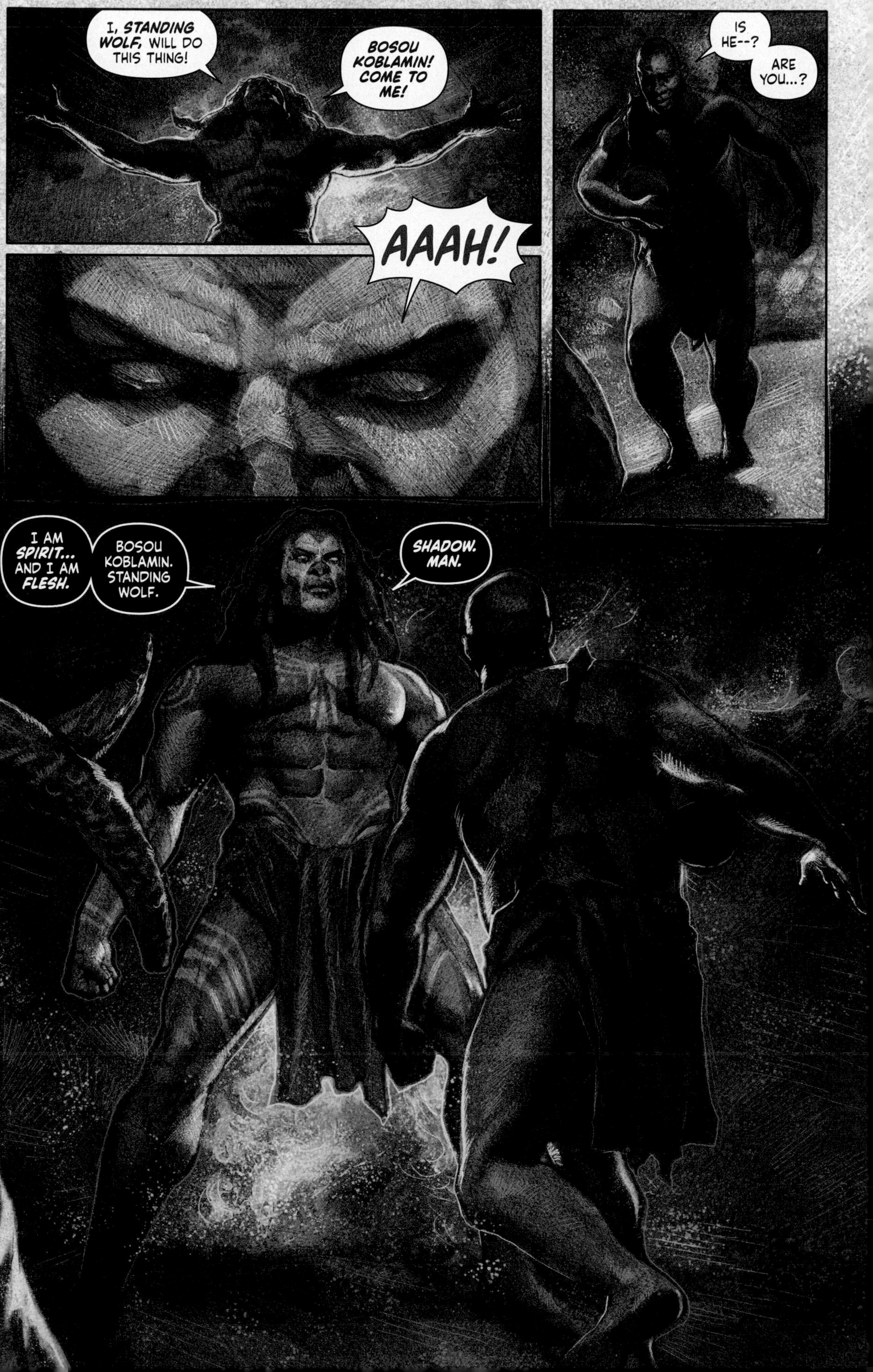
I, STANDING WOLF, WILL DO THIS THING!
BOSOU KOBLAMIN! COME TO ME!
IS HE--?
ARE YOU...?
AAAH!
I AM SPIRIT... AND I AM FLESH.
BOSOU KOBLAMIN. STANDING WOLF.
SHADOW. MAN.

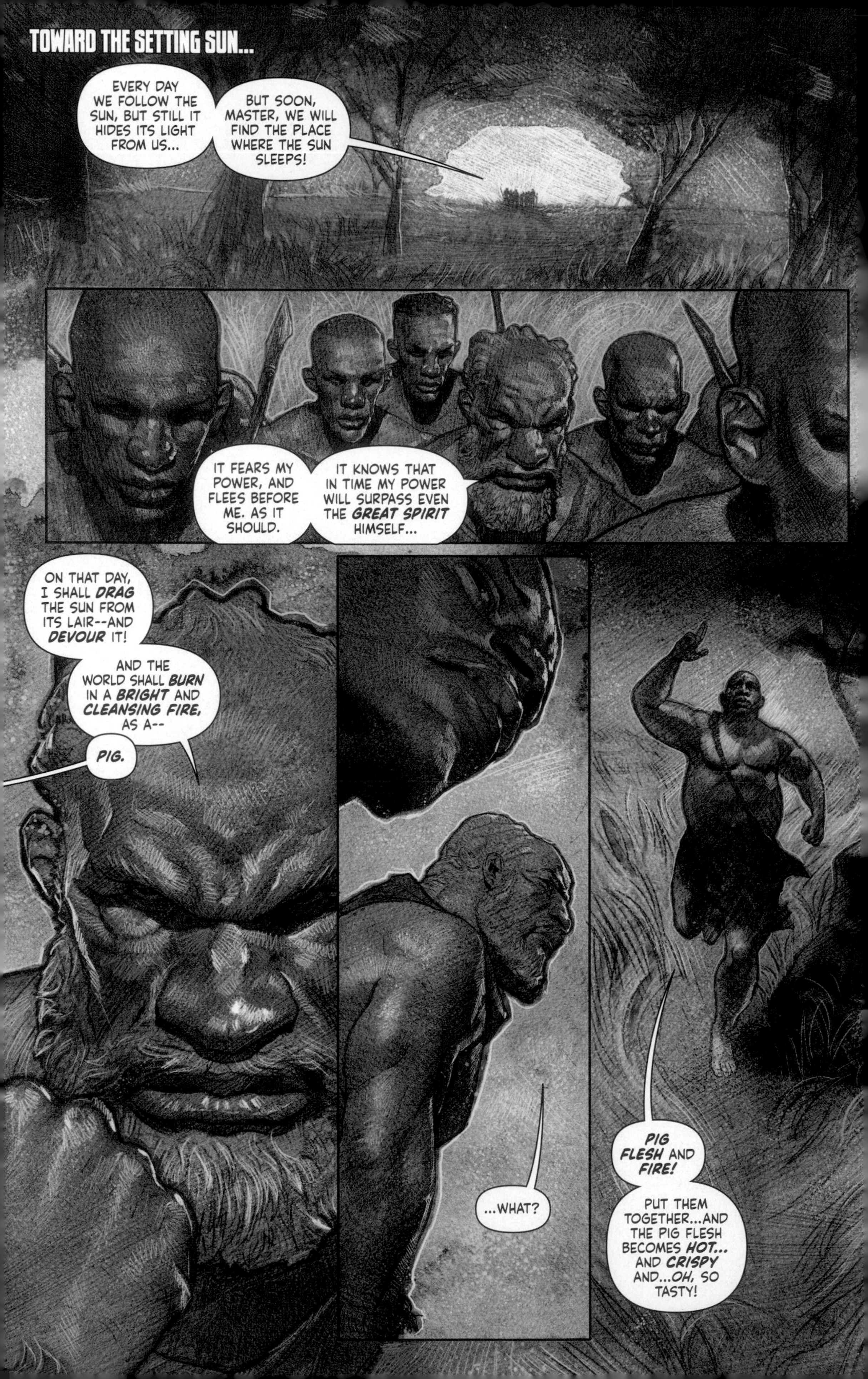
TOWARD THE SETTING SUN...
EVERY DAY WE FOLLOW THE SUN, BUT STILL IT HIDES ITS LIGHT FROM US...
BUT SOON, MASTER, WE WILL FIND THE PLACE WHERE THE SUN SLEEPS!
IT FEARS MY POWER, AND FLEES BEFORE ME. AS IT SHOULD.
IT KNOWS THAT IN TIME MY POWER WILL SURPASS EVEN THE GREAT SPIRIT HIMSELF...
ON THAT DAY, I SHALL DRAG THE SUN FROM ITS LAIR--AND DEVOUR IT!
AND THE WORLD SHALL BURN IN A BRIGHT AND CLEANSING FIRE, AS A--
PIG.
...WHAT?
PIG FLESH AND FIRE!
PUT THEM TOGETHER...AND THE PIG FLESH BECOMES HOT... AND CRISPY AND...OH, SO TASTY!

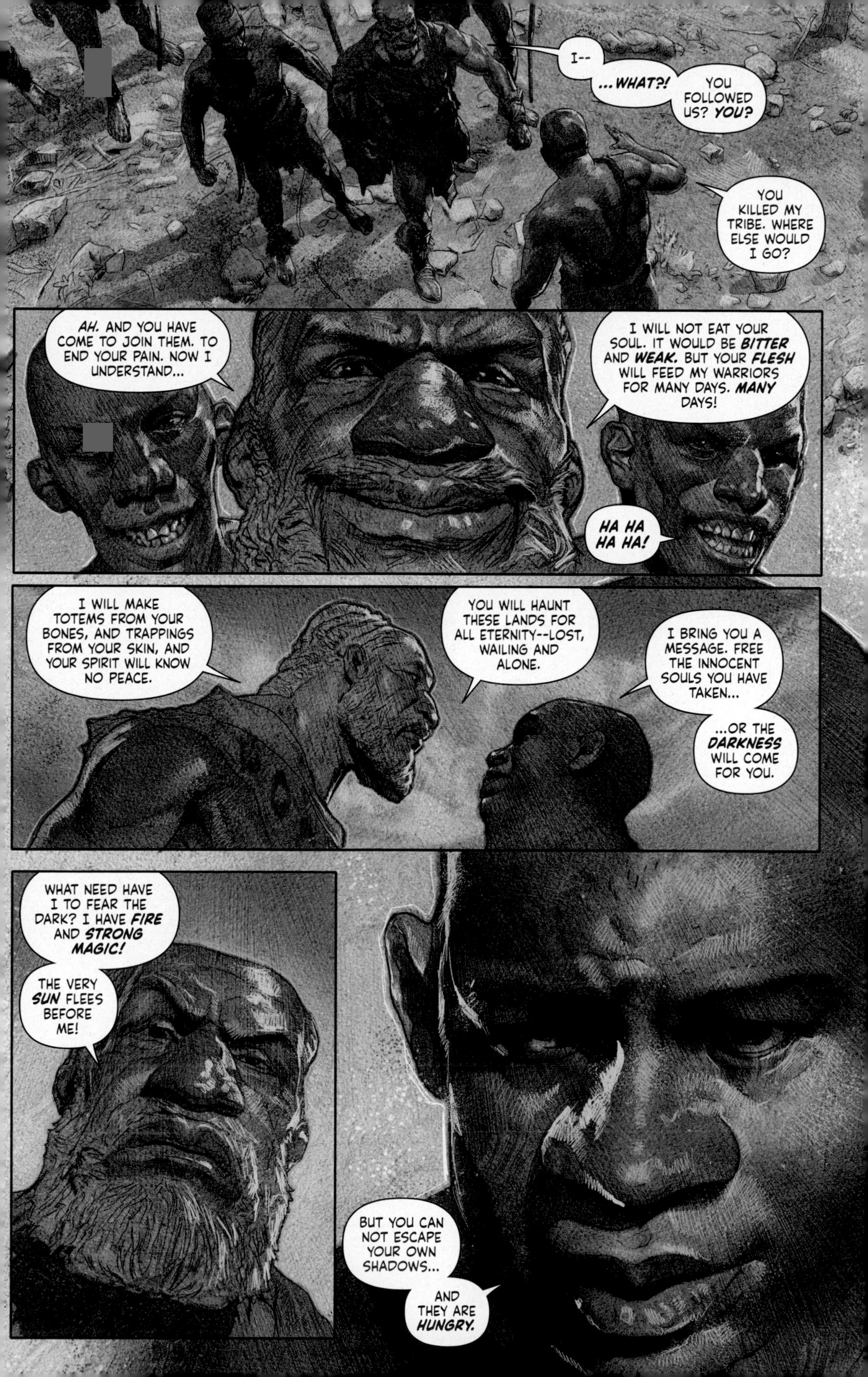
I--
...WHAT?!
YOU FOLLOWED US? YOU?
YOU KILLED MY TRIBE. WHERE ELSE WOULD I GO?
AH. AND YOU HAVE COME TO JOIN THEM. TO END YOUR PAIN. NOW I UNDERSTAND...
I WILL NOT EAT YOUR SOUL. IT WOULD BE BITTER AND WEAK. BUT YOUR FLESH WILL FEED MY WARRIORS FOR MANY DAYS. MANY DAYS!
HA HA HA HA!
I WILL MAKE TOTEMS FROM YOUR BONES, AND TRAPPINGS FROM YOUR SKIN, AND YOUR SPIRIT WILL KNOW NO PEACE.
YOU WILL HAUNT THESE LANDS FOR ALL ETERNITY--LOST, WAILING AND ALONE.
I BRING YOU A MESSAGE. FREE THE INNOCENT SOULS YOU HAVE TAKEN...
...OR THE DARKNESS WILL COME FOR YOU.
WHAT NEED HAVE I TO FEAR THE DARK? I HAVE FIRE AND STRONG MAGIC!
THE VERY SUN FLEES BEFORE ME!
BUT YOU CAN NOT ESCAPE YOUR OWN SHADOWS...
AND THEY ARE HUNGRY.

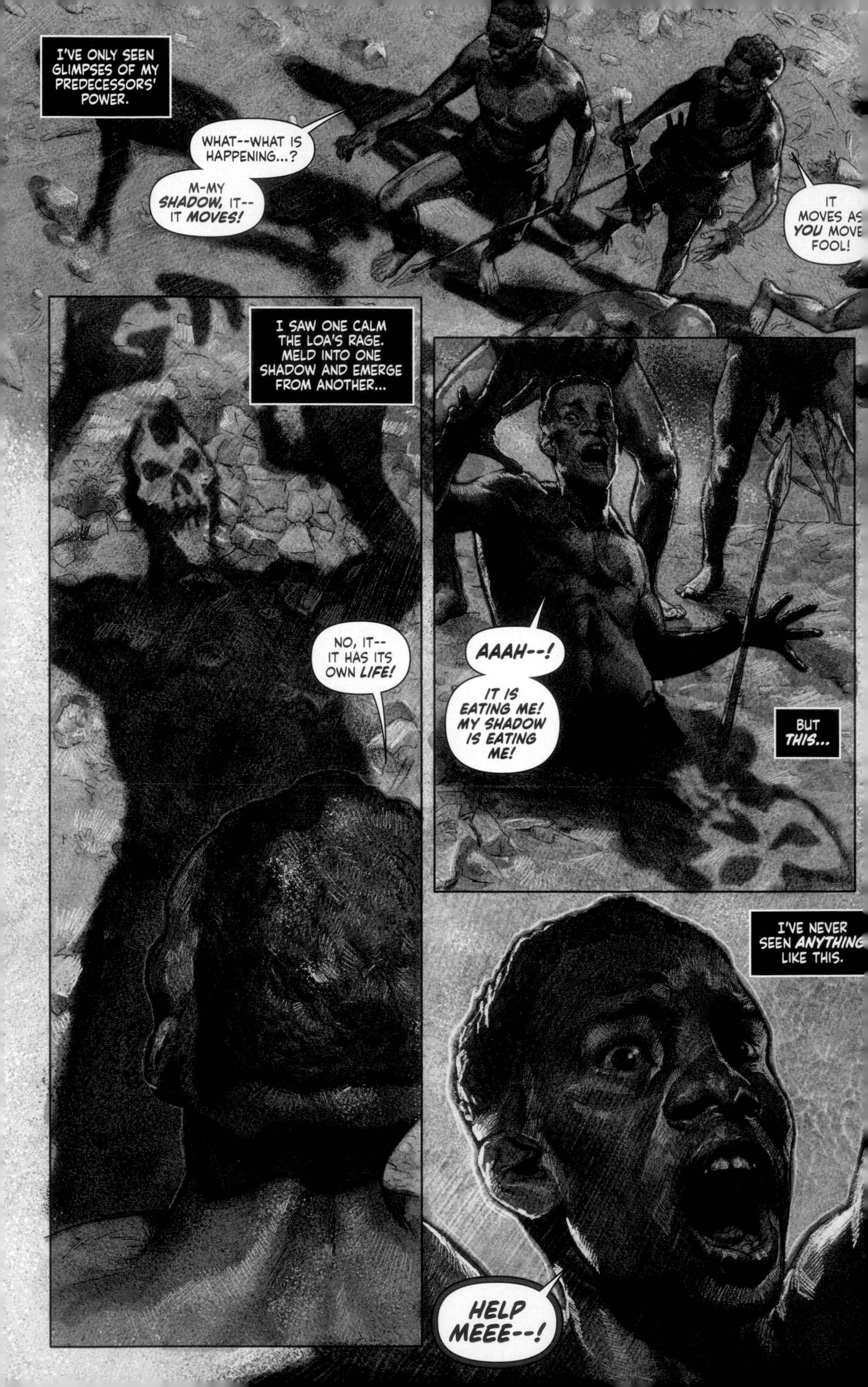
I'VE ONLY SEEN GLIMPSES OF MY PREDECESSORS' POWER.
WHAT--WHAT IS HAPPENING...?
M-MY SHADOW, IT-- IT MOVES!
IT MOVES AS YOU MOVE FOOL!
I SAW ONE CALM THE LOA'S RAGE. MELD INTO ONE SHADOW AND EMERGE FROM ANOTHER...
NO, IT-- IT HAS ITS OWN LIFE!
AAAH--!
IT IS EATING ME! MY SHADOW IS EATING ME!
BUT THIS...
I'VE NEVER SEEN ANYTHING LIKE THIS.
HELP MEEE--!

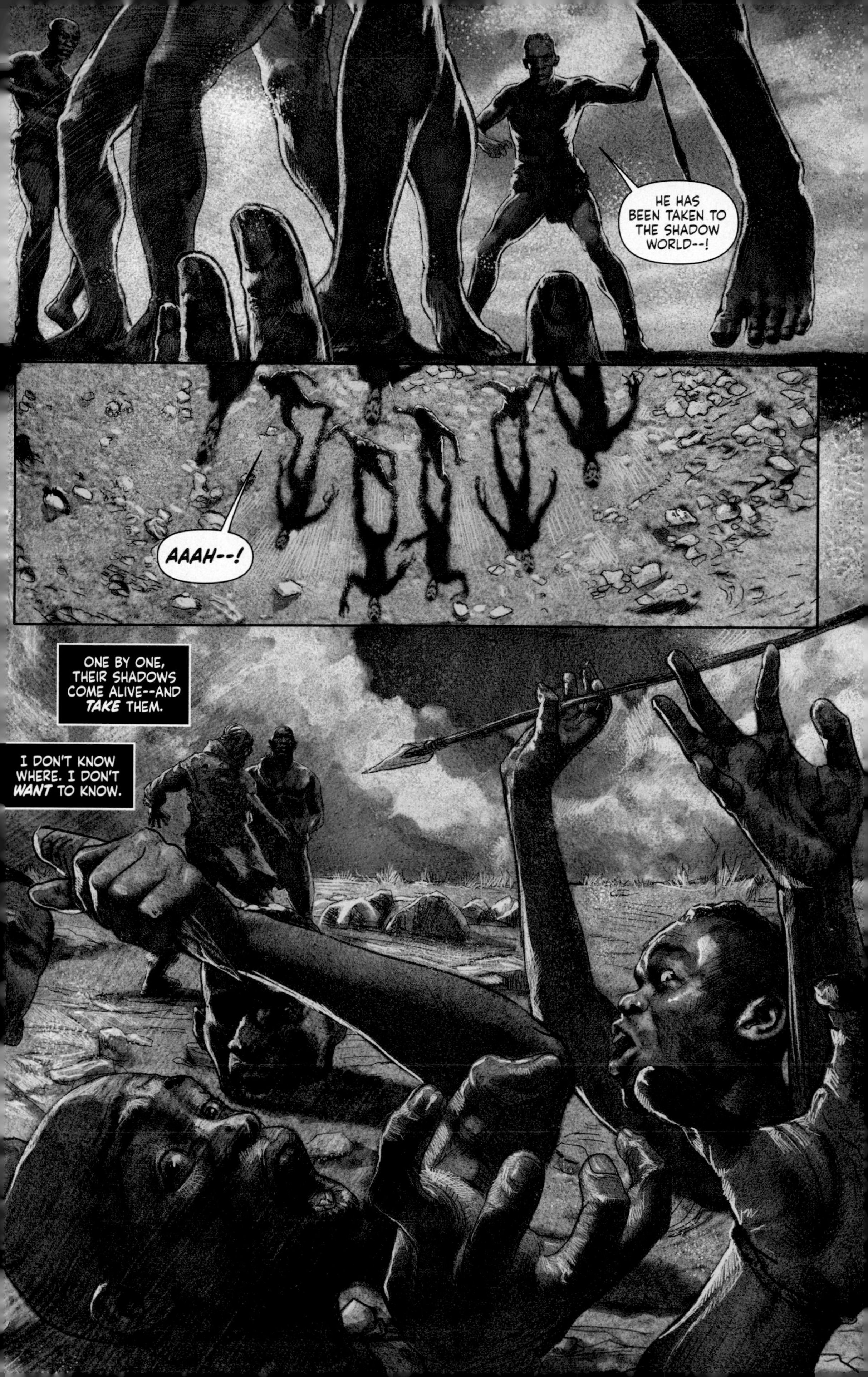
HE HAS BEEN TAKEN TO THE SHADOW WORLD--!
AAAH--!
ONE BY ONE, THEIR SHADOWS COME ALIVE--AND *TAKE* THEM.
I DON'T KNOW WHERE. I DON'T *WANT* TO KNOW.

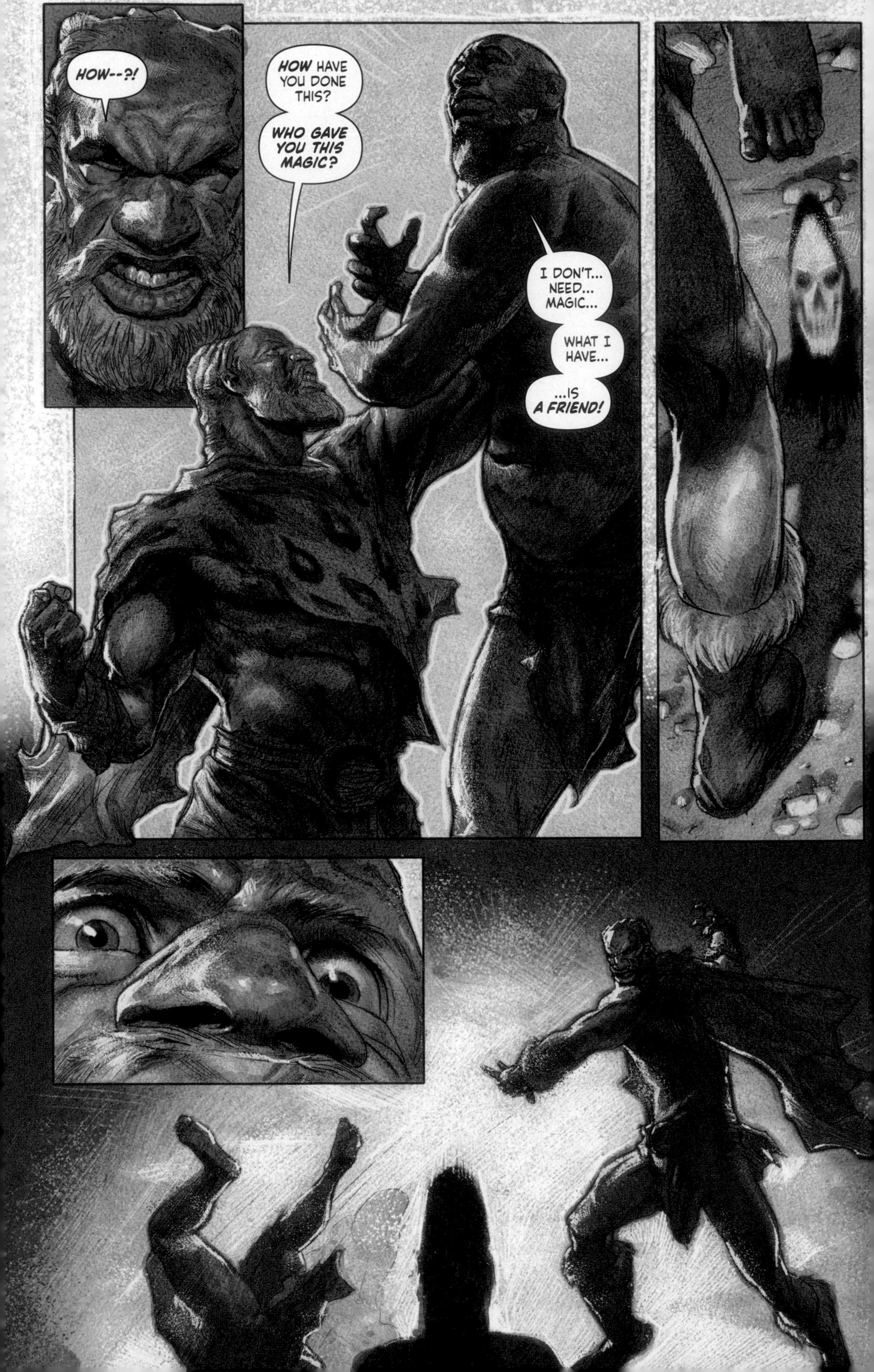
HOW--?!
HOW HAVE YOU DONE THIS?
WHO GAVE YOU THIS MAGIC?
I DON'T... NEED... MAGIC...
WHAT I HAVE...
...IS A FRIEND!

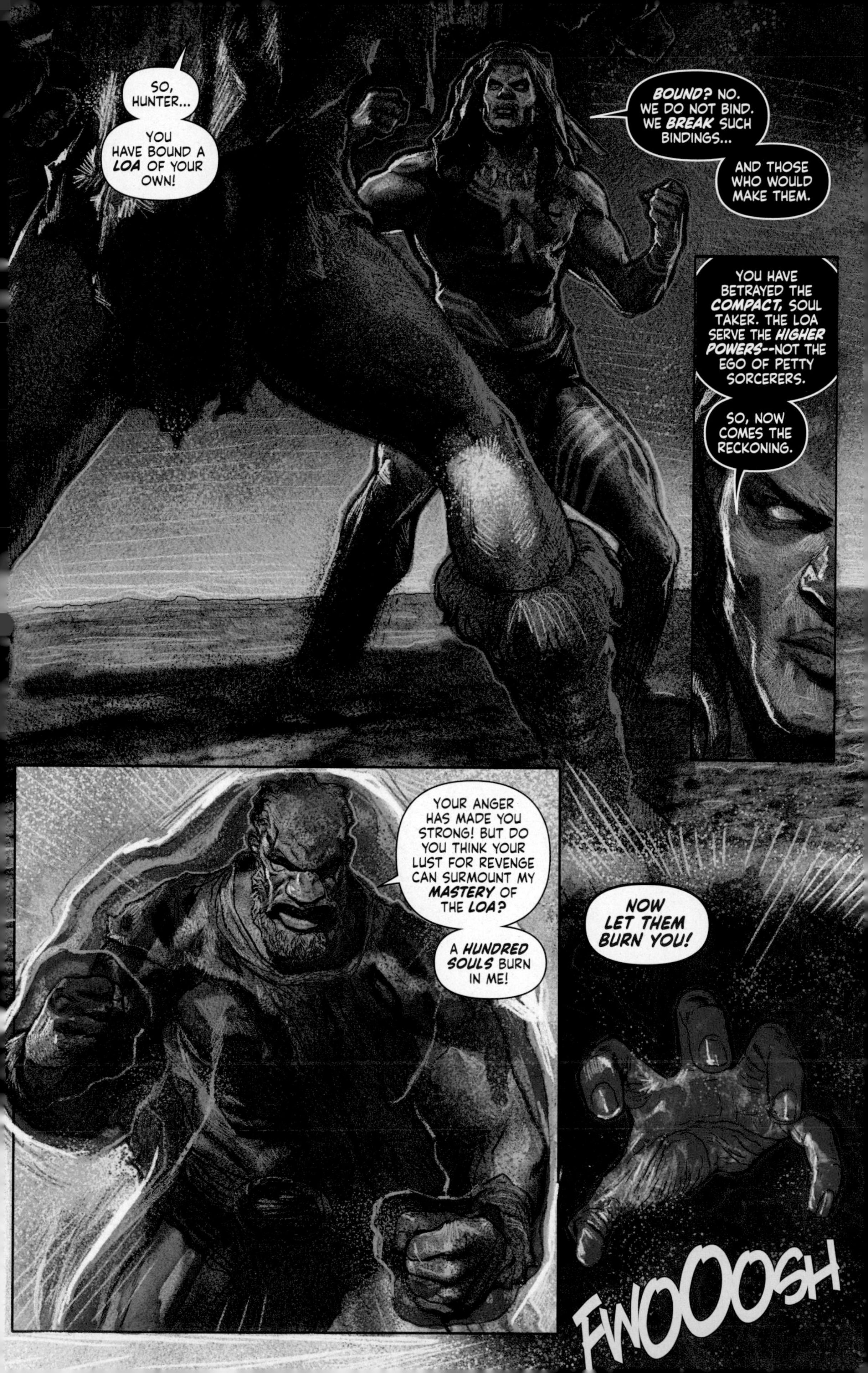
SO, HUNTER...
YOU HAVE BOUND A LOA OF YOUR OWN!
BOUND? NO. WE DO NOT BIND. WE BREAK SUCH BINDINGS...
AND THOSE WHO WOULD MAKE THEM.
YOU HAVE BETRAYED THE COMPACT, SOUL TAKER. THE LOA SERVE THE HIGHER POWERS--NOT THE EGO OF PETTY SORCERERS.
SO, NOW COMES THE RECKONING.
YOUR ANGER HAS MADE YOU STRONG! BUT DO YOU THINK YOUR LUST FOR REVENGE CAN SURMOUNT MY MASTERY OF THE LOA?
A HUNDRED SOULS BURN IN ME!
NOW LET THEM BURN YOU!
FWOOOSH

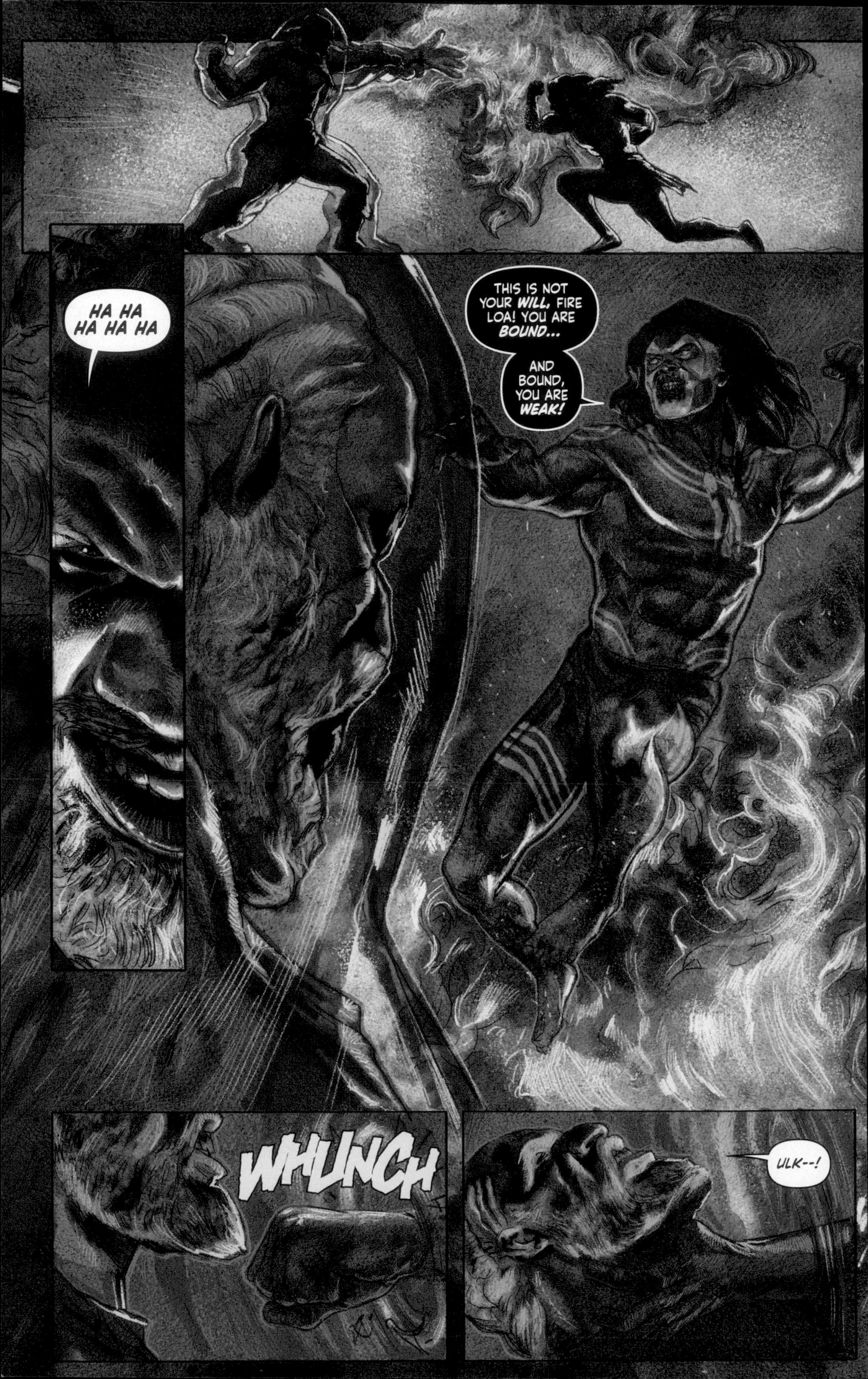
HA HA HA HA HA
THIS IS NOT YOUR WILL, FIRE LOA! YOU ARE BOUND...
AND BOUND, YOU ARE WEAK!
WHUNCH
ULK--!

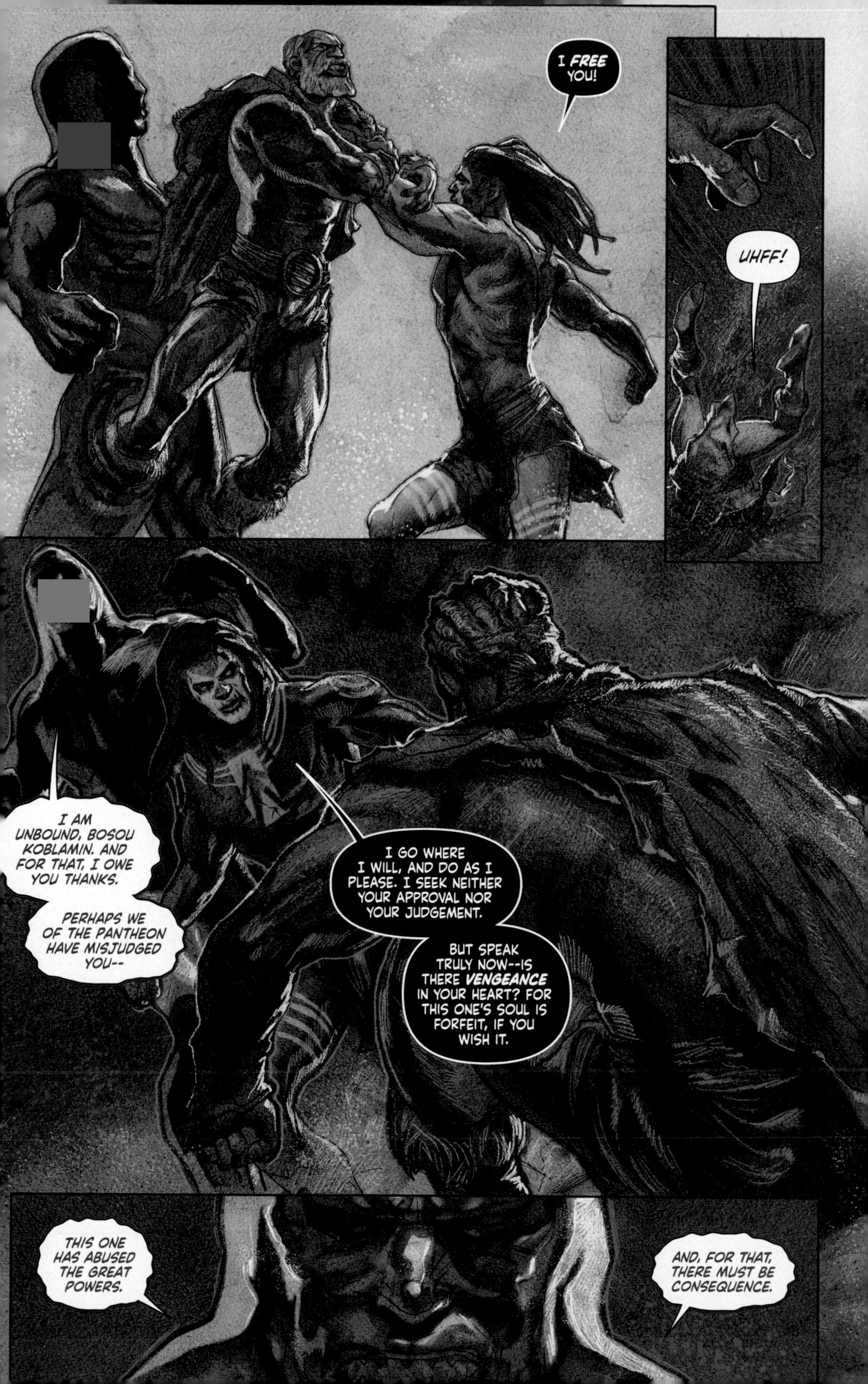
I FREE YOU!
UHFF!
I AM UNBOUND, BOSOU KOBLAMIN. AND FOR THAT, I OWE YOU THANKS.
PERHAPS WE OF THE PANTHEON HAVE MISJUDGED YOU--
I GO WHERE I WILL, AND DO AS I PLEASE. I SEEK NEITHER YOUR APPROVAL NOR YOUR JUDGEMENT.
BUT SPEAK TRULY NOW--IS THERE VENGEANCE IN YOUR HEART? FOR THIS ONE'S SOUL IS FORFEIT, IF YOU WISH IT.
THIS ONE HAS ABUSED THE GREAT POWERS.
AND, FOR THAT, THERE MUST BE CONSEQUENCE.

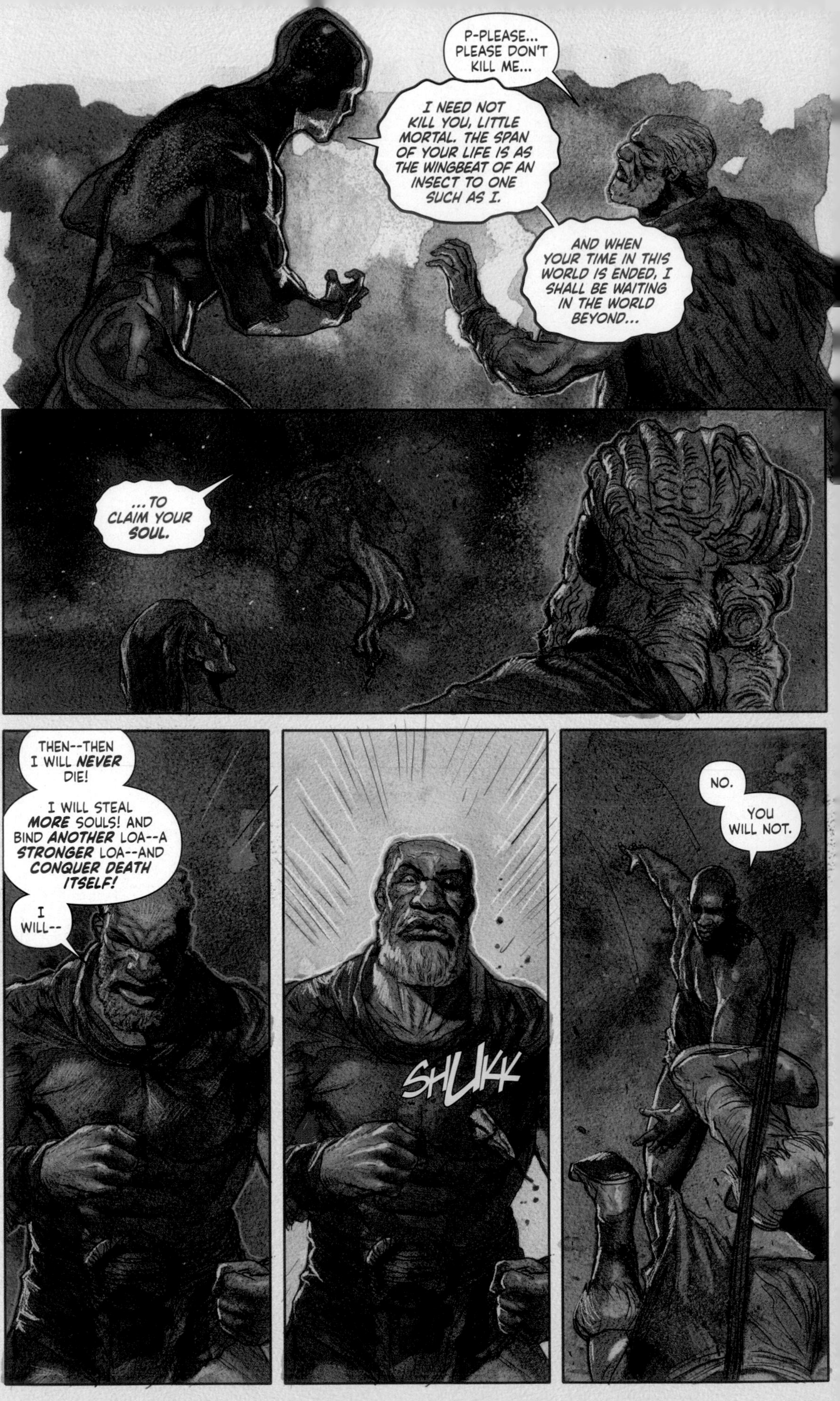
P-PLEASE... PLEASE DON'T KILL ME...
I NEED NOT KILL YOU, LITTLE MORTAL. THE SPAN OF YOUR LIFE IS AS THE WINGBEAT OF AN INSECT TO ONE SUCH AS I.
AND WHEN YOUR TIME IN THIS WORLD IS ENDED, I SHALL BE WAITING IN THE WORLD BEYOND...
...TO CLAIM YOUR SOUL.
THEN--THEN I WILL NEVER DIE!
I WILL STEAL MORE SOULS! AND BIND ANOTHER LOA--A STRONGER LOA--AND CONQUER DEATH ITSELF!
I WILL--
SHUKK
NO.
YOU WILL NOT.

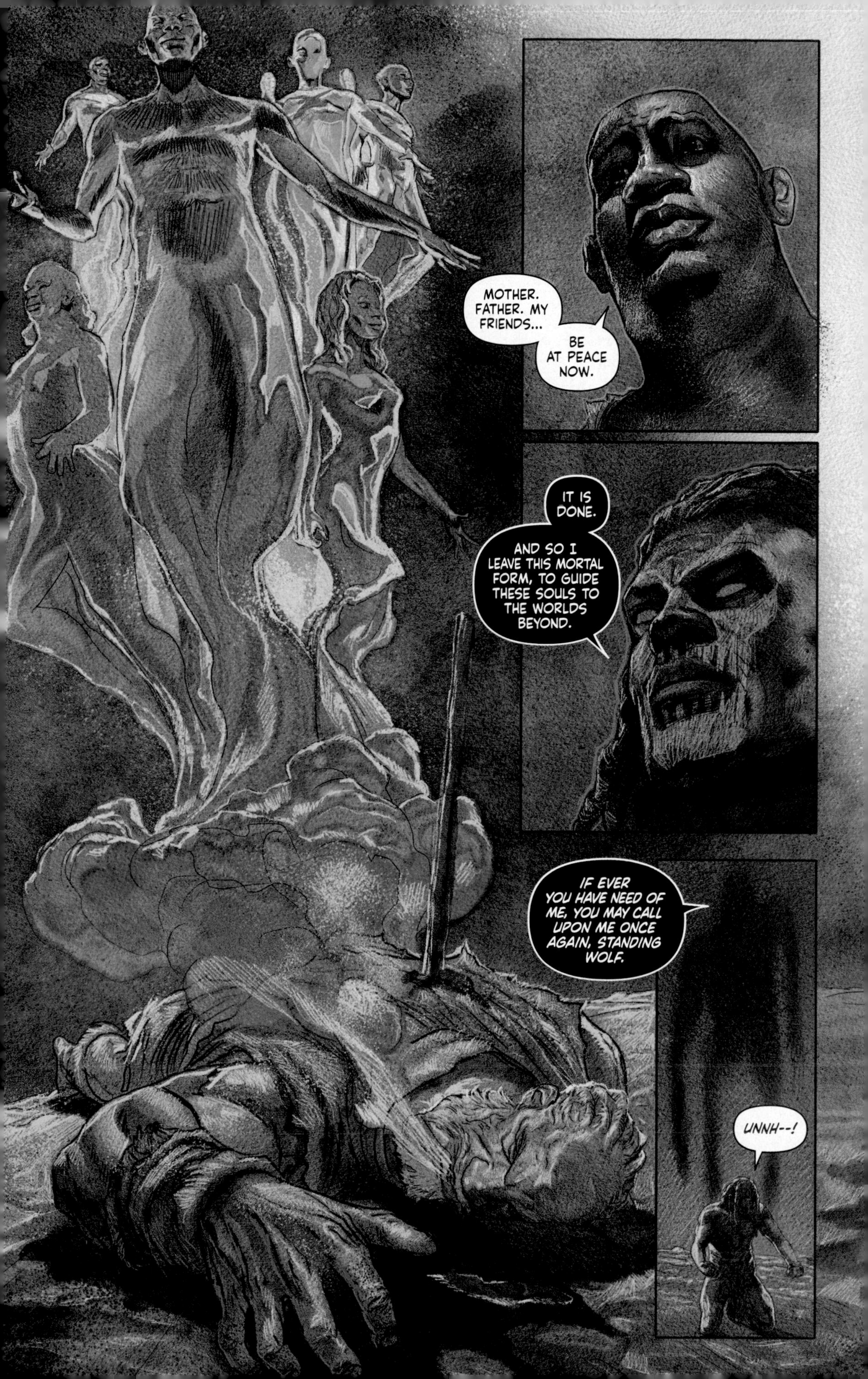
MOTHER. FATHER. MY FRIENDS...
BE AT PEACE NOW.
IT IS DONE.
AND SO I LEAVE THIS MORTAL FORM, TO GUIDE THESE SOULS TO THE WORLDS BEYOND.
IF EVER YOU HAVE NEED OF ME, YOU MAY CALL UPON ME ONCE AGAIN, STANDING WOLF.
UNNH--!

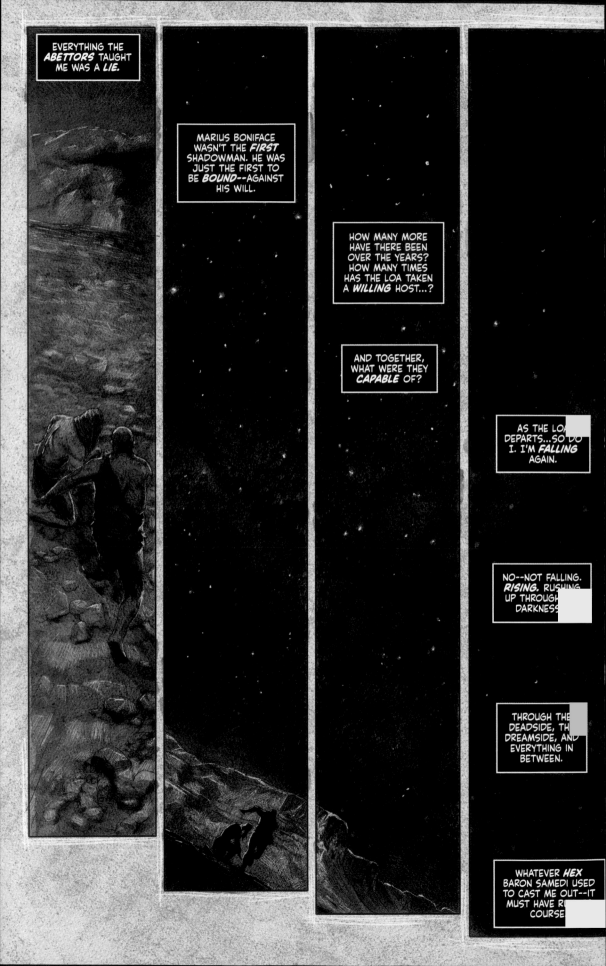

EVERYTHING THE *ABETTORS* TAUGHT ME WAS A *LIE.*

MARIUS BONIFACE WASN'T THE *FIRST* SHADOWMAN. HE WAS JUST THE FIRST TO BE *BOUND*--AGAINST HIS WILL.

HOW MANY MORE HAVE THERE BEEN OVER THE YEARS? HOW MANY TIMES HAS THE LOA TAKEN A *WILLING* HOST...?

AND TOGETHER, WHAT WERE THEY *CAPABLE* OF?

AS THE LOA DEPARTS...SO DO I. I'M *FALLING* AGAIN.

NO--NOT FALLING. *RISING.* RUSHING UP THROUGH DARKNESS

THROUGH THE DEADSIDE, THE DREAMSIDE, AND EVERYTHING IN BETWEEN.

WHATEVER *HEX* BARON SAMEDI USED TO CAST ME OUT--IT MUST HAVE RUN COURSE

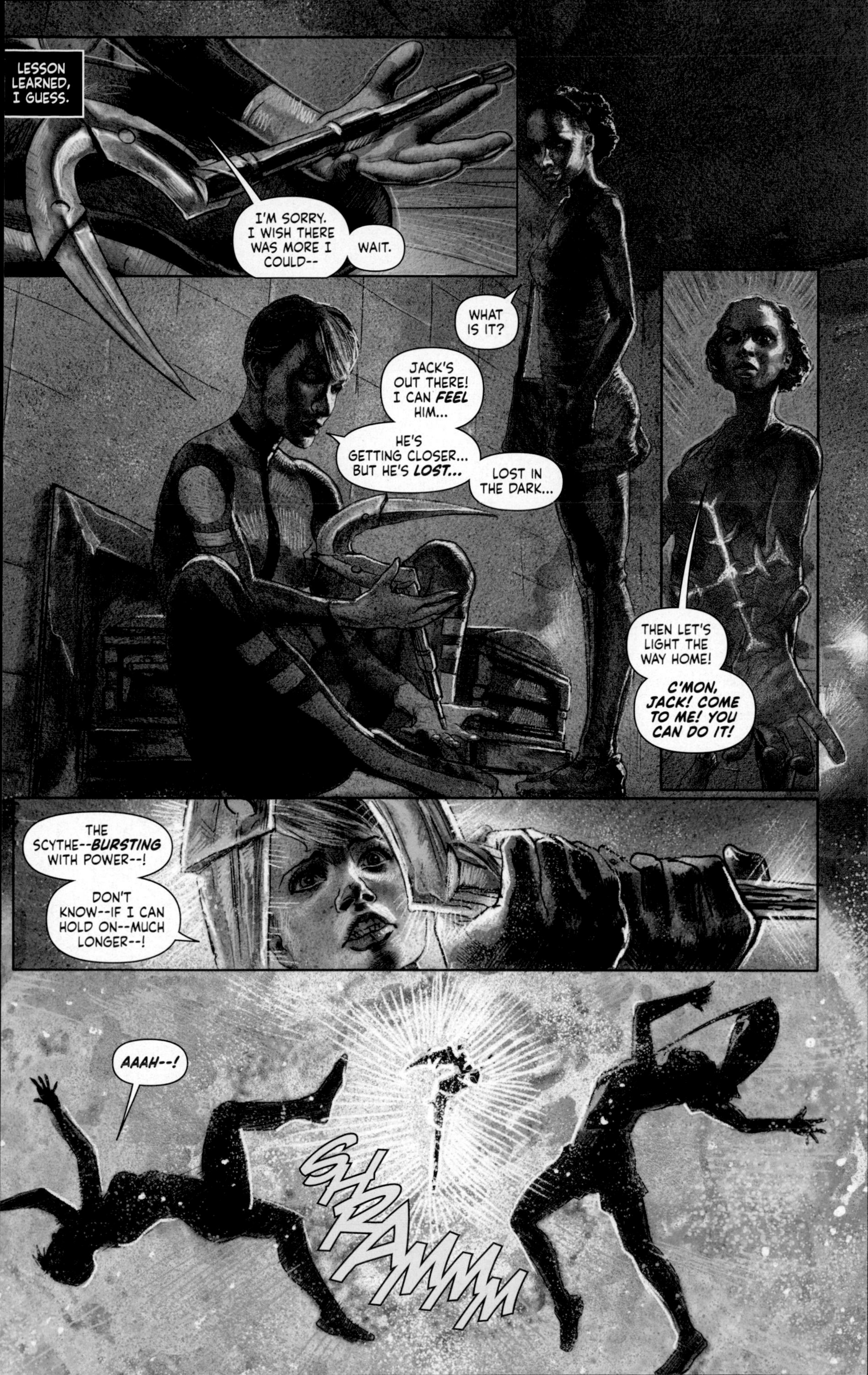
LESSON LEARNED, I GUESS.
I'M SORRY. I WISH THERE WAS MORE I COULD--
WAIT.
WHAT IS IT?
JACK'S OUT THERE! I CAN FEEL HIM...
HE'S GETTING CLOSER... BUT HE'S LOST...
LOST IN THE DARK...
THEN LET'S LIGHT THE WAY HOME!
C'MON, JACK! COME TO ME! YOU CAN DO IT!
THE SCYTHE--BURSTING WITH POWER--!
DON'T KNOW--IF I CAN HOLD ON--MUCH LONGER--!
AAAH--!
SHRAMMMM

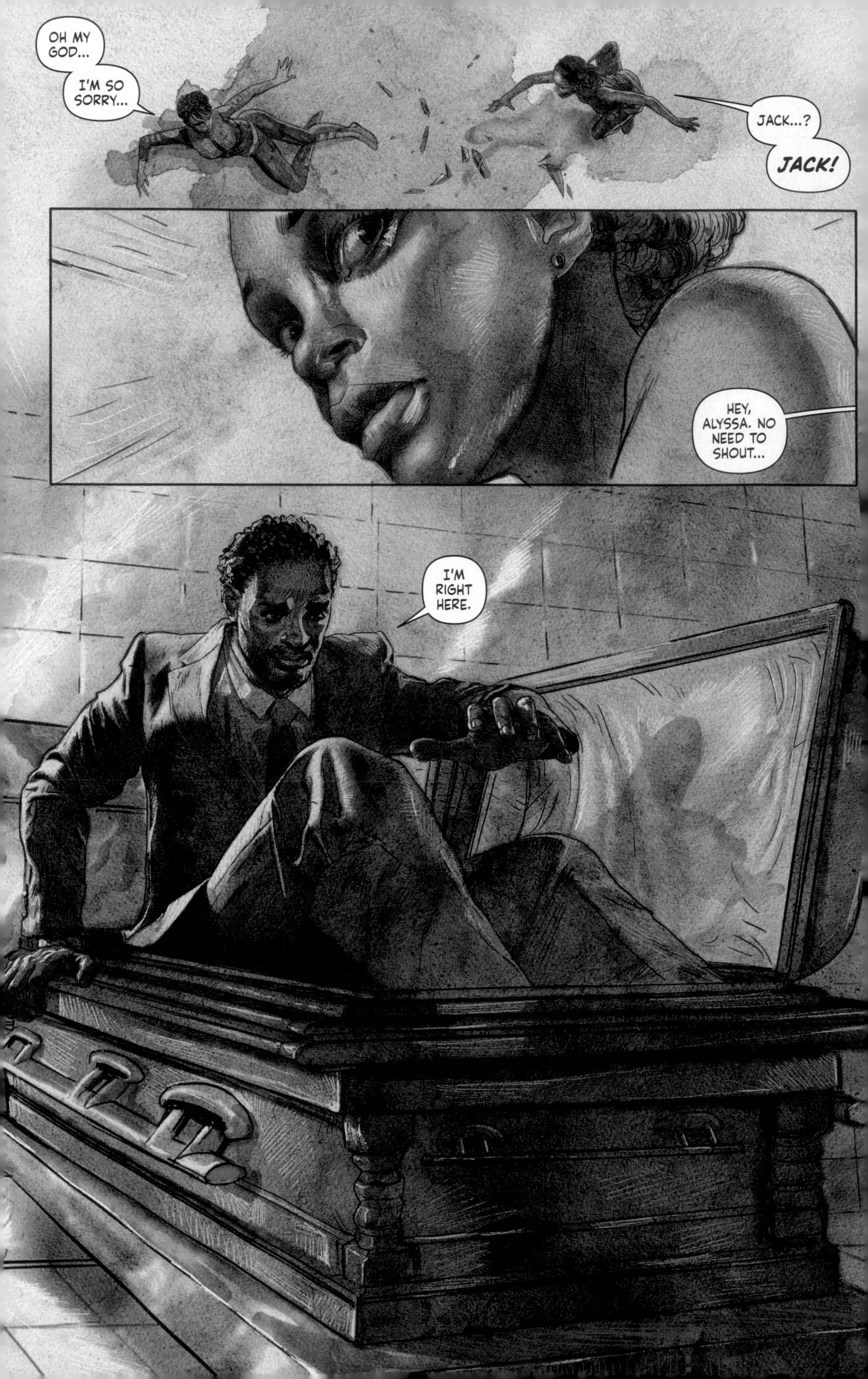
OH MY GOD...
I'M SO SORRY...
JACK...?
JACK!
HEY, ALYSSA. NO NEED TO SHOUT...
I'M RIGHT HERE.

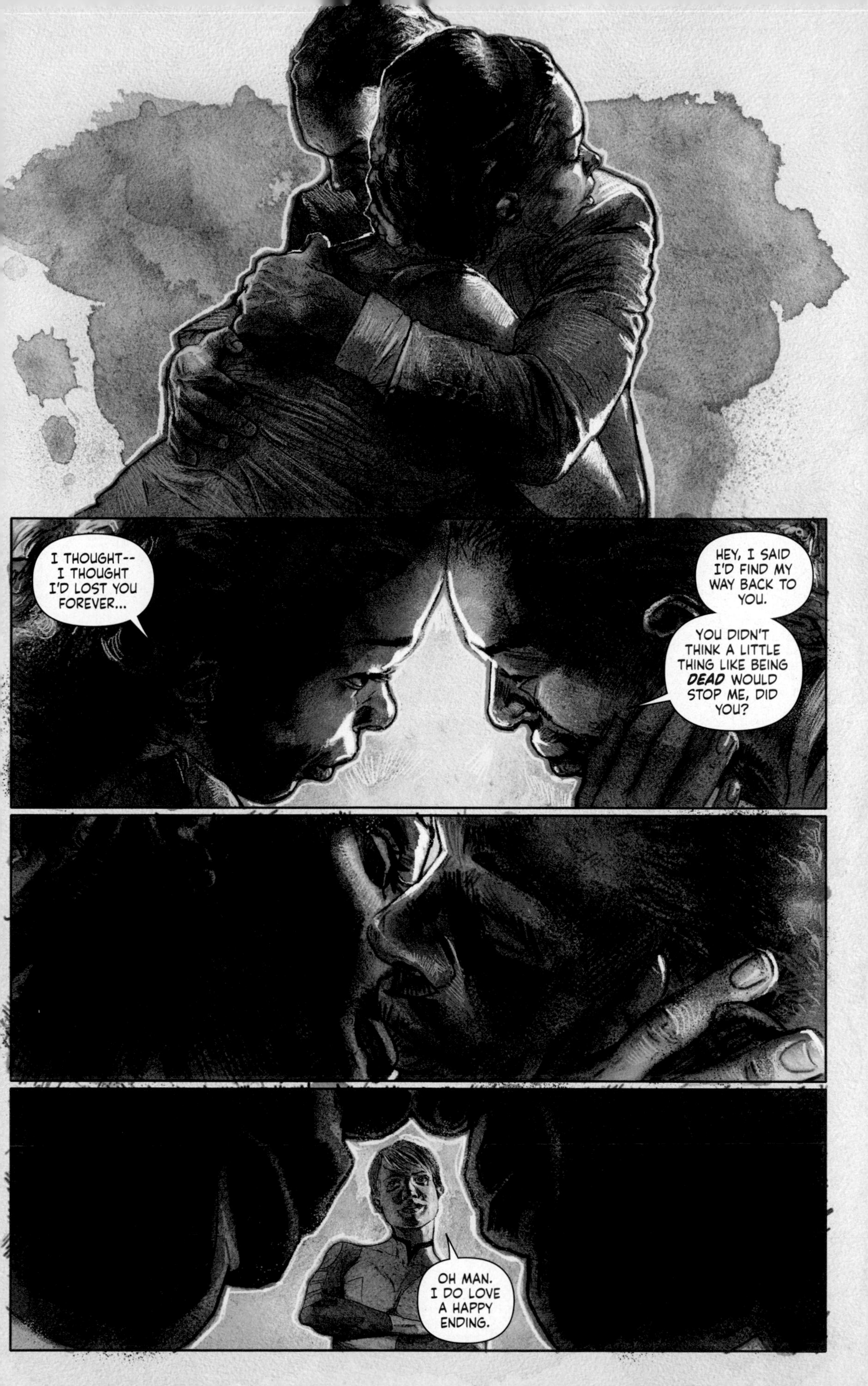
I THOUGHT-- I THOUGHT I'D LOST YOU FOREVER...
HEY, I SAID I'D FIND MY WAY BACK TO YOU.
YOU DIDN'T THINK A LITTLE THING LIKE BEING *DEAD* WOULD STOP ME, DID YOU?
OH MAN. I DO LOVE A HAPPY ENDING.

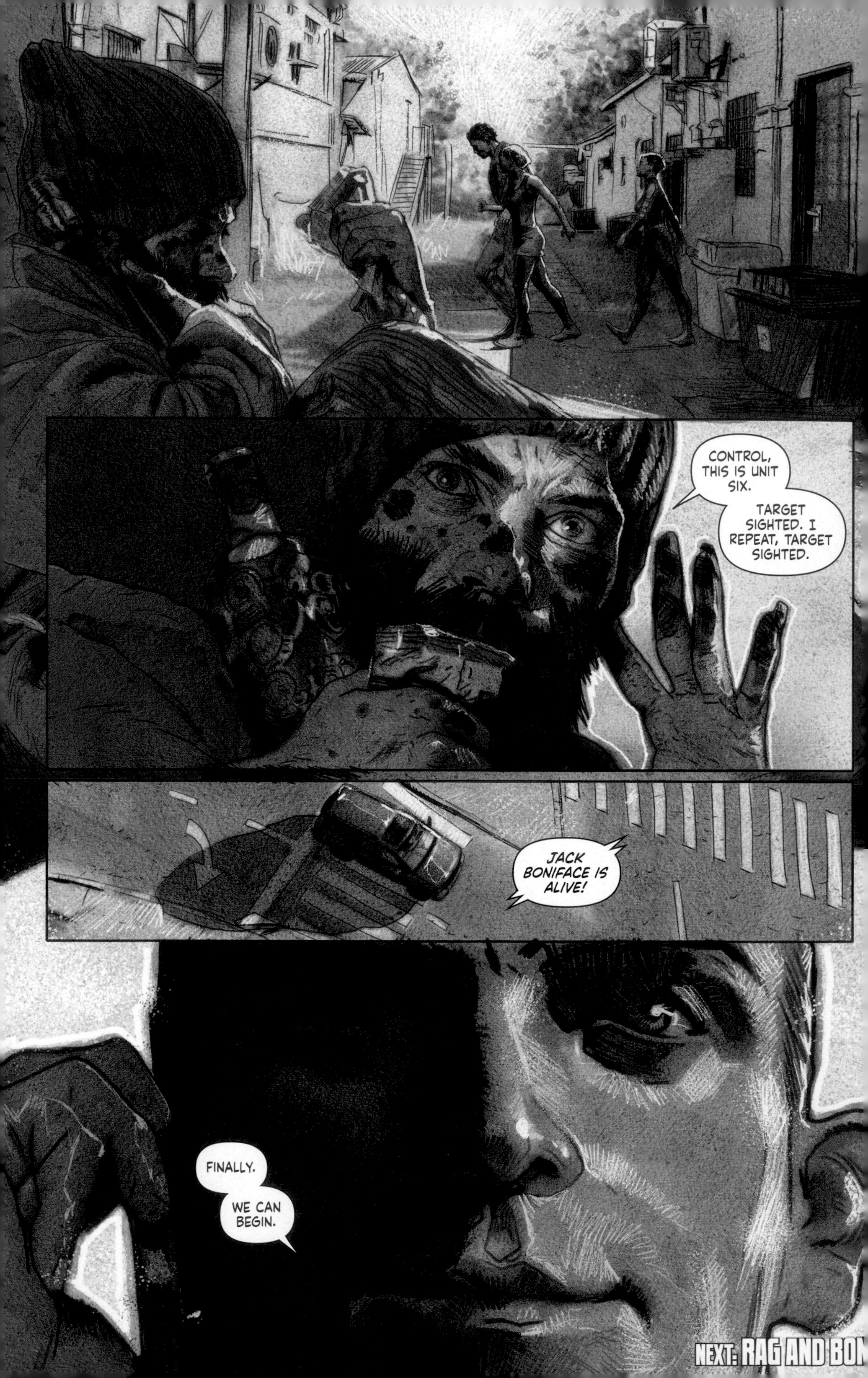
CONTROL, THIS IS UNIT SIX.
TARGET SIGHTED. I REPEAT, TARGET SIGHTED.
JACK BONIFACE IS ALIVE!
FINALLY.
WE CAN BEGIN.
NEXT: RAG AND BON

THE SHADOWMAN OF THE 1940s

SCRIPT EXCERPTS BY **ANDY DIGGLE**, ART BY **SHAWN MARTINBROUGH**,
1940s SHADOWMAN DESIGN BY **DAVE JOHNSON**

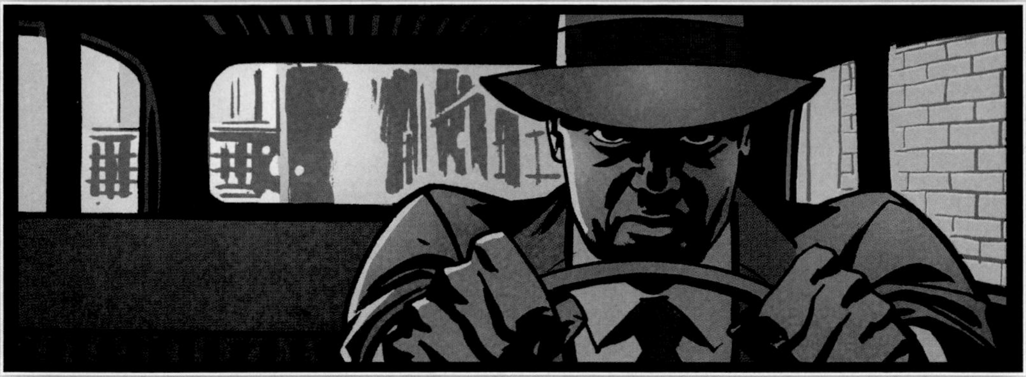

Widen to show Max sitting at the wheel of his parked car (high-end late 30s model). He's watching the Manhattan backstreet beyond, though our focus here is on Max. He's on a stakeout, and he's been sitting here a while. Max wears a wool coat over a smart '40s suit and tie.

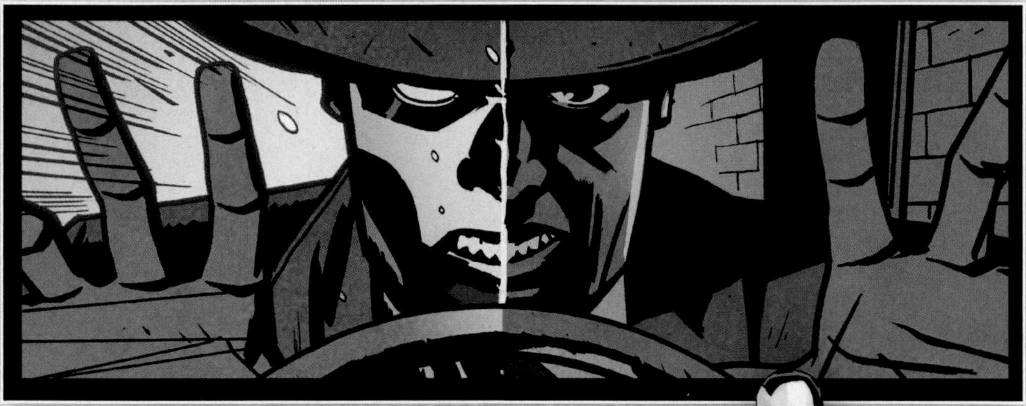

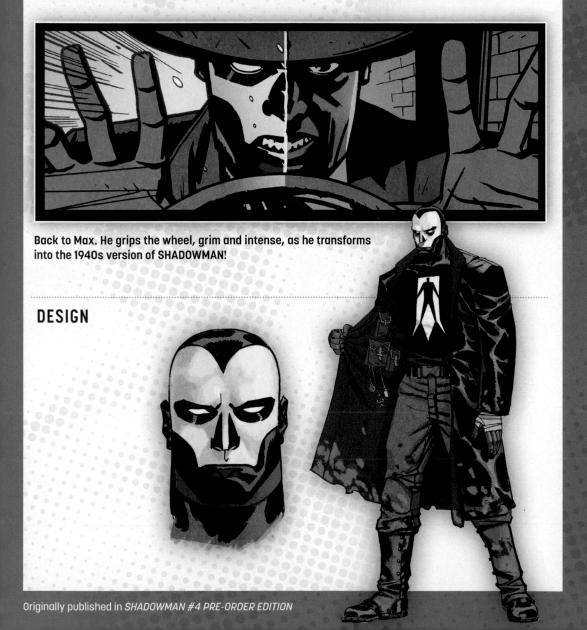

Back to Max. He grips the wheel, grim and intense, as he transforms into the 1940s version of SHADOWMAN!

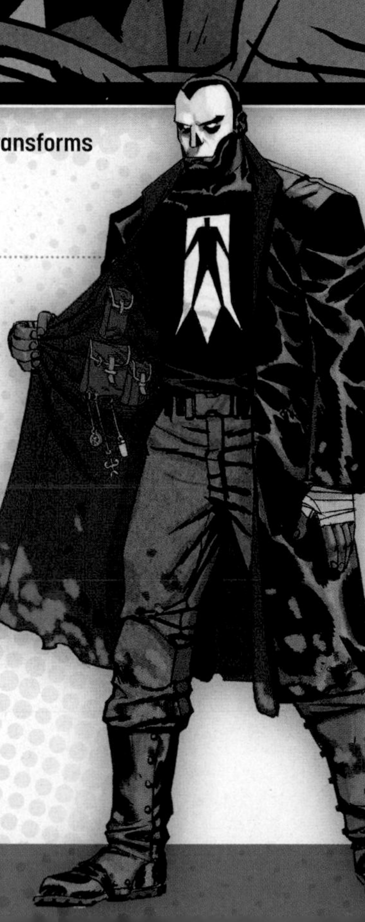

DESIGN

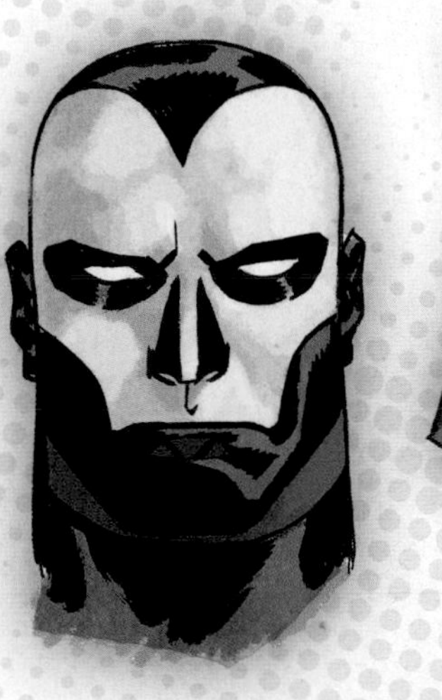

Originally published in *SHADOWMAN #4 PRE-ORDER EDITION*

FARMER IN THE HELL
SCRIPT EXCERPTS BY **ANDY DIGGLE**, ART BY **DOUG BRAITHWAITE**

The FARMER (seen here from behind) turns to see FOUR COWBOYS approaching on horseback, kicking up dust. The farmer is MARIUS BONIFACE, the first Shadowman. He was a hero in the Civil War, but the years have not been kind. Now he's older, and dirt-poor. Grim, embittered, stoic. He wears a grubby granddad shirt, pants and bracers, work boots.

RAKE looks down on MARIUS. Rake is 60, lean, tough and cruel, with a gray goatee beard. He and his men each have a different PLAYING CARD in their hat-bands. His men are KICKER, OMAHA and SHORT STACK - all terrible men. Each has a rifle and bed roll on their saddle. Everything dusty from travel.

Marius gives us a hard-eyed look. He knows these men are sons of bitches and he doesn't want trouble. But he is not afraid.

Originally published in *SHADOWMAN #5 PRE-ORDER EDITION*

THE DAWN OF SHADOWS

SCRIPT EXCERPTS BY **ANDY DIGGLE**, ART BY **RENATO GUEDES**

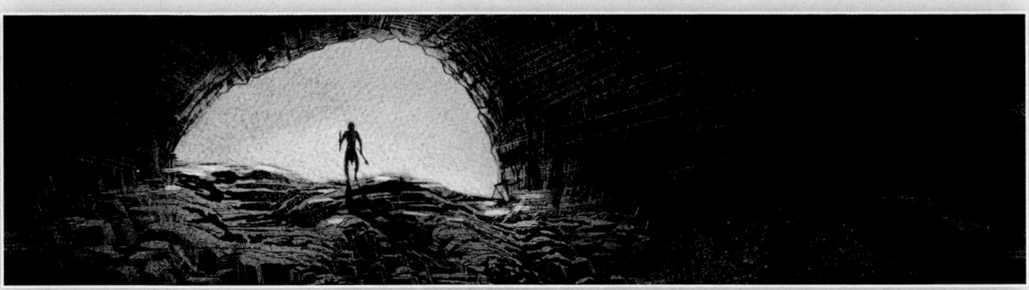

Wide slot panel. We're looking up the long, throat-like cave tunnel from deep inside it. Daylight is just a distant glimmer at the far end. STANDING WOLF creeps toward us, his burning torch casting only the faintest flicker of light. Deep shadow all around...

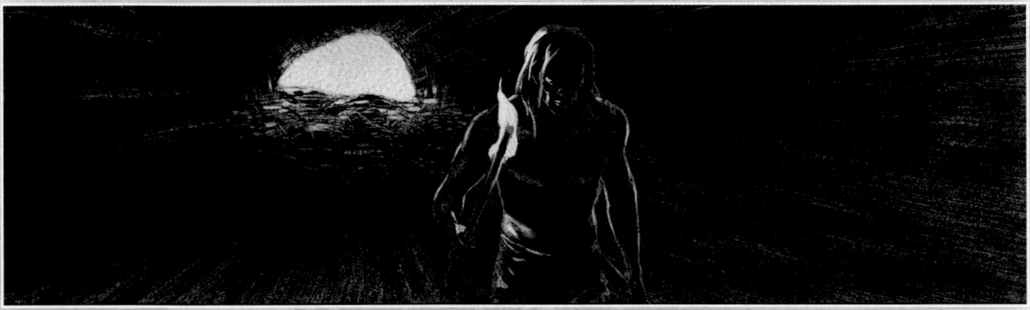

We're far from daylight now; STANDING WOLF's burning torch is the only light source. He has moved close to us. Holding the torch in one hand, he reaches his other hand up towards us, as if to touch us. Superstitious awe and reverence in his wide eyes...

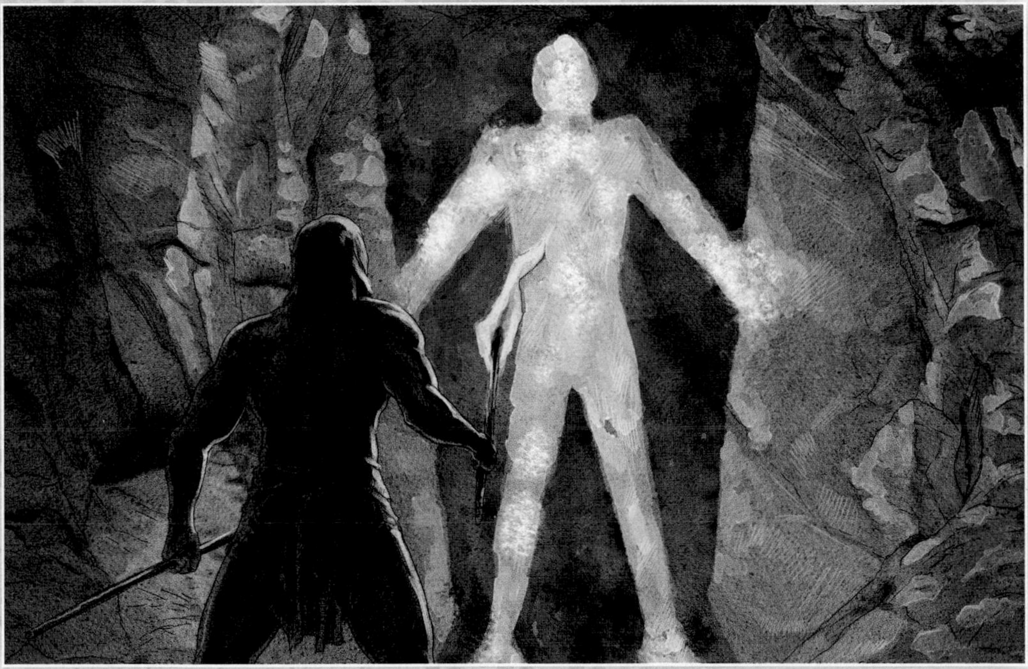

BIG! Reverse angle, so our POV is now close behind STANDING WOLF. He is reaching up to touch a HUGE CAVE PAINTING on the wall, bigger than he is. Daubed on the rock in pale clay is a primitive rendering of the SHADOWMAN symbol!

Originally published in *SHADOWMAN #6 PRE-ORDER EDITION*

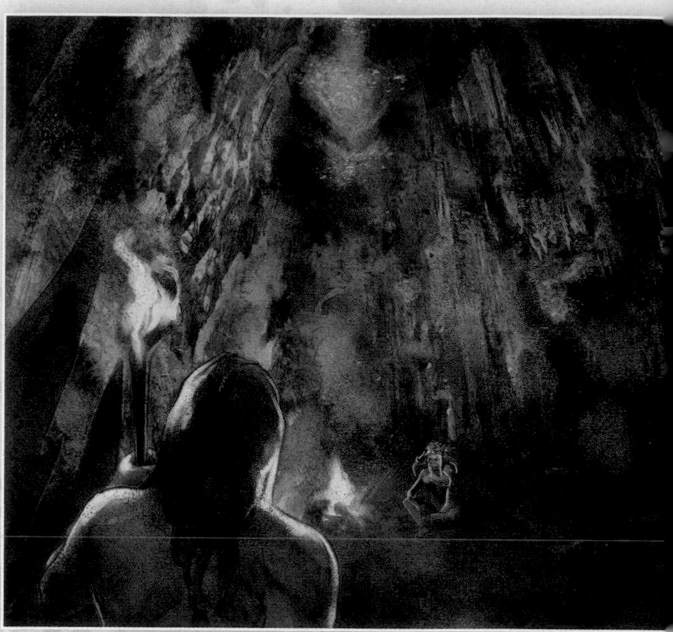

SHADOW CAVERN:
STANDING WOLF emerges into a large central cavern. A small FIRE PIT at the center of the chamber, ringed with small rocks. THE KEEPER OF THE DEAD sits cross-legged at the fire, dramatically underlit by the flames. She is a wiry, old gray-haired woman; a SHAMAN, wearing primitive totems and bangles made of BONE, horned headdress, etc. Deep black shadow behind her. This might work as a POV looking over Standing Wolf's shoulder as he enters.

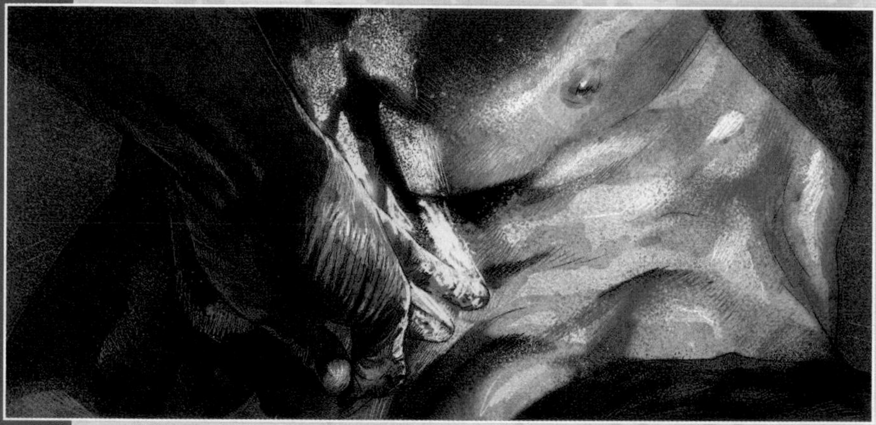

FINGER PAINTING:
The Keeper paints the Shadowman doorway-silhouette logo onto Standing Wolf's chest with her fingertips. It's a primitive design, closer to African tribal art than the modern version. Softer edges, flowing lines. Sh uses three fingertips to mark the three spikes of light that stick down from the bottom of the symbol.

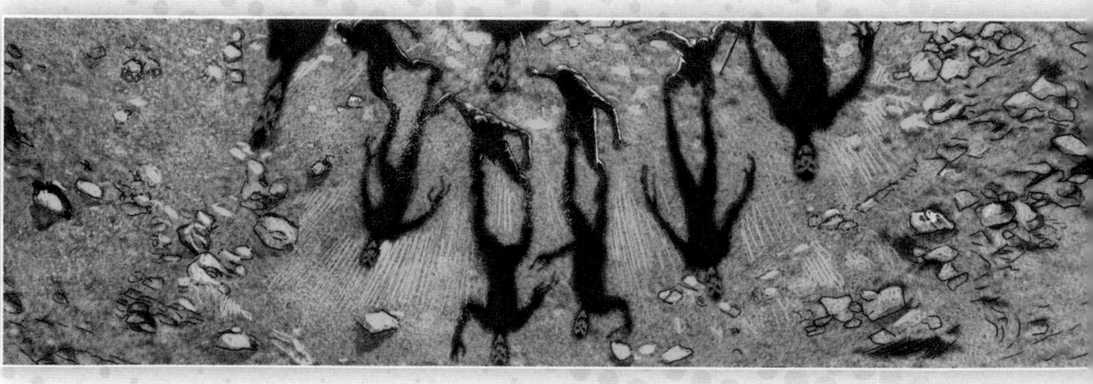

DEATH FROM BELOW:
Bird's eye POV, so we're looking STRAIGHT DOWN on the warriors. Their shadows stretch across the ground before them. NOW EVERY SHADOW HAS A SKULL FACE!

Originally published in *SHADOWMAN #7 PRE-ORDER EDITION*

SAND THEN THERE WERE NONE:
The warriors thrash and flail as they are dragged down into their own shadows! Chaos and terror. Some try to brace themselves against the ground; others stab at their own shadows with spears. But it's hopeless. They're sinking into oblivion.

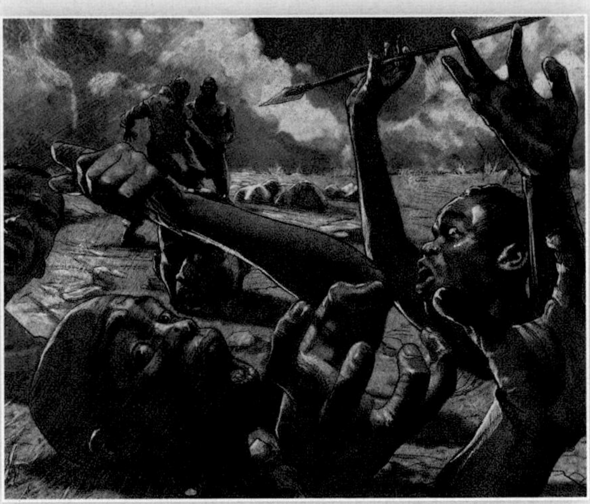

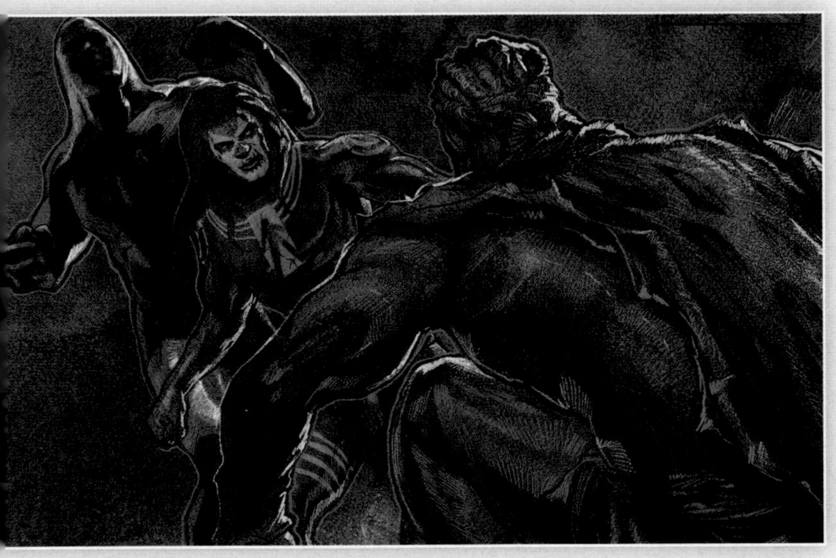

ONCE BURNED:
Pull back to reveal the FIRE LOA standing behind and slightly to one side of Shadowman. The fire loa is huge, taller than Shadowman. They stand together, both facing us, fearsome and vengeful, allies now. Soul Taker lies sprawled in the dust before them. Wisps of smoke rise from Shadowman, but he doesn't notice or care.

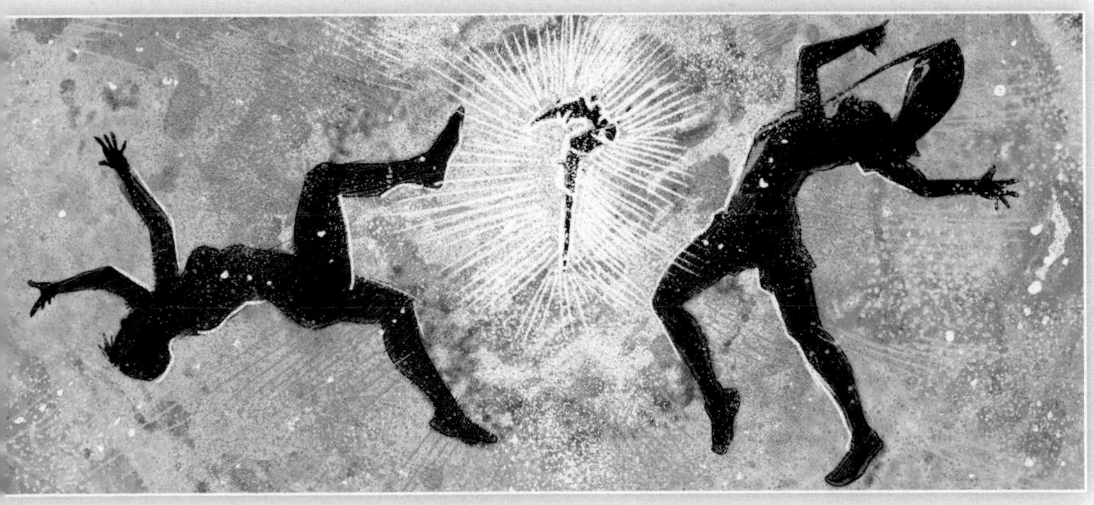

CYTHE BRIGHT:
he scythe EXPLODES in a flash of dazzlingly bright magical energy! Doctor Mirage and Alyssa are thrown back.

SHADOW STRIKE
SCRIPT EXCERPTS BY **ANDY DIGGLE**, ART BY **RENATO GUEDES**

Angle on the group of warriors. One of them is staring down, ALARMED at the sight of HIS OWN SHADOW. One of his companions scowls, mocking his stupidity.

POV looking down over the scared warrior's shoulder, so we can see his own long shadow cast on the ground by the setting sun. His SHADOW has Shadowman's SKULL MASK where its face would be, like a skull-shaped hole cut out of the silhouette. The shadow raises its claw-like hands threateningly. It is indeed moving independently of the warrior who casts it...

The warrior SCREAMS in terror as he begins to SINK INTO THE GROUND up to his waist! Or, rather, he is sinking into his own SHADOW where it touches his flesh. The shadow stretches before us with its skull face. The other warriors jump back in fear --

The hapless warrior has sunk up to the shoulders, sinking into his shadow where it meets his body. He reaches for us imploringly, terror on his face --

Originally published in *SHADOWMAN #7 PRE-ORDER EDITION*

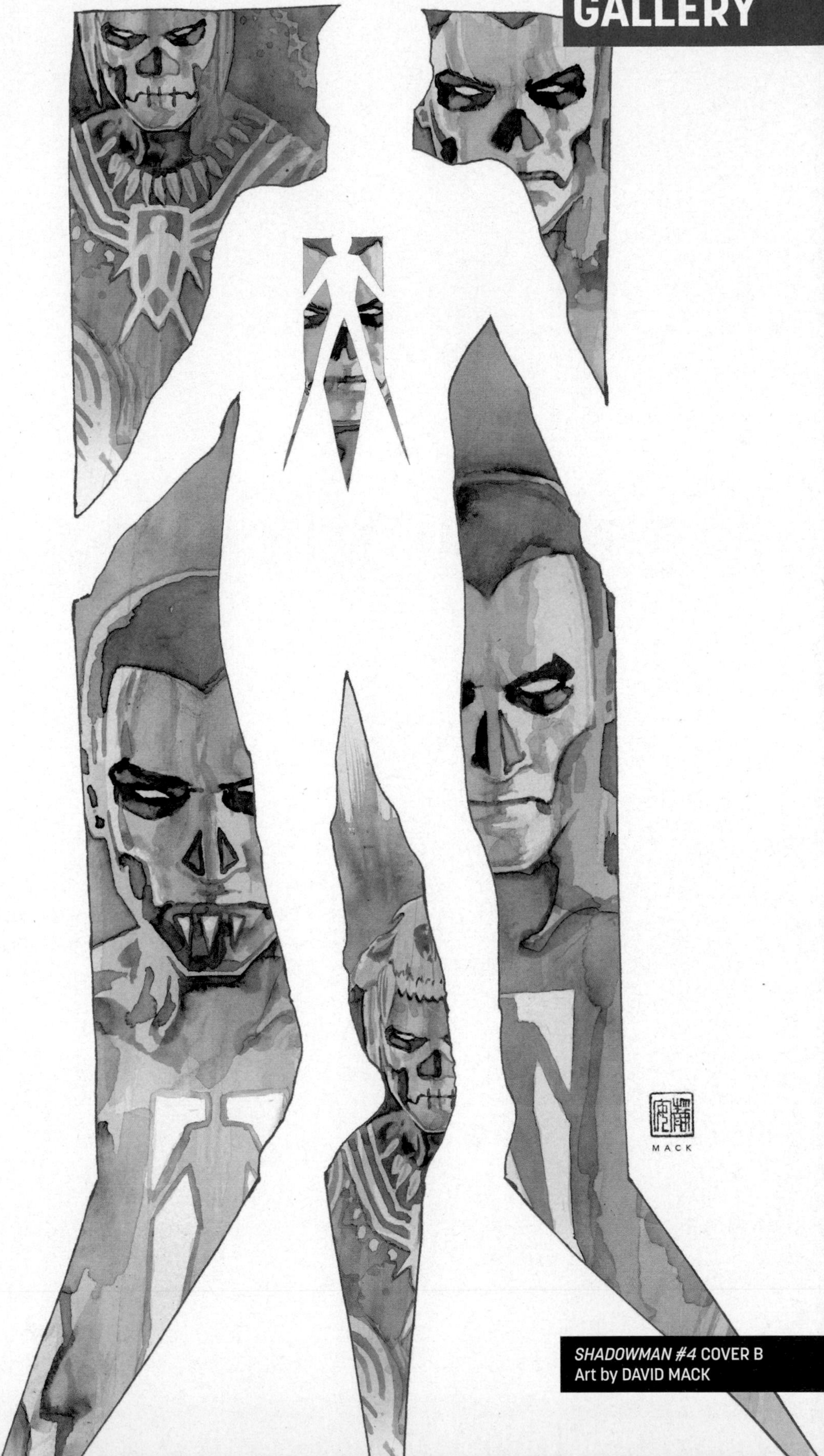
MACK

SHADOWMAN #4 COVER B
Art by DAVID MACK

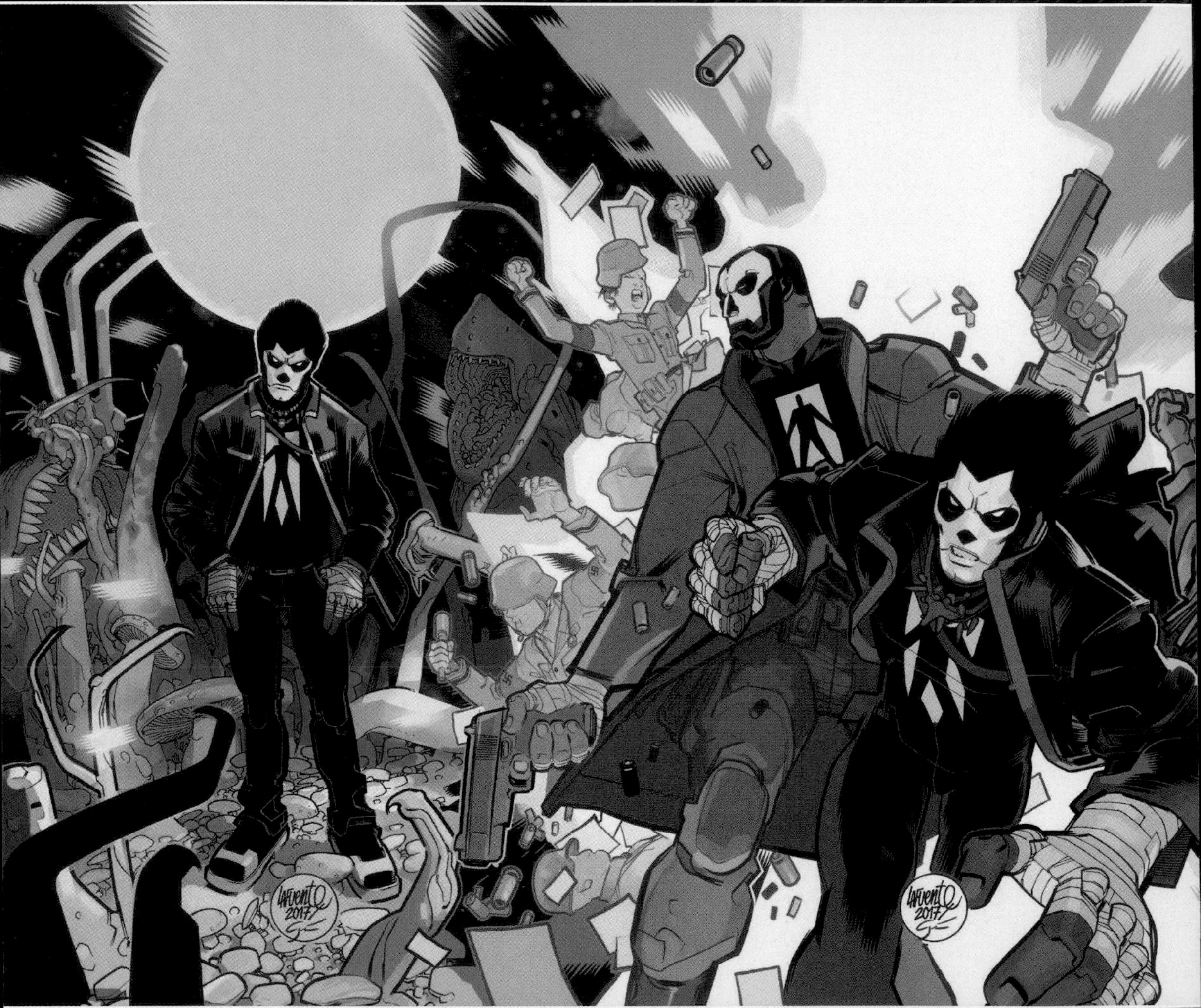

SHADOWMAN #4-7 INTERLOCKING VARIANT COVERS
Art by DAVID LAFUENTE with GERMAN GARCIA

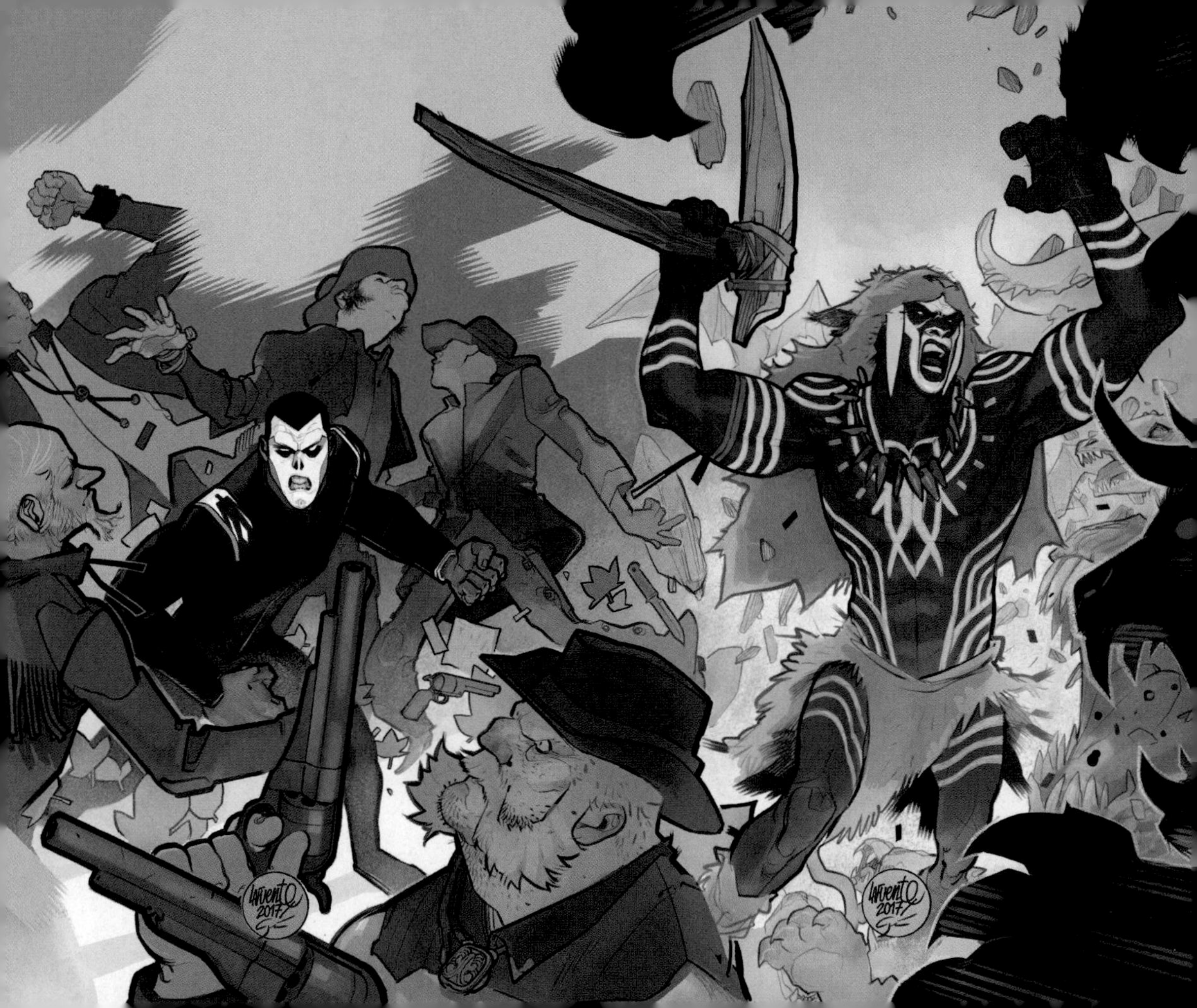

SHADOWMAN #4 ICON VARIANT COVER
Art by DAVE JOHNSON

SHADOWMAN #5 COVER B
Art by DAVID MACK

SHADOWMAN #4 PRE-ORDER EDITION COVER (facing)
Art by HANNAH TEMPLER

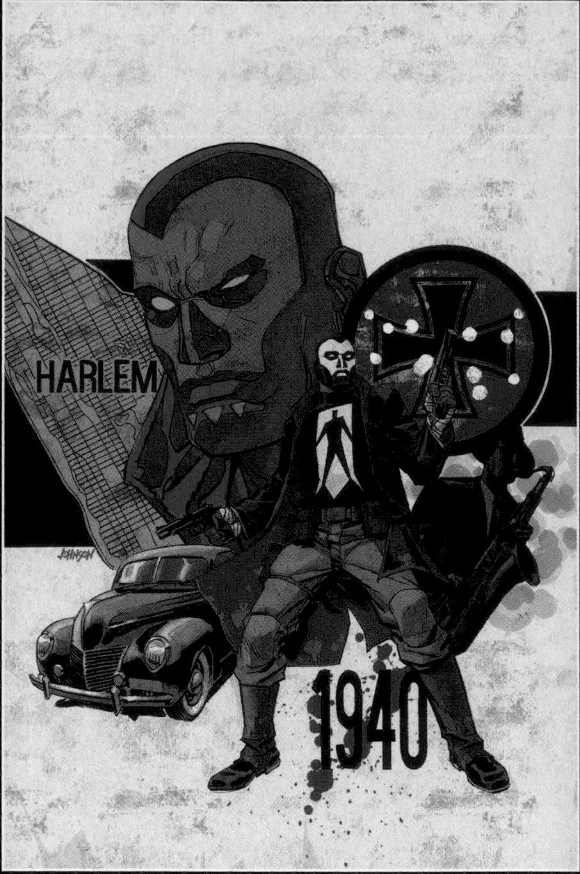
HARLEM
JOHNSON
1940

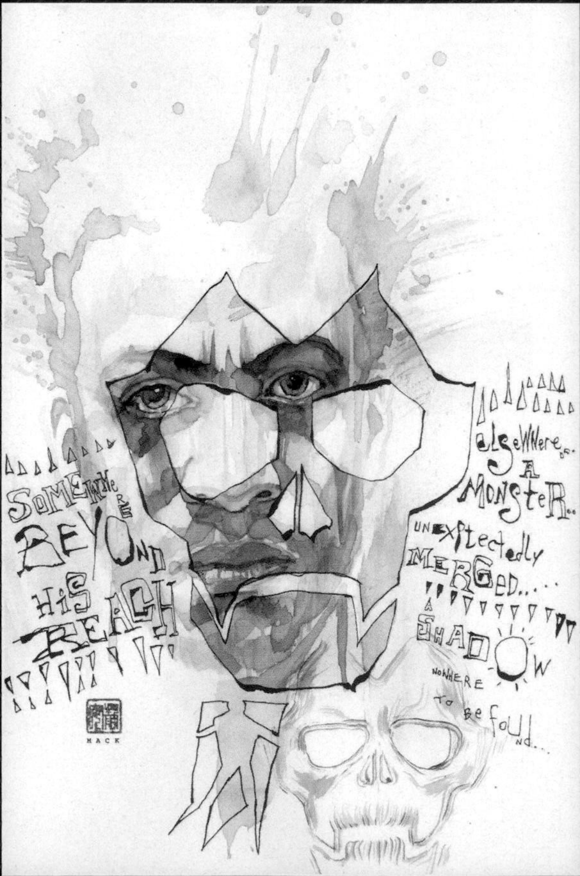
SOMEWHERE
BEYOND
HIS REACH
ELSEWHERE...
A
MONSTER...
UNEXPECTEDLY
MERGED....
A
SHADOW
NOWHERE
TO BE FOUND...
MACK

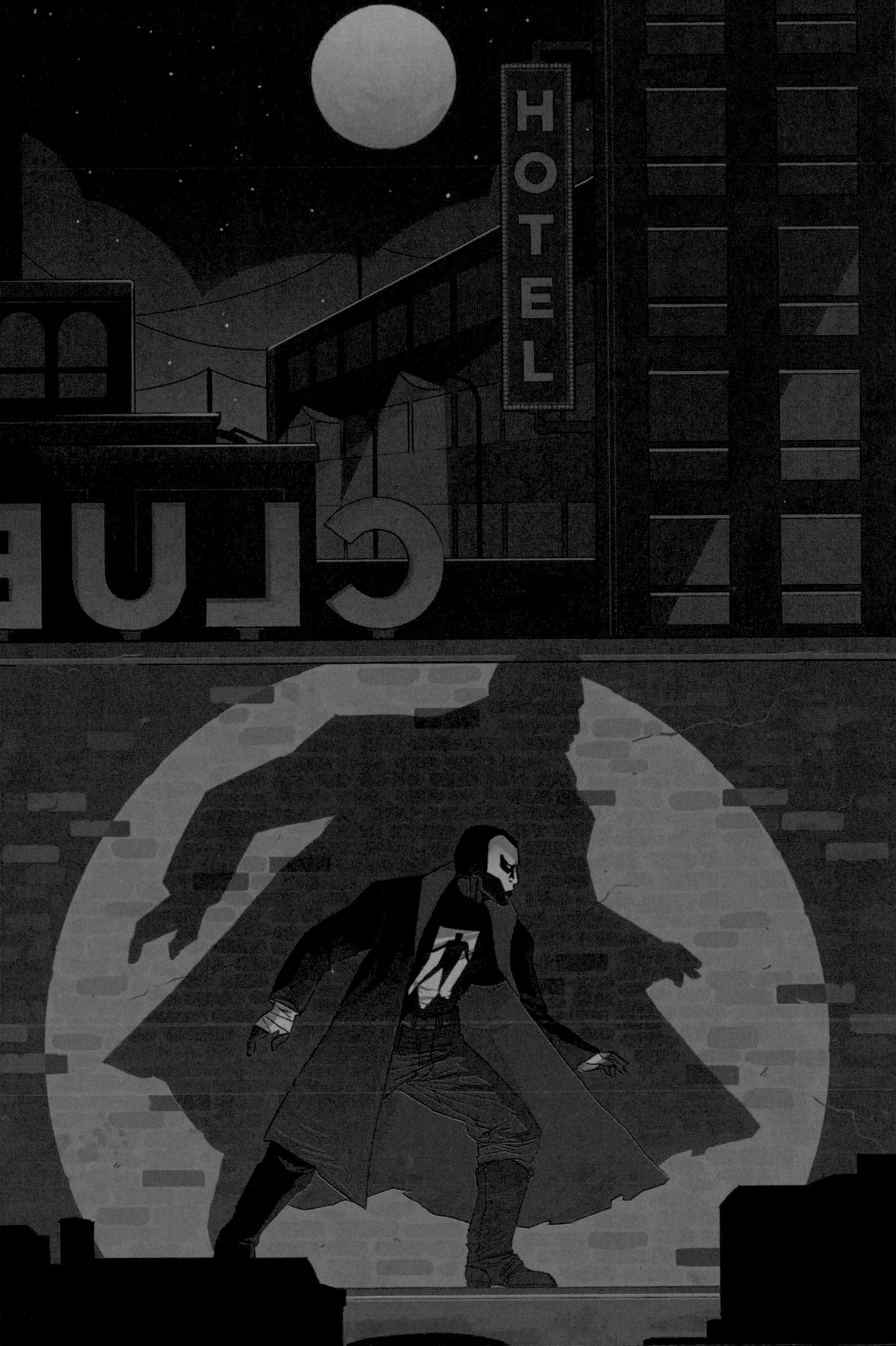
HOTEL

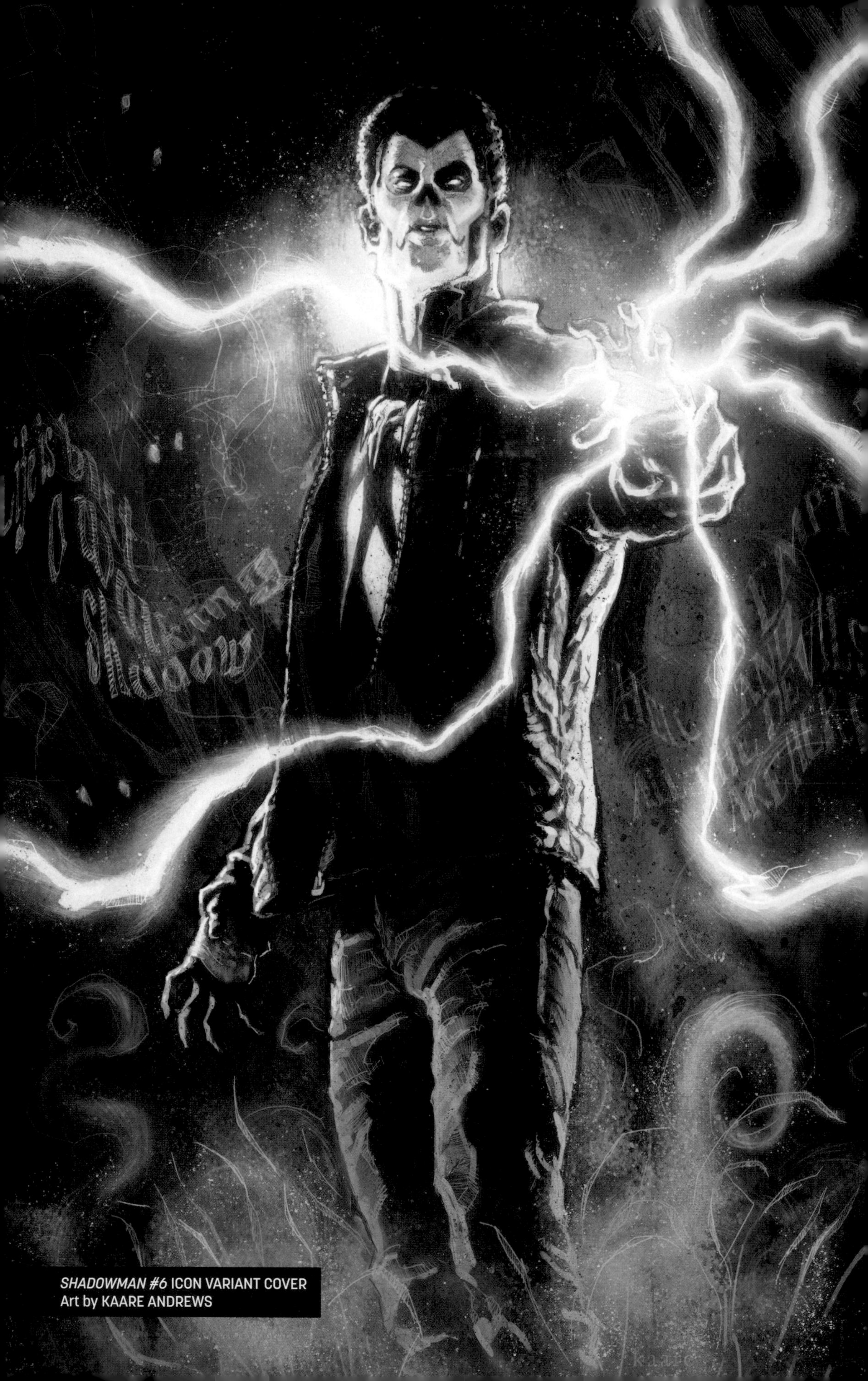

SHADOWMAN #6 ICON VARIANT COVER
Art by KAARE ANDREWS

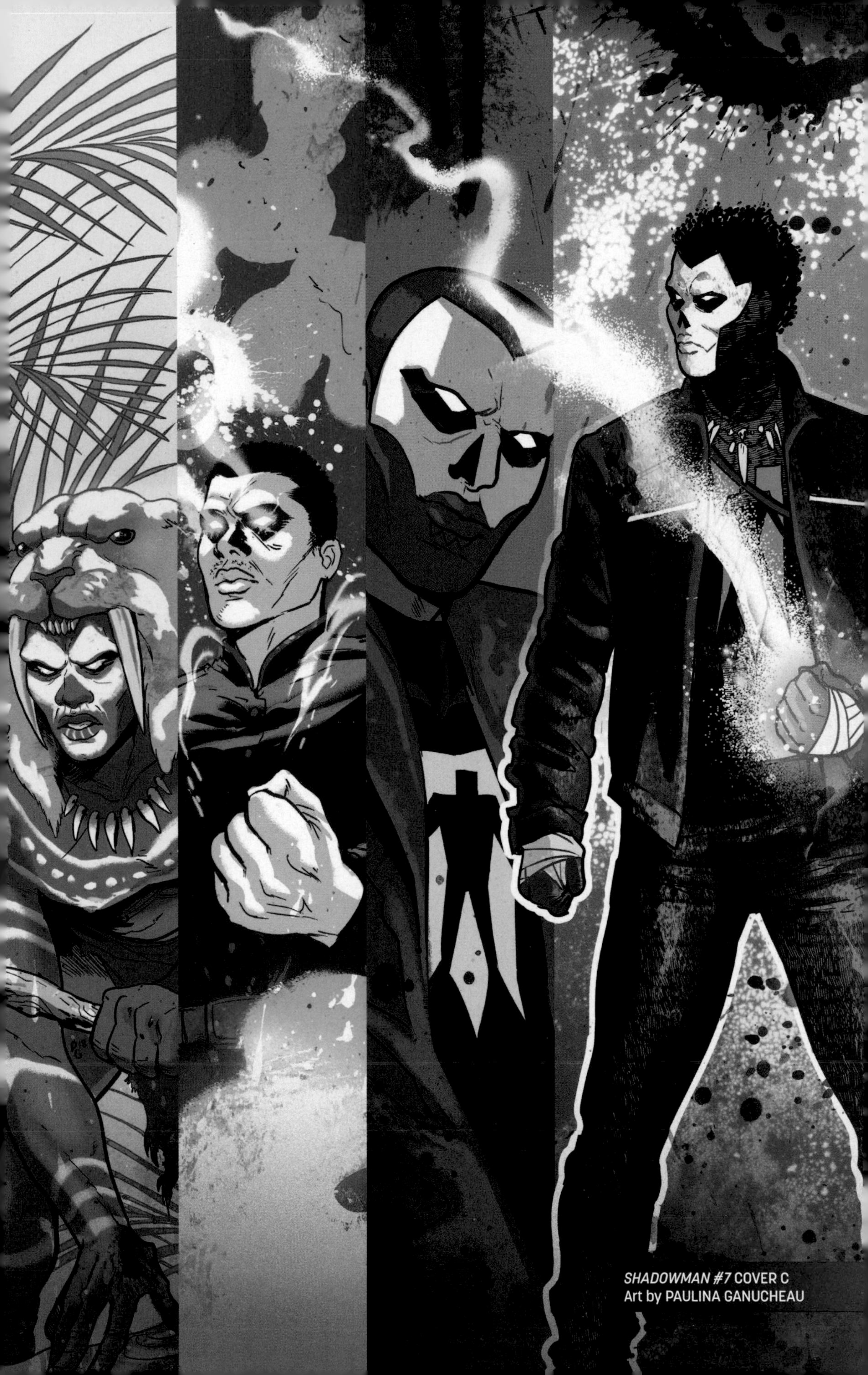

SHADOWMAN #7 COVER C
Art by PAULINA GANUCHEAU

SHADOWMAN #4, pages 2, 3, and 4 (facing)
Art by SHAWN MARTINBROUGH

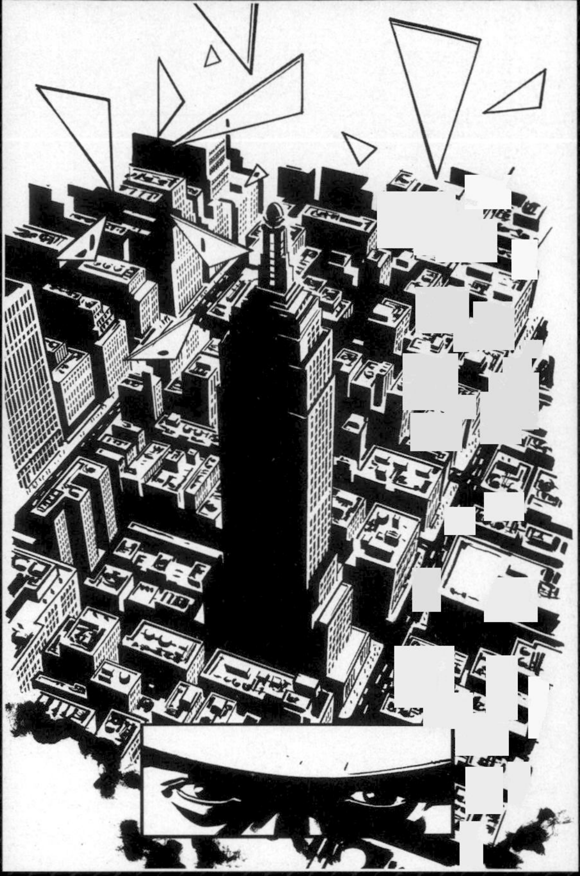

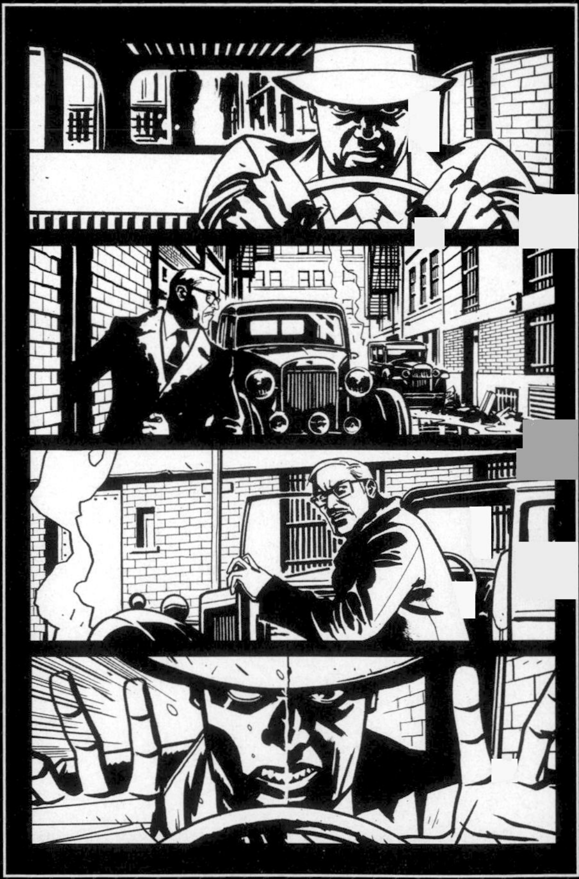

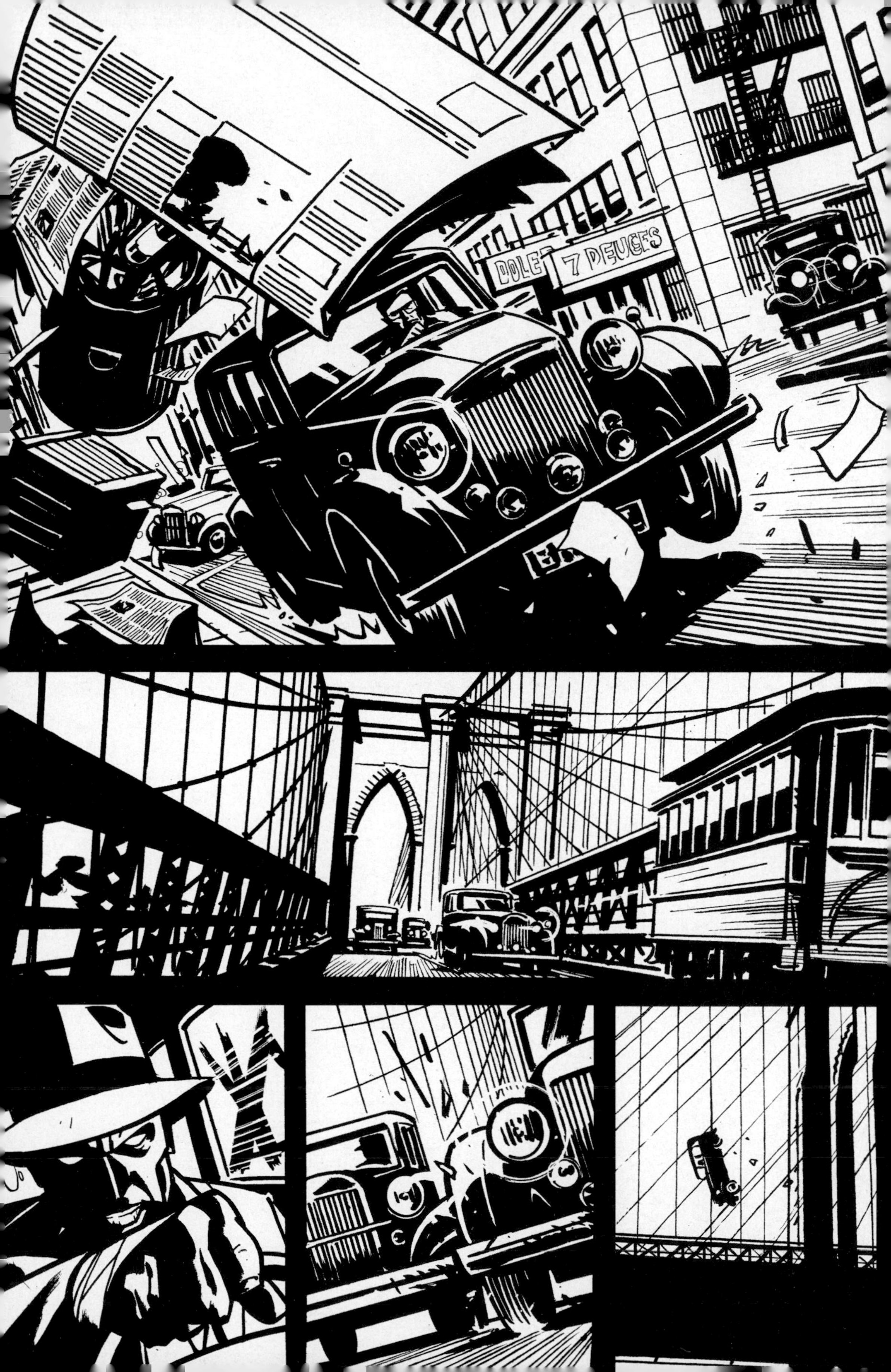
DOLE
7 DEUCES

SHADOWMAN #4, pages 17, 18, and 19 (facing)
Art by STEPHEN SEGOVIA

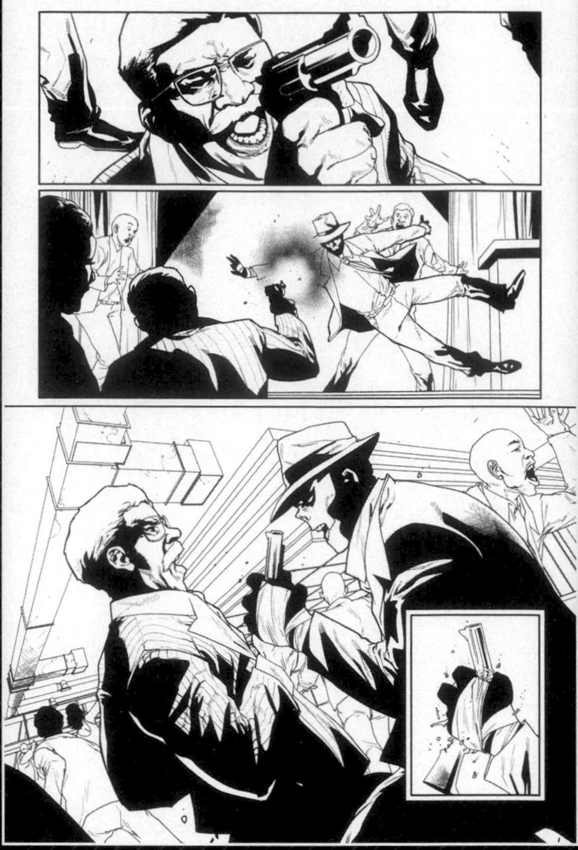

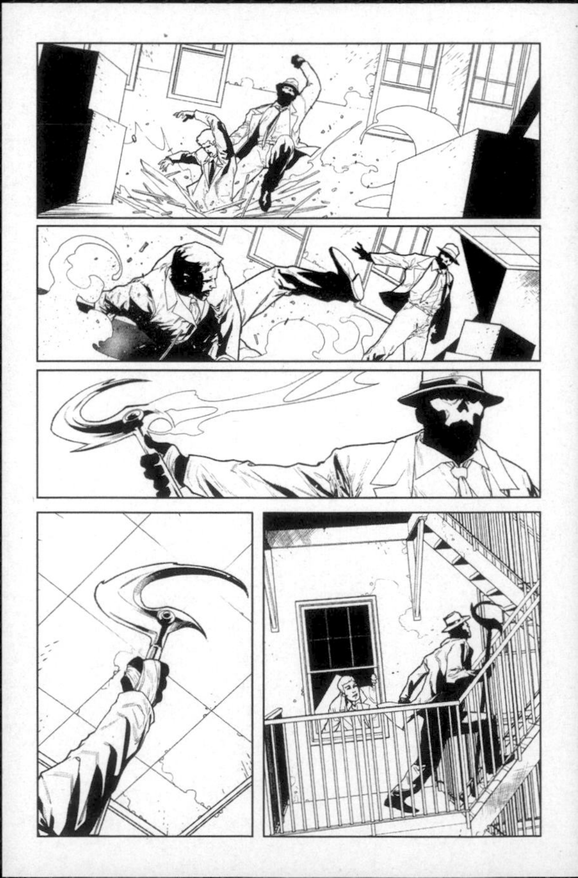

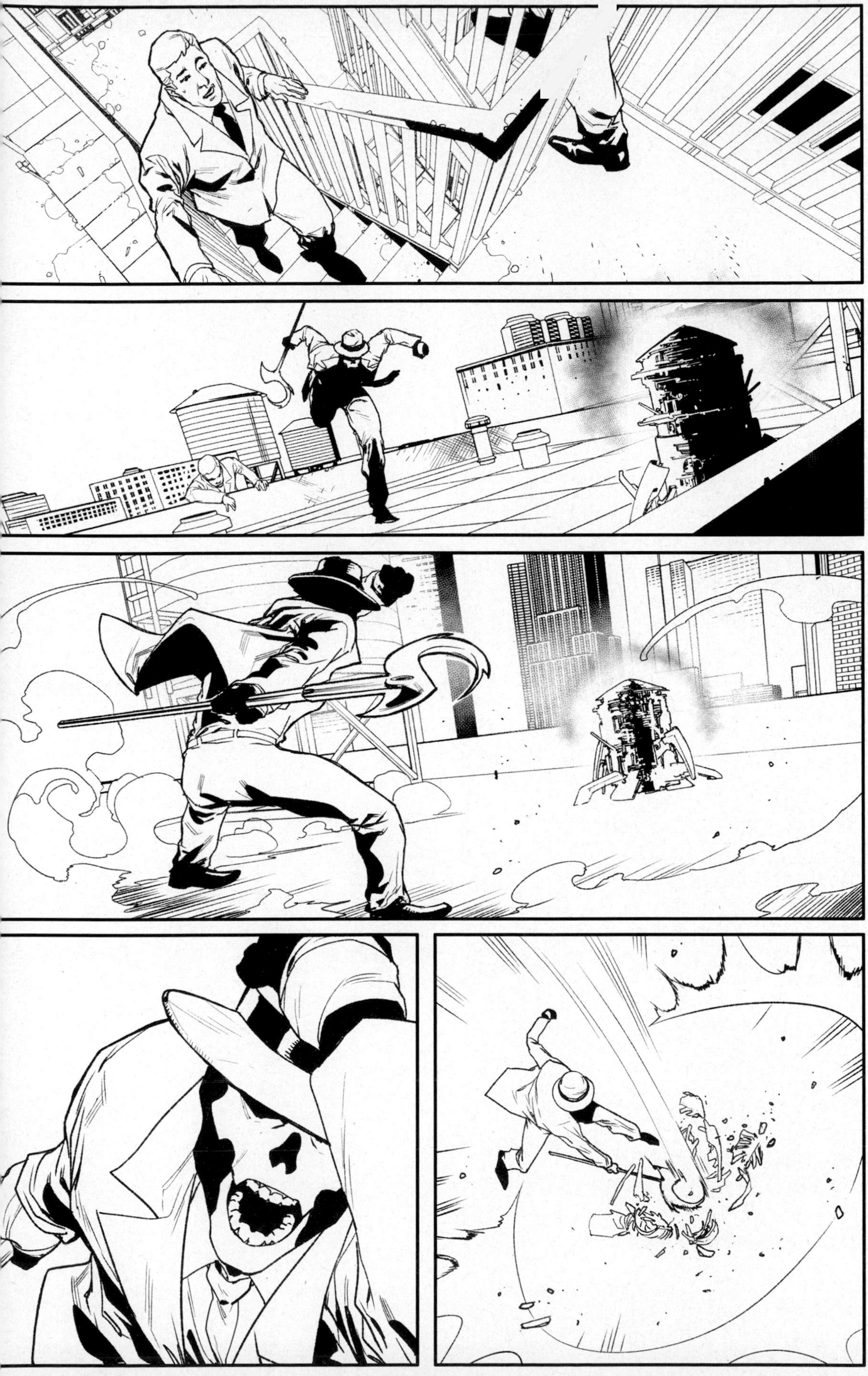

SHADOWMAN #5, pages 6, 7, and 8 (facing)
Art by DOUG BRAITHWAITE

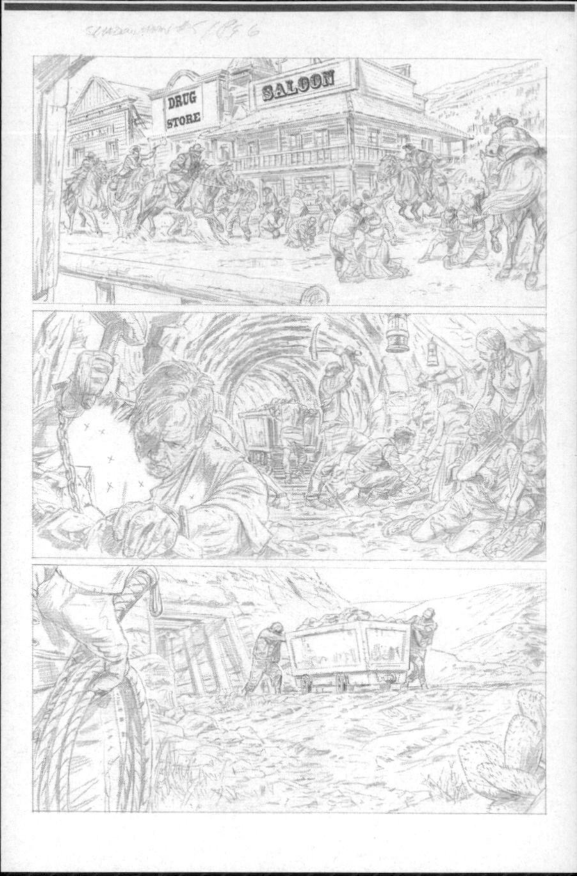
DRUG STORE
SALOON

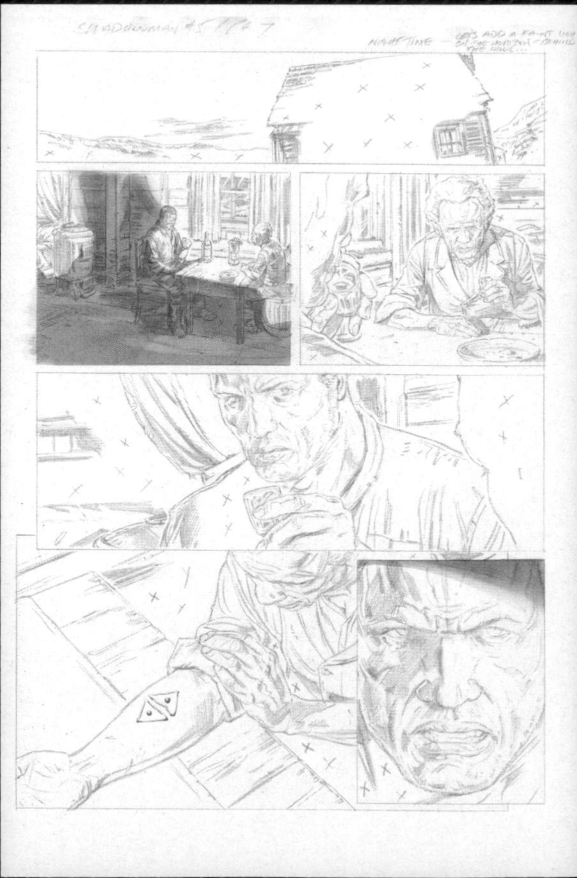
NIGHT TIME

SHADOWMAN #5 / PG 8

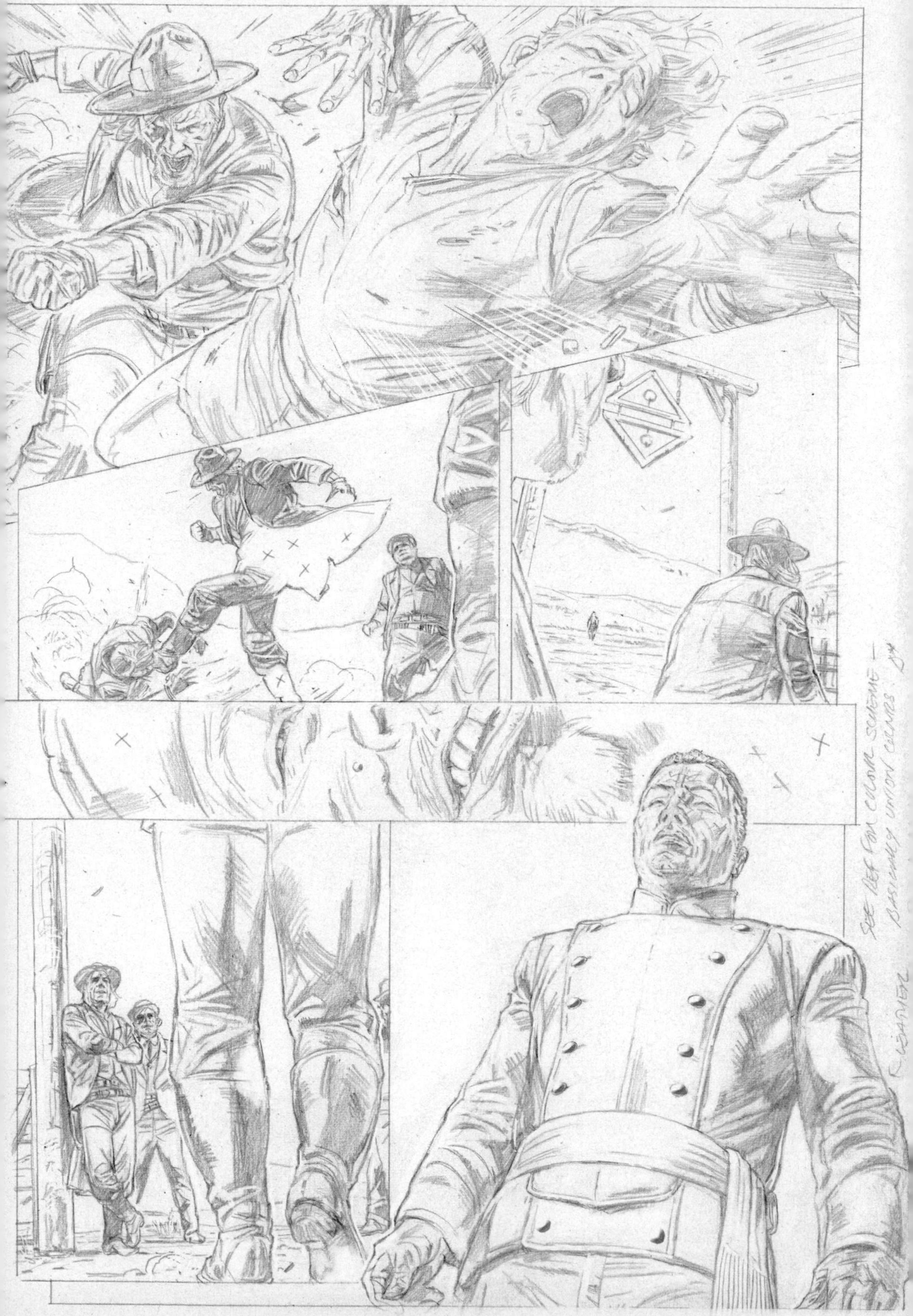

SEE REF FOR COLOUR SCHEME —
BASICALLY UNION COLOURS

SHADOWMAN #5, pages 11, 12, and 13 (facing)
Art by DOUG BRAITHWAITE

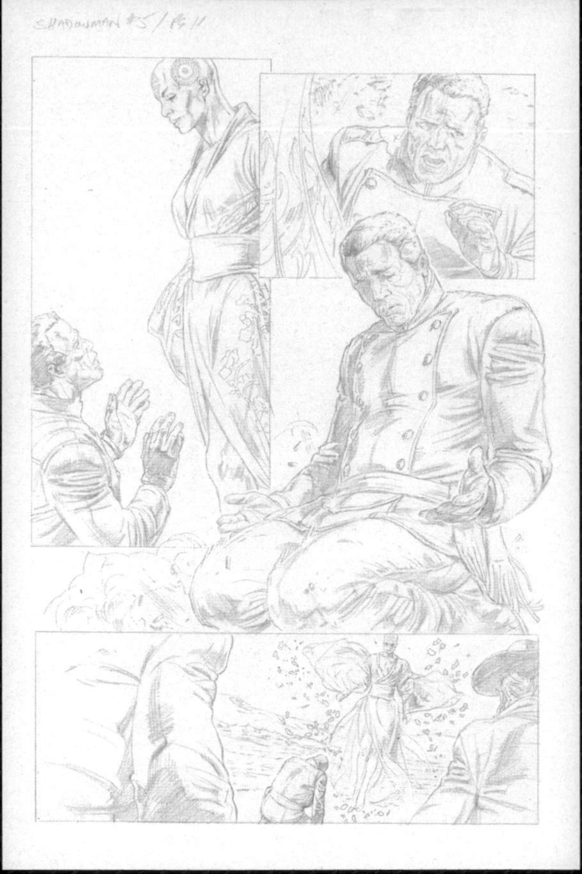
SHADOWMAN #5 / PG 11

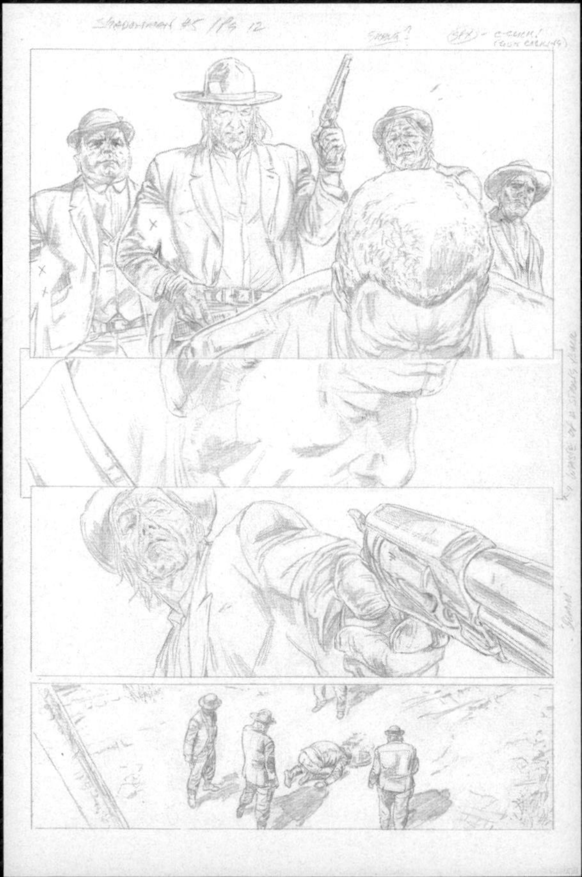
SHADOWMAN #5 / PG 12

103 13

LARGE
LEAVE / RED SUNSET

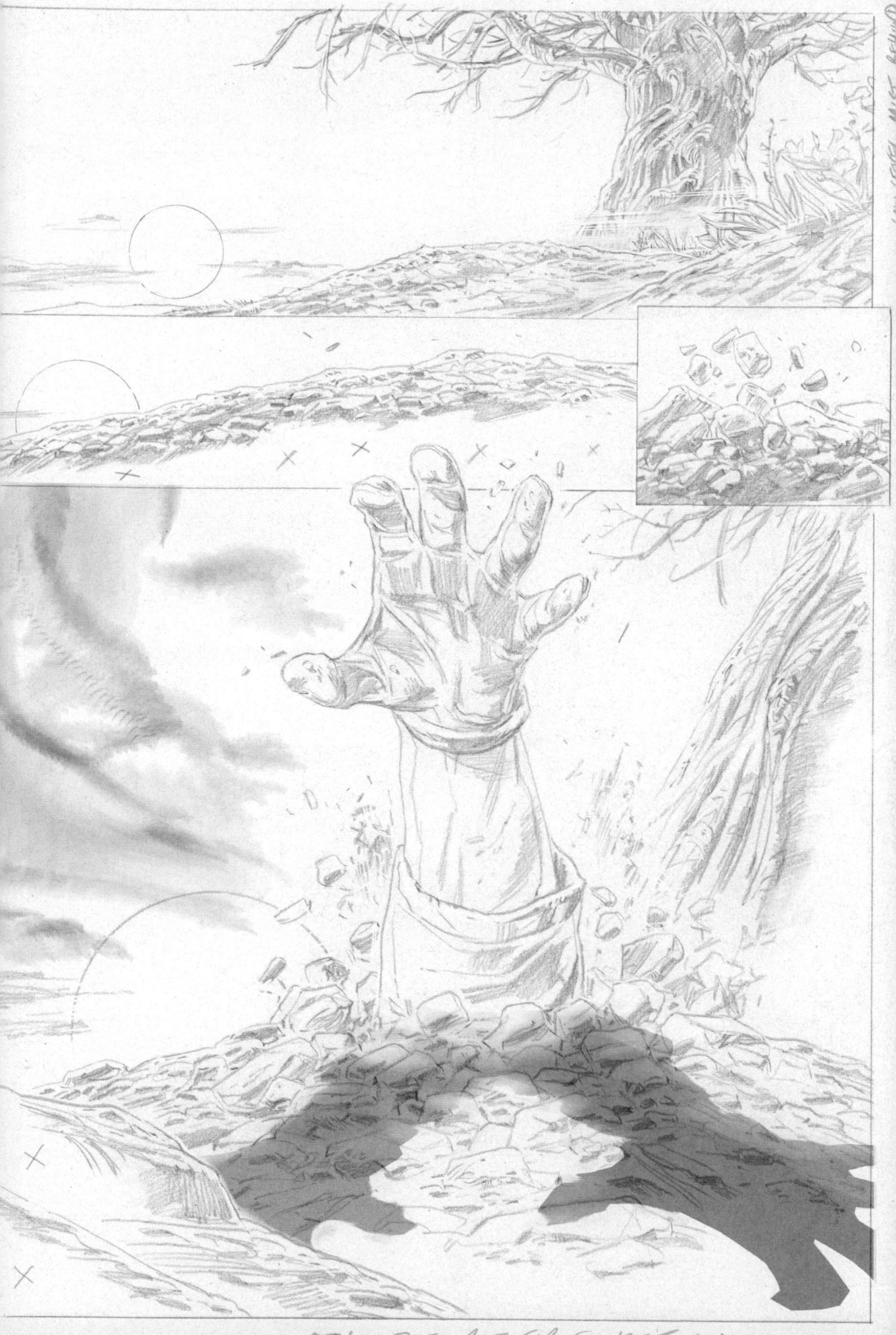

NOTE:- SEE REF FOR SUNSET GUIDE...

SHADOWMAN #5, pages 16, 17, and 18 (facing)
Art by DOUG BRAITHWAITE

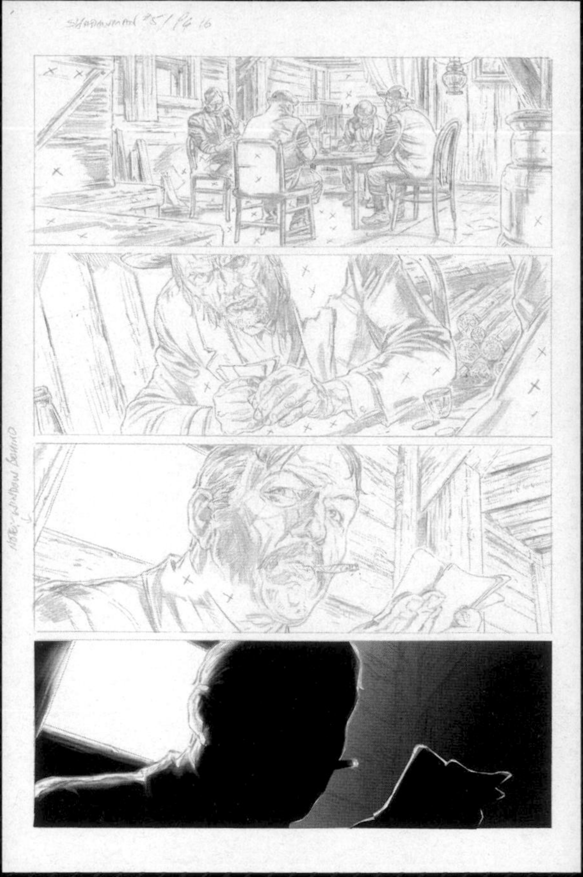
SHADOWMAN #5 / PG 16

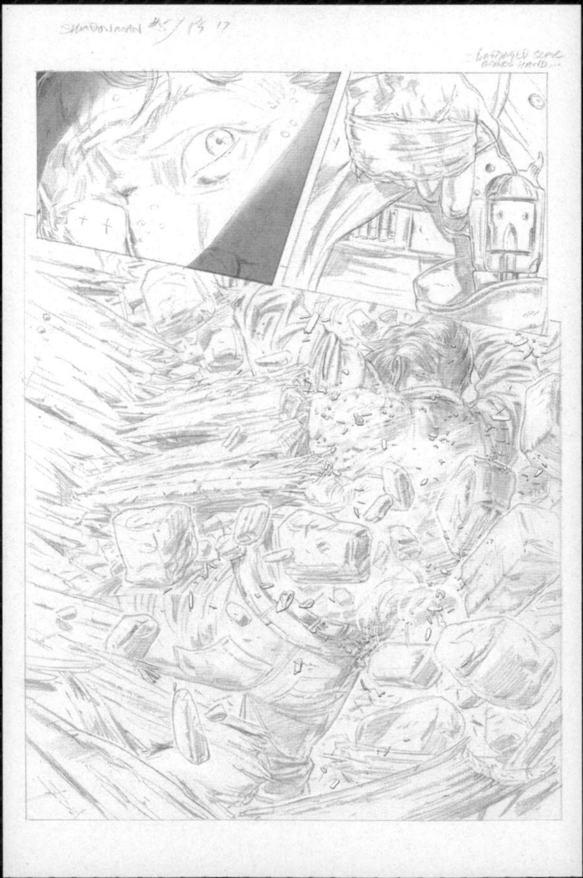
SHADOWMAN #5 / PG 17

SHADOWMAN #5 / 1.05.18

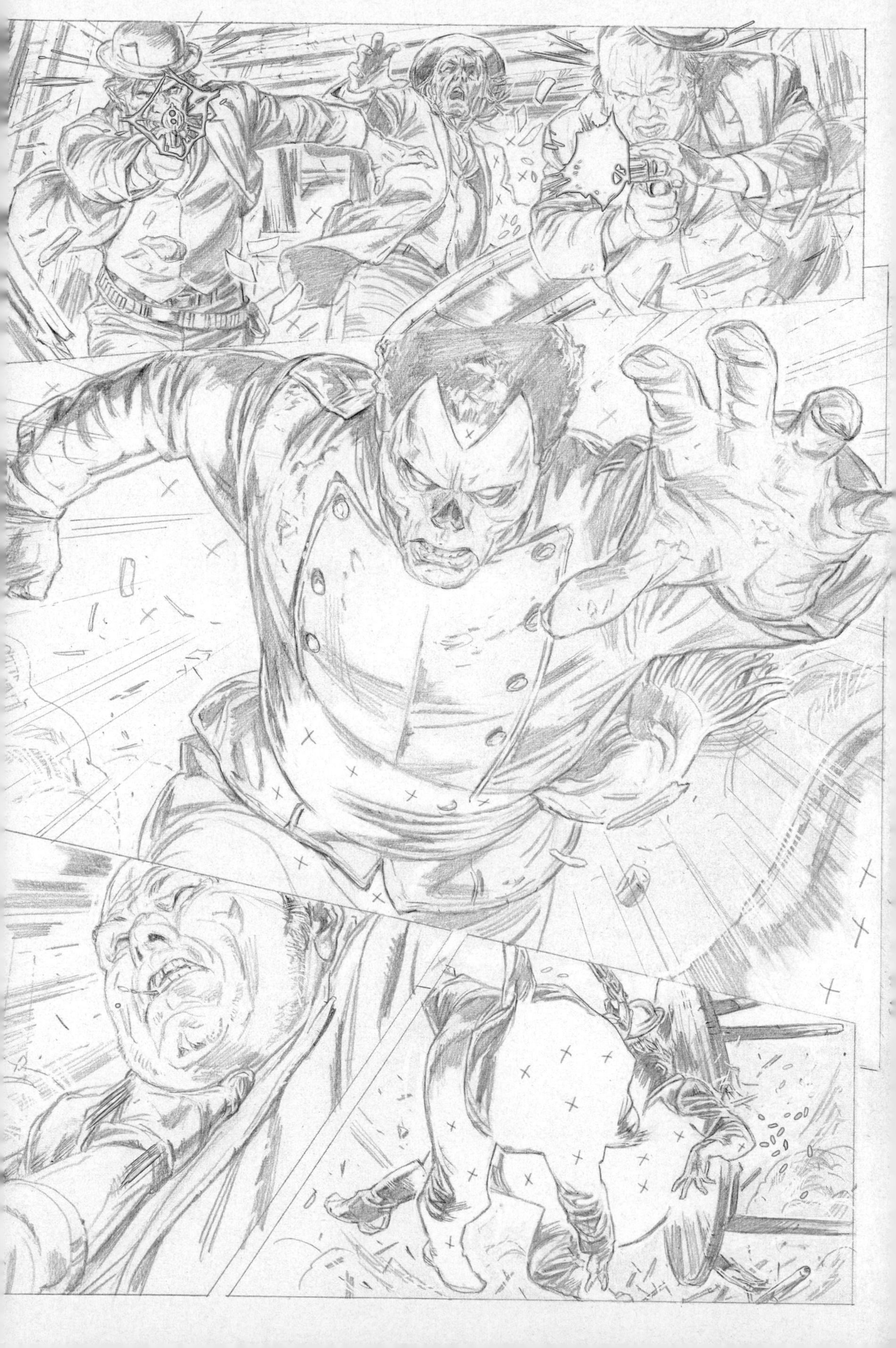

EXPLORE THE VALIANT UNIVERSE

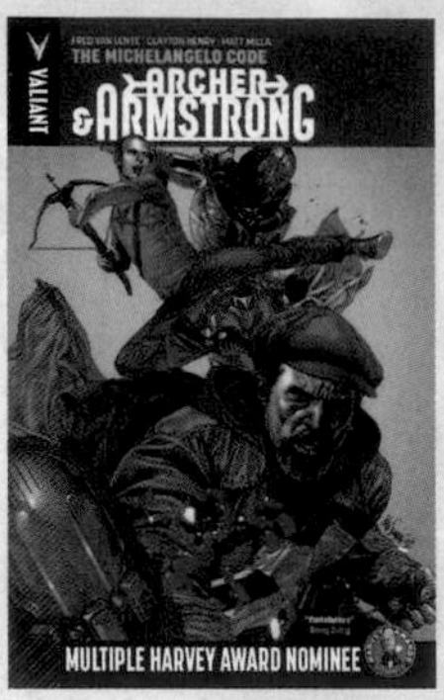
THE MICHELANGELO CODE
ARCHER & ARMSTRONG
MULTIPLE HARVEY AWARD NOMINEE

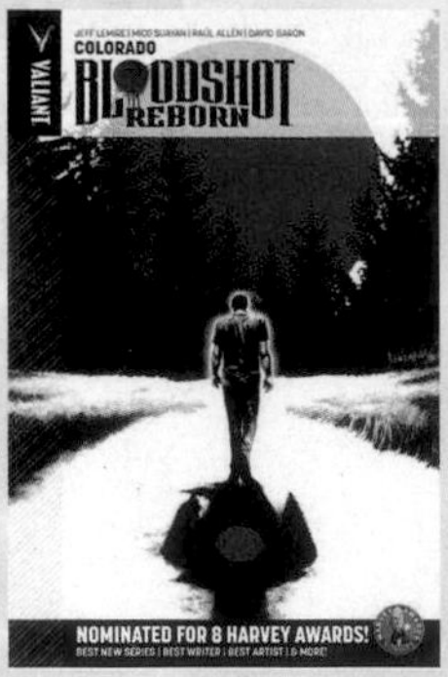
COLORADO
BLOODSHOT REBORN
NOMINATED FOR 8 HARVEY AWARDS!

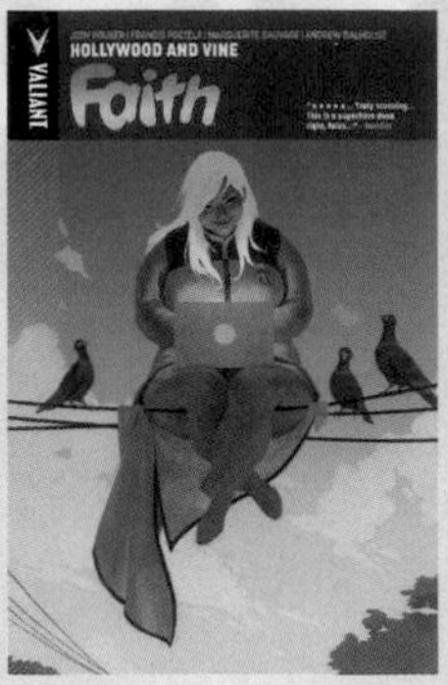
HOLLYWOOD AND VINE
Faith

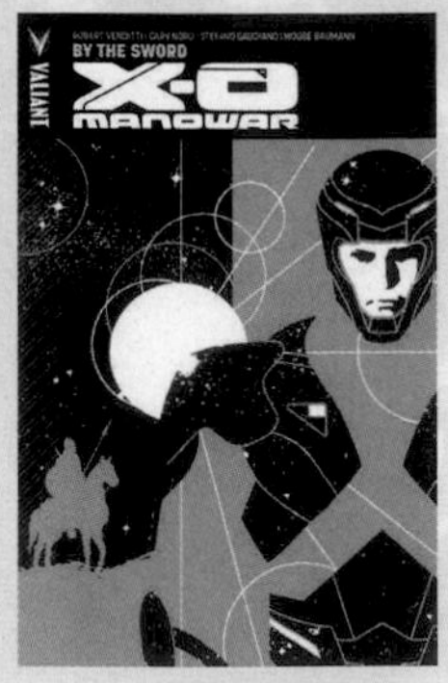
BY THE SWORD
X-O MANOWAR

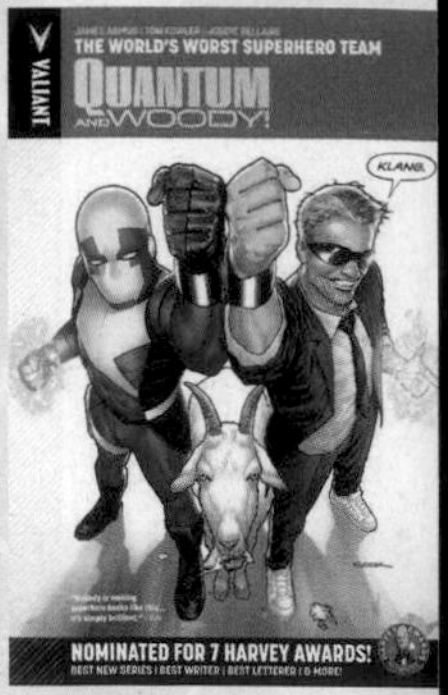
THE WORLD'S WORST SUPERHERO TEAM
QUANTUM AND WOODY!
KLANG
NOMINATED FOR 7 HARVEY AWARDS!

4001 A.D.

4001 A.D.
ISBN: 9781682151433
4001 A.D.: Beyond New Japan
ISBN: 9781682151464
Rai Vol 4: 4001 A.D.
ISBN: 9781682151471

A&A: THE ADVENTURES OF ARCHER AND ARMSTRONG

Volume 1: In the Bag
ISBN: 9781682151495
Volume 2: Romance and Road Trips
ISBN: 9781682151716
Volume 3: Andromeda Estranged
ISBN: 9781682152034

ARCHER & ARMSTRONG

Volume 1: The Michelangelo Code
ISBN: 9780979640988
Volume 2: Wrath of the Eternal Warrior
ISBN: 9781939346049
Volume 3: Far Faraway
ISBN: 9781939346148
Volume 4: Sect Civil War
ISBN: 9781939346254
Volume 5: Mission: Improbable
ISBN: 9781939346353
Volume 6: American Wasteland
ISBN: 9781939346421
Volume 7: The One Percent and Other Tales
ISBN: 9781939346537

ARMOR HUNTERS

Armor Hunters
ISBN: 9781939346452
Armor Hunters: Bloodshot
ISBN: 9781939346469
Armor Hunters: Harbinger
ISBN: 9781939346506
Unity Vol. 3: Armor Hunters
ISBN: 9781939346445
X-O Manowar Vol. 7: Armor Hunters
ISBN: 9781939346476

BLOODSHOT

Volume 1: Setting the World on Fire
ISBN: 9780979640964
Volume 2: The Rise and the Fall
ISBN: 9781939346032
Volume 3: Harbinger Wars
ISBN: 9781939346124
Volume 4: H.A.R.D. Corps
ISBN: 9781939346193
Volume 5: Get Some!
ISBN: 9781939346315
Volume 6: The Glitch and Other Tales
ISBN: 9781939346711

BLOODSHOT REBORN

Volume 1: Colorado
ISBN: 9781939346674
Volume 2: The Hunt
ISBN: 9781939346827
Volume 3: The Analog Man
ISBN: 9781682151334
Volume 4: Bloodshot Island
ISBN: 9781682151952

BLOODSHOT SALVATION

Volume 1: The Book of Revenge
ISBN: 9781682152553

BLOODSHOT U.S.A.

ISBN: 9781682151952

BOOK OF DEATH

Book of Death
ISBN: 9781939346971
Book of Death: The Fall of the Valiant Universe
ISBN: 9781939346988

BRITANNIA

Volume 1
ISBN: 9781682151853
Volume 2: We Who Are About to Die
ISBN: 9781682152133

DEAD DROP

ISBN: 9781939346858

THE DEATH-DEFYING DOCTOR MIRAGE

Volume 1
ISBN: 9781939346490
Volume 2: Second Lives
ISBN: 9781682151297

THE DELINQUENTS

ISBN: 9781939346513

DIVINITY

Divinity I
ISBN: 9781939346766
Divinity II
ISBN: 9781682151518
Divinity III
ISBN: 9781682151914
Divinity III: Glorious Heroes of the Stalinverse
ISBN: 9781682152072

ETERNAL WARRIOR

Volume 1: Sword of the Wild
ISBN: 9781939346209
Volume 2: Eternal Emperor
ISBN: 9781939346292
Volume 3: Days of Steel
ISBN: 9781939346742

WRATH OF THE ETERNAL WARRIOR

Volume 1: Risen
ISBN: 9781682151235
Volume 2: Labyrinth
ISBN: 9781682151594
Volume 3: Deal With a Devil
ISBN: 9781682151976

ETERNITY

ISBN: 9781682152652

FAITH

Volume 1: Hollywood and Vine
ISBN: 9781682151402
Volume 2: California Scheming
ISBN: 9781682151631
Volume 3: Superstar
ISBN: 9781682151990
Volume 4: The Faithless
ISBN: 9781682152195
Faith and the Future Force:
ISBN: 9781682152331

GENERATION ZERO

Volume 1: We Are the Future
ISBN: 9781682151754
Volume 2: Heroscape
ISBN: 9781682152096

HARBINGER

Volume 1: Omega Rising
ISBN: 9780979640957
Volume 2: Renegades
ISBN: 9781939346025
Volume 3: Harbinger Wars
ISBN: 9781939346117
Volume 4: Perfect Day
ISBN: 9781939346155
Volume 5: Death of a Renegade
ISBN: 9781939346339
Volume 6: Omegas
ISBN: 9781939346384

HARBINGER RENEGADE

Volume 1: The Judgment of Solomon
ISBN: 9781682151693
Volume 2: Massacre
ISBN: 9781682152232

EXPLORE THE VALIANT UNIVERSE

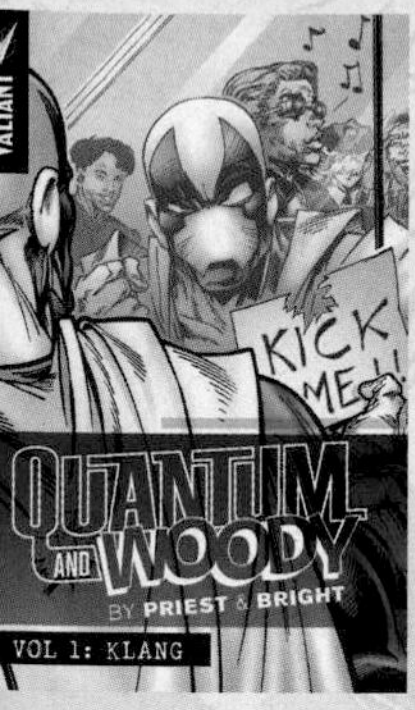
KICK ME
QUANTUM AND WOODY
BY PRIEST & BRIGHT
VOL 1: KLANG

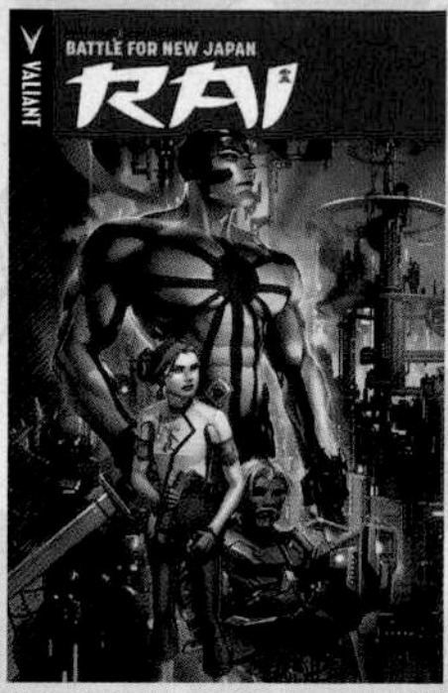
VALIANT
BATTLE FOR NEW JAPAN
RAI

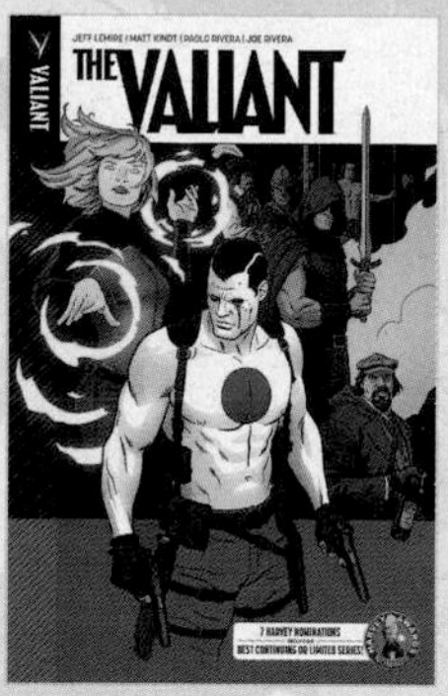
VALIANT
THE VALIANT

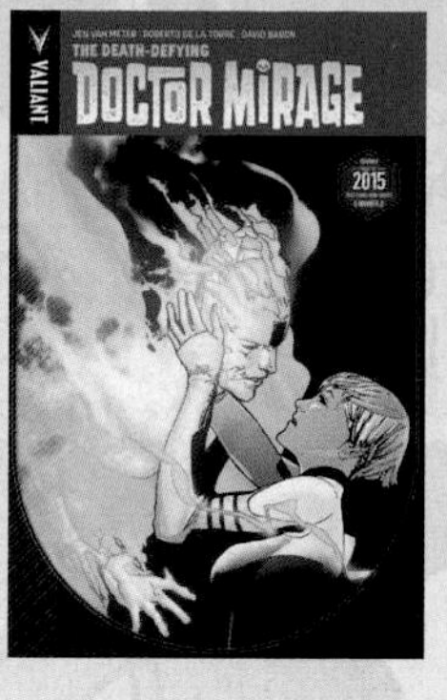
VALIANT
THE DEATH-DEFYING
DOCTOR MIRAGE
2015

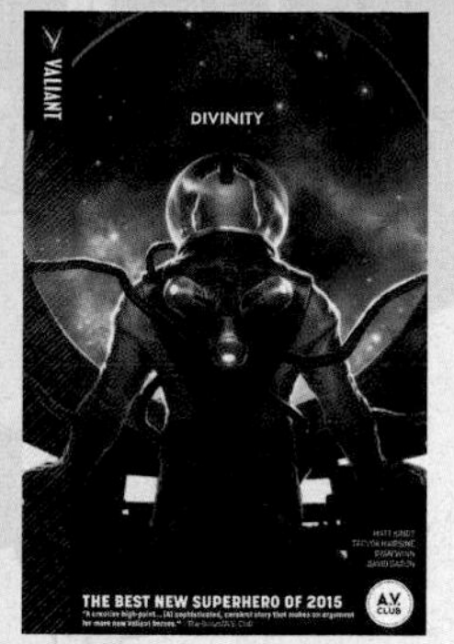
VALIANT
DIVINITY
THE BEST NEW SUPERHERO OF 2015
A.V. CLUB

ARBINGER WARS
arbinger Wars
SBN: 9781939346094
loodshot Vol. 3: Harbinger Wars
SBN: 9781939346124
arbinger Vol. 3: Harbinger Wars
SBN: 9781939346117

MPERIUM
olume 1: Collecting Monsters
SBN: 9781939346759
olume 2: Broken Angels
SBN: 9781939346896
olume 3: The Vine Imperative
SBN: 9781682151112
olume 4: Stormbreak
SBN: 9781682151372

NINJAK
olume 1: Weaponeer
SBN: 9781939346667
olume 2: The Shadow Wars
SBN: 9781939346940
olume 3: Operation: Deadside
SBN: 9781682151259
olume 4: The Siege of King's Castle
SBN: 9781682151617
olume 5: The Fist & The Steel
SBN: 9781682151792
olume 6: The Seven Blades of Master Darque
SBN: 9781682152119

INJA-K
olume 1: The Ninja Files
SBN: 9781682152591
olume 2: The Coalition
SBN: 9781682152812

UANTUM AND WOODY
olume 1: The World's Worst Superhero Team
SBN: 9781939346186
olume 2: In Security
SBN: 9781939346230
olume 3: Crooked Pasts, Present Tense
SBN: 9781939346391
olume 4: Quantum and Woody Must Die!
SBN: 9781939346629

UANTUM AND WOODY!
olume 1: Kiss Kiss, Klang, Klang
SBN: 9781682152690

UANTUM AND WOODY Y PRIEST & BRIGHT
olume 1: Klang
SBN: 9781939346780

Volume 2: Switch
ISBN: 9781939346803
Volume 3: And So...
ISBN: 9781939346865
Volume 4: Q2 - The Return
ISBN: 9781682151099

RAI
Volume 1: Welcome to New Japan
ISBN: 9781939346414
Volume 2: Battle for New Japan
ISBN: 9781939346612
Volume 3: The Orphan
ISBN: 9781939346841
Volume 4: 4001 A.D.
ISBN: 9781682151471

RAPTURE
ISBN: 9781682151891

SAVAGE
ISBN: 9781682152256

SECRET WEAPONS
ISBN: 9781682152294

SHADOWMAN
Volume 1: Birth Rites
ISBN: 9781939346001
Volume 2: Darque Reckoning
ISBN: 9781939346056
Volume 3: Deadside Blues
ISBN: 9781939346162
Volume 4: Fear, Blood, And Shadows
ISBN: 9781939346278
Volume 5: End Times
ISBN: 9781939346377

SHADOWMAN BY ENNIS & WOOD
ISBN: 9781682151358

IVAR, TIMEWALKER
Volume 1: Making History
ISBN: 9781939346636
Volume 2: Breaking History
ISBN: 9781939346834
Volume 3: Ending History
ISBN: 9781939346995

UNITY
Volume 1: To Kill a King
ISBN: 9781939346261
Volume 2: Trapped by Webnet
ISBN: 9781939346346
Volume 3: Armor Hunters
ISBN: 9781939346445
Volume 4: The United
ISBN: 9781939346544

Volume 5: Homefront
ISBN: 9781939346797
Volume 6: The War-Monger
ISBN: 9781939346902
Volume 7: Revenge of the Armor Hunters
ISBN: 9781682151136

THE VALIANT
ISBN: 9781939346605

VALIANT HIGH
ISBN: 9781682152799

VALIANT ZEROES AND ORIGINS
ISBN: 9781939346582

WAR MOTHER
ISBN: 9781682152379

X-O MANOWAR
Volume 1: By the Sword
ISBN: 9780979640940
Volume 2: Enter Ninjak
ISBN: 9780979640995
Volume 3: Planet Death
ISBN: 9781939346087
Volume 4: Homecoming
ISBN: 9781939346179
Volume 5: At War With Unity
ISBN: 9781939346247
Volume 6: Prelude to Armor Hunters
ISBN: 9781939346407
Volume 7: Armor Hunters
ISBN: 9781939346476
Volume 8: Enter: Armorines
ISBN: 9781939346551
Volume 9: Dead Hand
ISBN: 9781939346650
Volume 10: Exodus
ISBN: 9781939346933
Volume 11: The Kill List
ISBN: 9781682151273
Volume 12: Long Live the King
ISBN: 9781682151655
Volume 13: Succession and Other Tales
ISBN: 9781682151754

X-O MANOWAR (2017)
Volume 1: Soldier
ISBN: 9781682152058
Volume 2: General
ISBN: 9781682152171
Volume 3: Emperor
ISBN: 9781682152355
Volume 4: Visigoth
ISBN: 9781682152638
Volume 5: Barbarians
ISBN: 9781682152836

EXPLORE THE VALIANT UNIVERSE

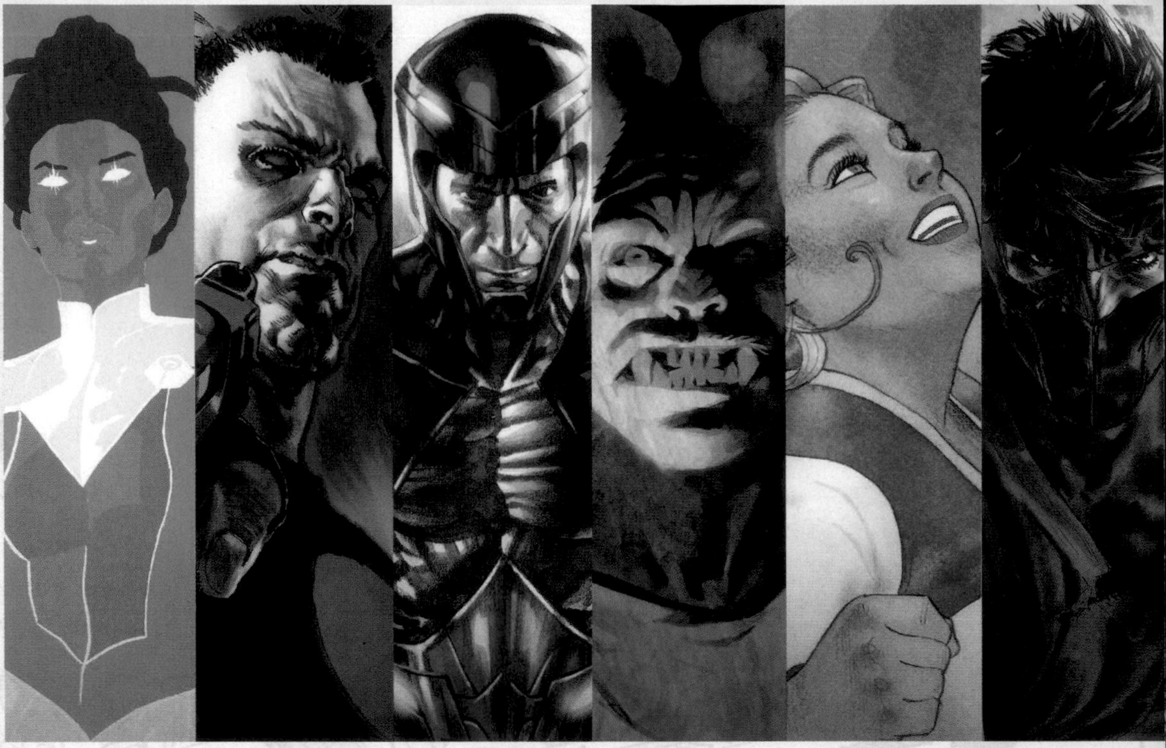

4001 A.D. DELUXE EDITION
ISBN: 978-1-68215-193-8

ARCHER & ARMSTRONG DELUXE EDITIONS
Book 1: ISBN: 978-1-939346-22-3
Book 2: ISBN: 978-1-939346-95-7

ARMOR HUNTERS DELUXE EDITION
ISBN: 978-1-939346-72-8

BLOODSHOT DELUXE EDITIONS
Book 1: ISBN: 978-1-939346-21-6
Book 2: ISBN: 978-1-939346-81-0

BLOODSHOT REBORN DELUXE EDITIONS
Book 1: ISBN: 978-1-68215-155-6
Book 2: ISBN: 978-1-68215-227-0

BOOK OF DEATH DELUXE EDITION
ISBN: 978-1-68215-115-0

THE DEATH-DEFYING DOCTOR MIRAGE DELUXE EDITION
ISBN: 978-1-68215-153-2

DIVINITY DELUXE EDITION
ISBN: 978-1-939346-92-6

FAITH: HOLLYWOOD & VINE DELUXE EDITION
ISBN: 978-1-68215-201-0

HARBINGER DELUXE EDITIONS
Book 1: ISBN: 978-1-939346-13-1
Book 2: ISBN: 978-1-939346-77-3

HARBINGER WARS DELUXE EDITION
ISBN: 978-1-939346-32-2

IVAR, TIMEWALKER DELUXE EDITION
Book 1: ISBN: 978-1-68215-119-8

NINJAK DELUXE EDITION
Book 1: ISBN: 978-1-68215-157-0
Book 2: ISBN: 978-1-68215-257-7

QUANTUM AND WOODY DELUXE EDITION
Book 1: ISBN: 978-1-939346-68-1

RAI DELUXE EDITION
Book 1: ISBN: 978-1-68215-117-4

SHADOWMAN DELUXE EDITION
Book 1: ISBN: 978-1-939346-43-8

UNITY DELUXE EDITION
Book 1: 978-1-939346-57-5

THE VALIANT DELUXE EDITION
ISBN: 978-1-939346-91-9

X-O MANOWAR DELUXE EDITIONS
Book 1: ISBN: 978-1-939346-10-0
Book 2: ISBN: 978-1-939346-52-0
Book 3 : ISBN: 978-1-68215-131-0
Book 4: ISBN: 978-1-68215-183-9
Book 5: ISBN: 978-1-68215-215-7

VALIANT CLASSIC

ARCHER & ARMSTRONG: THE COMPLETE CLASSIC OMNIBUS
ISBN: 978-1-939346-87-2

QUANTUM AND WOODY: THE COMPLETE CLASSIC OMNIBUS
ISBN: 978-1-939346-36-0

Q2: THE RETURN OF QUANTUM AND WOODY DELUXE EDITION
ISBN: 978-1-939346-56-8

VALIANT MASTERS: BLOODSHOT VOL. 1 - BLOOD OF THE MACHINE
ISBN: 978-0-9796409-3-3

VALIANT MASTERS: HARBINGER VOL. 1 - CHILDREN OF THE EIGHTH DAY
ISBN: 978-1-939346-48-3

VALIANT MASTERS: H.A.R.D. CORPS VOL. 1 - SEARCH AND DESTROY
ISBN: 978-1-939346-28-5

VALIANT MASTERS: NINJAK VOL. 1 - BLACK WATER
ISBN: 978-0-9796409-7-1

VALIANT MASTERS: RAI VOL. 1 - FROM HONOR TO STRENGTH
ISBN: 978-1-939346-07-0

VALIANT MASTERS: SHADOWMAN VOL. 1 - SPIRITS WITHIN
ISBN: 978-1-939346-01-8

X-O MANOWAR CLASSIC OMNIBUS
Vol. 1: ISBN: 978-1-939346-30-8

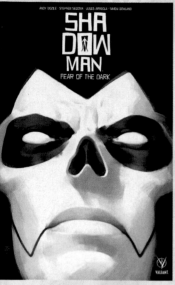

SHADOWMAN® READING ORDER

SHADOWMAN
FEAR OF THE DARK
VALIANT

Shadowman (2018)
Vol. 1: Fear of the Dark

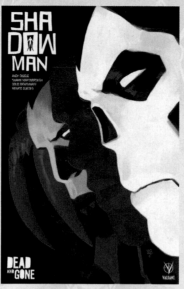

SHADOWMAN
DEAD AND GONE
VALIANT

Shadowman (2018)
Vol. 2: Dead and Gone

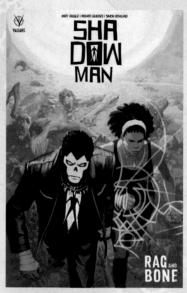

VALIANT
ANDY DIGGLE | RENATO GUEDES | SIMON BOWLAND
SHADOWMAN
RAG AND BONE

Shadowman (2018)
Vol. 3: Rag and Bone

Read the origins and first adventures of Valiant's supernatural icon!

VALIANT
BIRTH RITES
SHADOWMAN

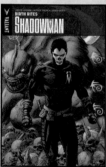

Shadowman Vol. 1:
Birth Rites

VALIANT
DARQUE RECKONING
SHADOWMAN

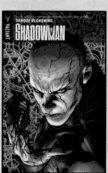

Shadowman Vol. 2:
Darque Reckoning

VALIANT
SHADOWMAN

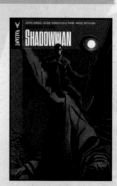

Shadowman Vol. 3:
Deadside Blues

VALIANT
FEAR, BLOOD, AND SHADOWS
SHADOWMAN

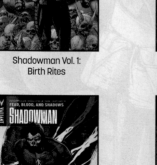

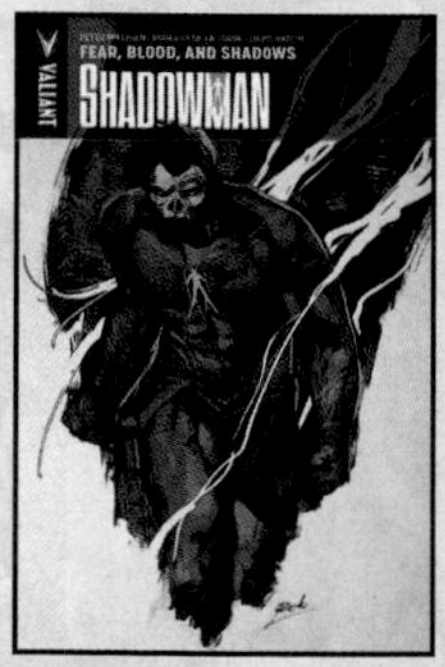

Shadowman Vol.4:
Fear, Blood, and Shadows

VALIANT
SHADOWMAN
END TIMES

Shadowman Vol. 5:
End Times

NINJAK • SHADOWMAN
RAPTURE

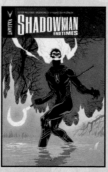

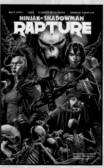

Rapture

SHADOWMAN®

VOLUME THREE: **RAG AND BONE**

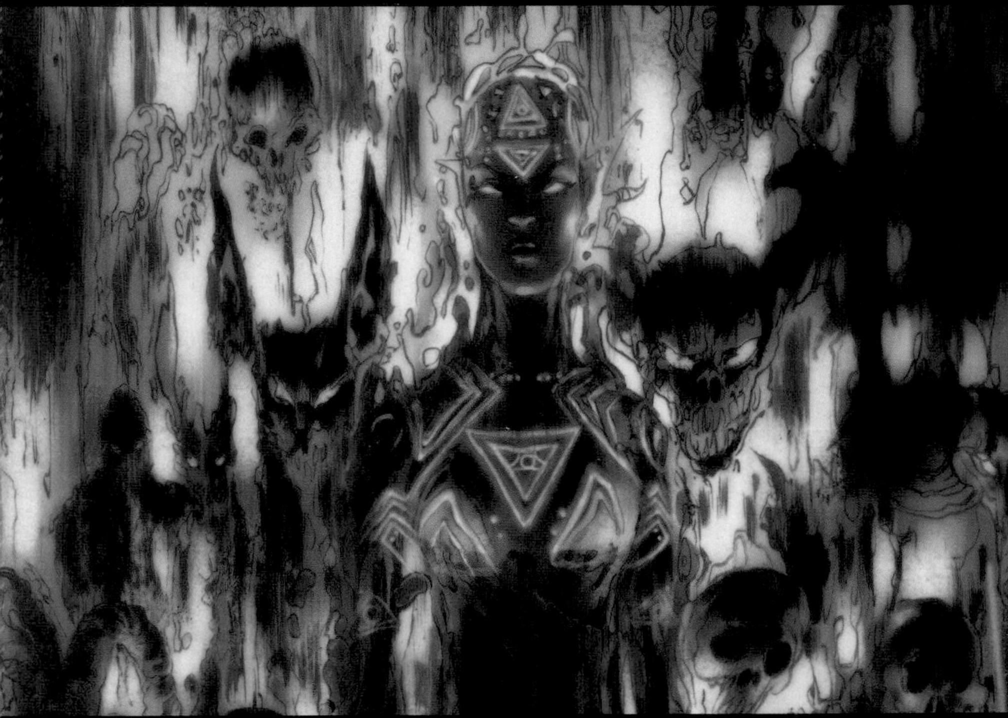

BONES ARE BURIED FOR A REASON...

As Shadowman returns to New Orleans with a revelatory new understanding of the immense abilities within himself, he won't have long to adjust...because a war for control of the ultimate magical artifact - the bones of Master Darque, his old arch-nemesis - is about to erupt out of the underground and into the harsh view of day!

On one side: The Brethren, a society of wealthy and powerful occultists obsessed with Darque's resurrection and ushering in a millennia-long reign of darkness. On the other: Shadowman's old allies from The Abettors... and Darque's own sister, Sandria, who would like nothing more than to grind her brother's bones to dust...

The endless cycle of death and rebirth stops here as Shadowman and the Darque clan usher in the reckoning they've waited ten lifetimes to achieve - with massive repercussions for the future of the Valiant Universe - as renowned writer Andy Diggle (*Green Arrow: Year One*) and high-octane artist Renato Guedes (*Action Comics*) return to heed the call of "RAG AND BONE"!

Collecting SHADOWMAN (2018) #8-11.

TRADE PAPERBACK
ISBN: 978-1-68215-314-7

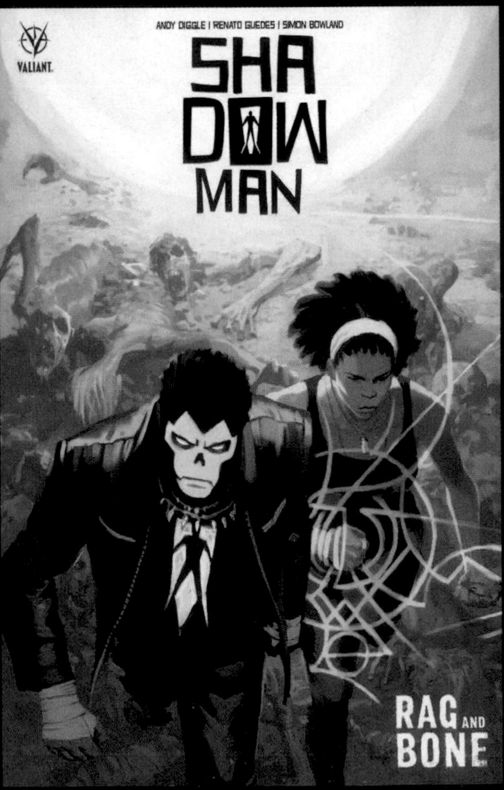
ANDY DIGGLE | RENATO GUEDES | SIMON BOWLAND
VALIANT
SHA DOW MAN
RAG AND BONE